UX for the Web

Build websites for user experience and usability

Marli Ritter
Cara Winterbottom

BIRMINGHAM - MUMBAI

UX for the Web

First published: September 2017

Production reference: 1250917

Published by Packt Publishing Ltd.
Livery Place
35 Livery Street
Birmingham
B3 2PB, UK.

ISBN 978-1-78712-847-7

www.packtpub.com

Credits

Authors
Marli Ritter
Cara Winterbottom

Reviewer
Alipta Ballav

Commissioning Editor
Ashwin Nair

Acquisition Editor
Shweta Pant

Content Development Editor
Onkar Wani

Technical Editor
Murtaza Tinwala

Copy Editor
Safis Editing

Project Coordinator
Devanshi Doshi

Proofreader
Safis Editing

Indexer
Rekha Nair

Graphics
Jason Monteiro

Production Coordinator
Shraddha Falebhai

About the Authors

Marli Ritter is a UX specialist and web accessibility evangelist who started off as a basic web designer in the '90s. Creating websites, she recognized the critical link between branding and design early on and spent the next couple of years studying brand communication at Vega School of Brand Leadership in Gauteng, South Africa.

During this time, she discovered her passion for education and decided to focus on lecturing web design and development at a selection of private educational institutions within the AdvTech group.

This love for sharing knowledge did not stop at lecturing, however, as Marli also worked closely with the Independent Institute of Education (IIE) to develop the curriculum for the revised web design and development qualification. Her time spent in education was invaluable, but her desire to explore new avenues guided her back to the industry.

Marli took a leap into the e-commerce sector by joining the Comair Limited team, creating brand-focused digital designs, while doing frontend development on travel brands such as kulula.com, Holiday Tours, mtbeds, GoTravel24, and African Dream Holidays.

Once again in search of new adventures, Marli found herself drawn to the vibrant brand and international presence of Travelstart. She joined this dynamic team to help improve UX across multiple countries and languages. This exposure to complex e-commerce systems catering to a broad user base made her more determined to learn design and development techniques that will enhance a user's experience.

This intricate dance between branding, design, development, and the end user is ultimately where her love affair with UX started. Her passion for the field is driven even further by her interest in cultural anthropology, psychology, and human behavior as well as her need to understand a user's behavior when interacting with digital products.

The past couple of years have seen Marli actively raising awareness by giving talks at local MeetUps as well as presenting a paper on the importance of web accessibility for everyday digital products at the annual South African UX Conference.

Her mission is to remove the divide between users that are fully able and users with limited abilities, to create a mindset that usability is, in fact, for everyone despite their limitations.

I would like to thank my family and friends for their support, understanding, and patience when I couldn't join for that hike or glass of wine because "I had to work", and of course when the grumpiness peeks through from lack of sleep. Now we can have as many glasses of wine as we can comfortably stomach and let's go climb that mountain!

Cara Winterbottom has a lifelong fascination with people, ideas, and data. This first led her toward the fields of psychology and philosophy. During this time, she discovered an interest in technology, especially how it can enable research and design around people, ideas, and data. These two strands converged when she discovered the field of user experience.

Cara has a strong academic background, with degrees in psychology and computer science. Her PhD in computer science was earned through designing, building, and user testing an authoring tool for novices to create 3D interactions for virtual environments. This sparked her interest in user experience. After an academic career of over a decade, Cara joined Flow Interactive, a leading UX agency in Cape Town, South Africa. Here, she learned how to deliver quality research and design work that leverages the best parts of academic rigor and business requirements and processes. For the past 6 years, she has worked as a freelance consultant, further developing these skills in a variety of settings and for a variety of products. The areas of user experience in which she is most interested are qualitative and quantitative research methods, especially usability testing and analysis, information architecture, and interaction design.

I would like to thank my partner, Andrew Smith, and my parents, Rosie and Peter Winterbottom, for their unwavering support while I have been immersed in writing this book. I would also like to thank my co-writer, Marli Ritter, for allowing me to share this experience with her, and for the lovely conversations we had along the way. Finally, I would like to thank Packt for giving me this opportunity, in particular, my editors, Onkar Wani and Shweta Pant, for their support and for making my writing better.

About the Reviewer

Alipta Ballav is a thought leader, mentor, and an individual contributor at times. He is a UX researcher with over 18 years of industry experience. A graduate in Visual Arts from the Rabindra Bharati University, Kolkata, he has been instrumental in defining meaningful experiences for global customers across multiple domains. In the recent past, Alipta was a UX researcher at the Stanford Crowd Research Collective--an initiative led by professors and students at Stanford--where he invested time building a sustainable crowdsourcing platform by teaming up with researchers across the globe. Alipta additionally does independent research in the territory of web accessibility and looking into approaches to minimize human computer interaction challenges through multi-modality. He also takes an interest in data science, quantitative techniques, and predictive modeling.

www.PacktPub.com

For support files and downloads related to your book, please visit www.PacktPub.com.

Did you know that Packt offers eBook versions of every book published, with PDF and ePub files available? You can upgrade to the eBook version at www.PacktPub.com and as a print book customer, you are entitled to a discount on the eBook copy. Get in touch with us at service@packtpub.com for more details.

At www.PacktPub.com, you can also read a collection of free technical articles, sign up for a range of free newsletters and receive exclusive discounts and offers on Packt books and eBooks.

https://www.packtpub.com/mapt

Get the most in-demand software skills with Mapt. Mapt gives you full access to all Packt books and video courses, as well as industry-leading tools to help you plan your personal development and advance your career.

Why subscribe?

- Fully searchable across every book published by Packt
- Copy and paste, print, and bookmark content
- On demand and accessible via a web browser

Customer Feedback

Thanks for purchasing this Packt book. At Packt, quality is at the heart of our editorial process. To help us improve, please leave us an honest review on this book's Amazon page at https://www.amazon.com/dp/1787128474.

If you'd like to join our team of regular reviewers, you can e-mail us at customerreviews@packtpub.com. We award our regular reviewers with free eBooks and videos in exchange for their valuable feedback. Help us be relentless in improving our products!

Table of Contents

Preface

User Experience (UX) is one of the most important factors to keep in mind when creating a digital product. With a highly competitive world where brands fight for the user's attention, loyalty, and money, the usability and enjoyment of a product play a fundamental role in its success. It sounds simple enough to create a product that's loved by millions of users, but there's a lot more to UX than creating an easy-to-use, aesthetically pleasing user interface. UX is a broad discipline with an intricate set of interlinked components that contribute to the overall experience a user will have with a digital product; however, the core focus is usability. Usability is one of the key components that drives an enjoyable user experience.

This book will introduce you to the core UX principles and practical methods for creating websites that are not only beautiful, but easy to use and fully accessible. Understanding the core principles of UX will enable a true understanding of the user, their behavior and needs, as well as how to effectively satisfy these needs. This understanding will help enhance your brand by creating a golden thread from your product to the user and establishing a trust relationship. Following practical UX methodologies will enable you to apply this understanding to product research, design, and development and testing so that you create an effective and user-friendly web product. UX research methods provide clear direction and guidelines for conducting research on a concept or product. This can then be tested and improved to increase user retention. By bringing your UX strategy to life with task flows, wireframes, and prototypes, it's easy to find holes in user journeys that can potentially sabotage the relationship. Implementing conventional web accessibility technical standards will ensure that the product complies with usability requirements and is accessible for all users, including users with special needs.

What this book covers

Chapter 1, *The Fundamentals of UX*, discusses the core principles of UX, such as Design Thinking, Human-Centered Design (HCD), and the User-Centered Design (UCD) process, and how these principles are connected with software development methodologies. The reader will learn the core principles of UX to understand the different aspects of UX within the life cycle of a project, the environment, and the people involved.

Chapter 2, *Stand Out from Your Competitors*, gives an overview of basic brand theory with the focus on the importance of UX for a brand and how this relationship can build a strong brand that stands out from its competitors. The reader will learn the significant role that UX plays in building a brand, and how applying basic UX principles can improve not only the brand's identity but also ensure the brand's superiority over its competitors.

Chapter 3, *Create an Emotional Connection with the User*, covers how to build a trust relationship with the user by creating a digital personality the user can relate to. Guidelines on how to use a tone of voice that is customary when communicating with the user as well as the use of subtle visual interactions within the user interface will be discussed. The reader will learn how to effectively communicate with the user to establish trust and credibility that will evolve in an emotional connection.

Chapter 4, *Best Practices for Usability Within the User Interface (UI)*, gives the essential guidelines to create a user interface that complies to the highest standard of usability on a digital platform. An overview of the design standards from the world's leading software giants--Apple and Google--will be discussed. The reader will learn how to create an aesthetically appealing and effective design that meets the usability standards for a quality digital product.

Chapter 5, *Set a Solid Foundation - Research and Analyze*, provides an overview of user research methodologies and processes. It will help the reader lay down a solid foundation of reliable data to build a user-friendly product. The reader will learn the importance of research and data for building a successful product, and how to conduct research effectively.

Chapter 6, *Create a UX Strategy - Users and Content*, looks at how to use research and data to create a UX strategy that includes the various users being catered to and the way information should be structured for these users to achieve their end goal within a digital product. The reader will learn how to focus on users' behavior and mould a smooth user journey that supports the UX strategy for a digital product.

Chapter 7, *Bring Your UX Strategy to Life with Wireframes and Prototypes*, explores the different stages of rolling out a product, from setting the look and feel to establishing what features and functionality will be included in the final product. This includes practical advice for creating effective moodboards, storyboards, wireframes, and prototypes. The reader will learn how to distinguish between the importance of wireframes and visual designs, and how to create effective prototypes for management and the development team.

Chapter 8, *Build Your Product - Devices, Browsers, and Assistive Technologies,* touches on the more technical aspects of catering for different technologies such as different devices, browsers, and assistive technologies people may use to interact with the product. The features and principles of responsive and universal design are explored. The reader will gain a high-level overview of how to develop a product for different devices, from desktop, tablet, and mobile to different browsers, for example, IE, Chrome, and Safari, based on the operating system the user uses as well as for different assistive technologies a person with special needs may use.

Chapter 9, *Optimize Your UX Strategy - Test, Test, Test,* focuses on practical UX methodologies to measure and test the web app with users. In particular, usability testing, analytics, and A/B testing are explored. The reader will learn to create a metric analysis and test all aspects of the UX strategy, while implementing the changes to build a successful digital product.

Chapter 10, *The Basics and Benefits of Web Accessibility,* looks at the fundamentals and benefits of web accessibility, the assistive technologies to cater for, and the legal implications if a digital product is not accessible to all users. The user will learn the basics of web accessibility, the impact it has on users and the digital product, and how to test products for accessibility.

Chapter 11, *A Practical Guide to Web Accessibility,* offers practical guidance on how to implement web accessibility guidelines such as the Web Content Accessibility Guidelines (WCAG) 2.0 to ensure that a digital product is accessible to all users, despite their limitations. The reader will learn about the fundamental technical standards for web accessibility, and WCAG 2.0 and WAI-ARIA to design and develop for user with special needs and assistive technology.

What you need for this book

UX is a discipline that has no software dependencies. Most of the exercises in this book can be done using a pen and paper only; however, you will need an internet browser with internet access to acquire the full extent of UX resources provided in the book.

Who this book is for

If you're a designer, developer, or just someone who has the desire to create websites that are not only beautiful to look at but also easy to use and fully accessible to everyone, including people with special needs, *UX for the Web* will provide you with the basic building blocks to achieve just that.

Conventions

In this book, you will find a number of text styles that distinguish between different kinds of information. Here are some examples of these styles and an explanation of their meaning.

Code words in text, database table names, folder names, filenames, file extensions, pathnames, dummy URLs, user input, and Twitter handles are shown as follows: "The bitmap graphic format (.bmp) for images."

A block of code is set as follows:

```
<form action="post">
 <label for="username">Username</label>
 <input id="username" type="text" aria-required="true" />
 <hr/>
 <label for="password">Password</label>
 <input id="password" type="text" aria-required="true" />
 <hr/>
```

When we wish to draw your attention to a particular part of a code block, the relevant lines or items are set in bold:

```
<button type="submit" aria-disabled="true" aria-describedby="usernameError
passwordError">Login</button>
```

New terms and important words are shown in bold. Words that you see on the screen, for example, in menus or dialog boxes, appear in the text like this: "Clicking the **Next** button moves you to the next screen."

Warnings or important notes appear in a box like this.

Tips and tricks appear like this.

Reader feedback

Feedback from our readers is always welcome. Let us know what you think about this book-what you liked or disliked. Reader feedback is important to us as it helps us develop titles that you will really get the most out of.

To send us general feedback, simply email `feedback@packtpub.com`, and mention the book's title in the subject of your message.

If there is a topic that you have expertise in and you are interested in either writing or contributing to a book, see our author guide at `www.packtpub.com/authors`.

Customer support

Now that you are the proud owner of a Packt book, we have a number of things to help you to get the most from your purchase.

Downloading the color images of this book

We also provide you with a PDF file that has color images of the screenshots/diagrams used in this book. The color images will help you better understand the changes in the output. You can download this file from `https://www.packtpub.com/sites/default/files/downloads/UXfortheWeb_ColorImages.pdf`.

Errata

Although we have taken every care to ensure the accuracy of our content, mistakes do happen. If you find a mistake in one of our books-maybe a mistake in the text or the code-- we would be grateful if you could report this to us. By doing so, you can save other readers from frustration and help us improve subsequent versions of this book. If you find any errata, please report them by visiting `http://www.packtpub.com/submit-errata`, selecting your book, clicking on the **Errata Submission Form** link, and entering the details of your errata. Once your errata are verified, your submission will be accepted and the errata will be uploaded to our website or added to any list of existing errata under the Errata section of that title.

To view the previously submitted errata, go to `https://www.packtpub.com/books/content/support` and enter the name of the book in the search field. The required information will appear under the **Errata** section.

Piracy

Piracy of copyrighted material on the Internet is an ongoing problem across all media. At Packt, we take the protection of our copyright and licenses very seriously. If you come across any illegal copies of our works in any form on the Internet, please provide us with the location address or website name immediately so that we can pursue a remedy.

Please contact us at copyright@packtpub.com with a link to the suspected pirated material.

We appreciate your help in protecting our authors and our ability to bring you valuable content.

Questions

If you have a problem with any aspect of this book, you can contact us at questions@packtpub.com, and we will do our best to address the problem.

1
The Fundamentals of UX

User experience (**UX**) is a popular term in the digital industry; everyone uses it freely in meetings. Business, marketing, design, and development all understand the importance of the user's experience with the digital product they're creating. Building a website or mobile app with an enjoyable user experience sounds simple enough, but this is where most organizations and teams get it wrong. When non-UX professionals speak of what they feel as a better user experience for a specific feature, they usually refer to their own experience as a user in terms of what makes sense to them personally when interacting with that feature, or it's merely their perception of what they feel the targeted user will enjoy and how they will interact with this feature. This perspective is not usually plausible because the person making these assumptions might not represent the actual target market, and their needs might not be the same as the intended user who will be using this feature.

Take, for example, a request that comes in from a business to implement search functionality on a travel website. A team of designers and developers are brainstorming this new feature. The designers feel a better user experience is to focus on UI elements, such as iconography, to give visual cues for guiding the user on how to use the search functionality, while the developers might focus on an additional filter component to narrow search results. Both of these approaches can definitely improve the user experience, but these are, in fact, only personal opinions based on their field of study and experience. The usability of the search component will only really be apparent if it's tested with real users that interact with this search functionality. The outcome of the user testing can potentially result in the iconography cluttering the UI or the additional filter component not being used at all to find the expected result.

UX is a broad discipline with an intricate set of interlinked components that contribute to the overall experience a user will have with a digital product, however, the core focus is usability. Usability is one of the key components that drive an enjoyable user experience. So what exactly is usability? According to *The International Organization for Standardization, ISO 9241 Ergonomics of Human-System Interaction*, the definition of usability is:

> *The effectiveness, efficiency, and satisfaction with which specified users achieve specified goals in particular environments.*
> *Effectiveness is the accuracy and completeness with which specified users can achieve specified goals in particular environments.*
> *Efficiency is the resources expended in relation to the accuracy and completeness of the goals achieved.*
> *Satisfaction is the comfort and acceptability of the work system to its users and other people affected by its use.*

From the preceding definition, it's clear that usability is not just related to technology, like the usability of websites or mobile apps, but is applicable to everything around us, such as the TV remote or the microwave oven. To understand how this term can be so broad, we'll look at a brief history of UX to discover the origins of human interaction with an object, be it a shovel or a computer. Before we get started following is a list of topics that will be covered in this chapter:

- History of UX and the rise of Human-Computer Interaction (HCI)
- Design Thinking and Human-Centered Design (HCD)
- User-Centered Design (UCD) Process and User-Driven Development (UDD)
- Software Development Methodologies
- Lean UX versus Agile UX
- UX & Design Disciplines
- Unique attributes of a User Experience (UX) Designer and a User Interface (UI) Designer

UX from the early 20th century

The origins of UX can be traced back centuries, but it was only in the early 19th century that UX started to mold into a distinct discipline. American engineer *Frederick Winslow Taylor* (1856-1915) pioneered the Industrial Revolution by giving birth to a movement called **Taylorism**, which focused on how workers interact with their tools to complete tasks efficiently. During the 1940s, Toyota developed a sociotechnical system, called the **Toyota Production System**, that was recognized as the first **Human Centered Production System** that focused on the interaction between humans and technology. Toyota's philosophy with this new system included constant improvement, no waste, and an emphasis on respecting team members. This approach included people as part of the improvement process, thus bringing back the human factor that was lost with Taylorism.

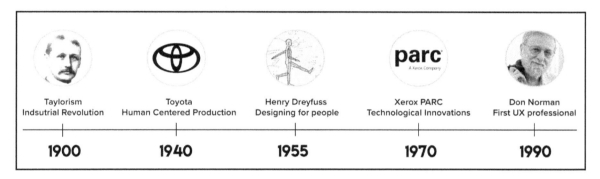

Taylorism	Toyota	Henry Dreyfuss	Xerox PARC	Don Norman
Indsutrial Revolution	Human Centered Production	Designing for people	Technological Innovations	First UX professional
1900	**1940**	**1955**	**1970**	**1990**

Fast forwarding to 1955, *Henry Dreyfuss*, an American industrial designer, wrote a classic design text called *Designing for People* in which he focused on people's experiences, good or bad, with the design of a product. One of the many useful points from his book is how to design for a variety of people with different sizes and abilities, to effortlessly use a service or product.

An excerpt from Dreyfuss's book:

When the point of contact between the product and the people becomes a point of friction, then the industrial designer has failed. On the other hand, if people are made safer, more comfortable, more eager to purchase, more efficient--or just plain happier--by contact with the product, then the designer has succeeded.

During the 1970s, a Xerox research center called *PARC (Palo Alto Research Center Incorporated)* explored the subject of innovations in workplace technology. This experimental project resulted in some groundbreaking technological innovations that we are still using today, for example, the **graphical user interface** (**GUI**), the bitmap graphic format (`.bmp`) for images, as well as the computer mouse to navigate with on a personal computer.

In the early 1980s, **human-computer interaction** (**HCI**) was established as a discipline that focused on computer science and human factors engineering, but has grown exponentially the past couple of decades into a broad discipline that focuses on a variety of specialties, such as ergonomics, sociology, cognitive processes of human behavior, accessibility, and human interface design, to name just a few.

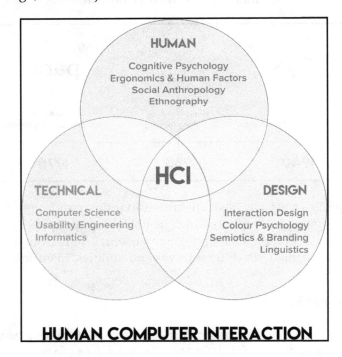

Before the rise of HCI as a discipline, the only people who interacted with computers were professionals in the field of information technology, but this changed with the first personal computer that was released in the late 1970s. Any person now had access to a personal computer and could use text editors, spreadsheets, and play computer games, and had the opportunity to learn programming languages. With the personal computer being a technological tool accessible to any person, the GUI, which is the visual interface the person uses to interact with the personal computer, was developed to make it easy to use. Soon after the GUI was implemented, computer screens became cluttered with hundreds of icons that made it hard to find files, and the first extension of HCI, the *search functionality*, was introduced for users to easily find what they were looking for. Another fundamental extension of HCI was in the 1980s when users were able to communicate with other users via email, which quickly expanded to instant messaging, online forums, and social networks, thus the interaction was not limited to using the computer to do personal tasks but to the computer becoming a *communication channel* with other humans. Throughout the 1980s, HCI expanded by introducing different devices. Users were not only using desktop computers but started using laptops and mobile phones that became available. From gradual *device expansion*, technology found its way into the daily lives of the user, such as in their cars and home appliances. It's clear from the path HCI has taken already that it will keep evolving with humans and become more integrated into their daily lives and in society.

Eventually, in the 90s, cognitive psychologist *Donald Norman* joined Apple as the vice president of the Advanced Technology Group and gave birth to the term *user experience* as we know it today.

> *Norman on creating the term user experience:*
>
> *I invented the term because I thought the human interface and usability were too narrow. I wanted to cover all aspects of the person's experience with a system, including industrial design, graphics, the interface, the physical interaction, and the manual.*

Norman's writings focus on the user's cognitive experience with products, especially with technological products. He wrote a widely influential text called *The Design of Everyday Things*. In this book, he promotes the usability and user experience, rather than aesthetics, of a product. Norman's focus on improving usability goes hand-in-hand with the person's perception of the product. Human-related sciences, technical advancement, and design focused disciplines all contribute to the improved interaction between a person and the technology they're using. People are different.

The way they learn and understand concepts, even their own personal perceptions of how they interact with technology, differ. American businessman and philanthropist *Charles Thomas Munger* established the theory of **mental models** in the early 90s in the business and finance realm and, from there, it's been expanded to many other industries, including UX. Due to mental models infiltrating many industries, there are many definitions. *Susan Carey* defined mental models in her 1986 journal article *Cognitive science and Science Education*, as follows:

> *A mental model represents a person's thought process for how something works (that is, a person's understanding of the surrounding world). Mental models are based on incomplete facts, past experiences, and even intuitive perceptions. They help shape actions and behavior, influence what people pay attention to in complicated situations, and define how people approach and solve problems.*

Carey's simplistic definition of mental models paves the way for UX professionals to create unique experiences that make sense to the user. The Nielsen Norman Group, one of the most influential leaders in the UX industry and founded by *Jakob Nielsen*, *Don Norman* and *Bruce Tognazzini* in 1998, highlights the following two points to keep in mind when working with the mental models and UX of a website:

1. **A mental model is based on belief, not facts**. Thus, the model is based on what the user knows or what they think they know about your website.
2. **Individual users each have their own mental model**. Different users will have different mental models of the same website.

The more the user interacts with your website, the more experience they will build up with the website, thus their mental model will change accordingly. The same way the user can interact with other websites that can also adjust to the user's mental model. It's imperative that the UI designer understands mental models and ensure their design patterns; layouts are consistent to reduce cognitive load. In the next chapter, we'll go into more detail on how to design accordingly regarding user's mental models to improve the user experience.

360° of UX

Now that we've covered the history of UX and understand the broad impact of UX as a usability measurement in a different context, we need to narrow it down to design thinking, human-centered design, and user-centered design as the core user-focused disciplines in which UX is rooted. At a quick glance, these disciplines all look the same, and they have similar steps and overlapping themes, but in essence, they have different outcomes. The type of project will determine the methodology used and required outcomes; there is no singular winning formula in UX.

Design thinking and human-centered design (HCD)

Design thinking is a methodology that was established in the late 60s to help businesses with creative problem-solving, and only became well known with the awareness of UX through IDEO, a global design company, during the early 90s. IDEO designed the first manufacturable mouse for Apple and was one of the market leaders in advancing HCD. According to IDEO, design thinking consists of five steps to creating anything of value (note that the focus is on anything of value, not necessarily a digital product, such as a website or mobile app).

1. **Empathize**: Understand the users you are designing a product or service for.
2. **Define**: From the research, define the user's needs.
3. **Ideate**: Generate as many ideas as possible to encourage innovation to solve the problem.
4. **Prototype**: Create a prototype to illustrate and test the idea.
5. **Test**: Use the prototype to test the idea with real users.

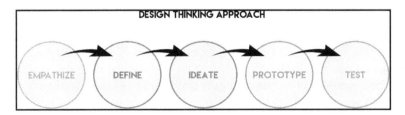

Design thinking is a methodology used on which to base UCD principles (which we'll discuss in more detail in the following section) and assist in the iterative process to problem solve and ensure the user's needs are met. IDEO has also developed useful toolkits to simplify design thinking in which one is to create a memorable acronym for HCD that is *hear*, *create*, and *deliver:*

1. **Hear**: It focuses on the people you're creating the solution for. What is it that the user desires? Is the proposed solution focusing on the needs of the user?
2. **Create**: It relates to the long-term benefits for the business. Is the solution that's being built for the user a viable option that's not just profitable but also a sustainable business model?
   1. **Deliver**: It relates to technology and the business' operational strength to create the solution. Does the solution strengthen the company's core operational capabilities as well as advance other areas of the company that are not as developed?

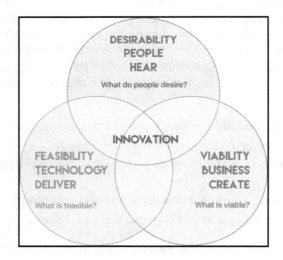

The focus is always on human-centered innovation to create practical and workable solutions for the user. These solutions are not limited to a digital product, such as a website or mobile app, but can be applied to any possible product the user interacts with, such as a bicycle, chair, or hairdryer. The terms design thinking, HCD, and UCD are used interchangeably in the industry and are commonly seen as the same thing. Even though they have some major overlapping similarities, they are indeed different. We've already discussed design thinking, so let's look at the definition of HCD before we dive into the UCD process.

Human-centered design (HCD) is an approach to interactive systems development that aims to make systems usable and useful by focusing on the users and their needs and requirements, and by applying human factors/ergonomics, usability knowledge, and techniques. This approach enhances effectiveness and efficiency; improves human well-being, user satisfaction, accessibility, and sustainability; and counteracts possible adverse effects of use on human health, safety, and performance. ISO 9241-210:2010(E)

HCD is the standard of usability based on the universal characteristics of people in general, while UCD is more focused on a segment of people and their personality traits and unique behavior.

User-centered design (UCD)

User-centered design (UCD) is the design philosophy that provides guidelines within the software development cycle to always focus on the user's wants, needs, and limitations to create the best possible end product for the user. This philosophy does not prescribe which tools to use and can thus be applied to waterfall or agile developments methodologies.

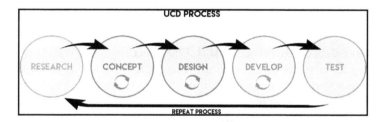

Even though many organizations adjust the UCD scope and the naming of steps, the basic foundation of the **UCD PROCESS** is always the same: **RESEARCH, CONCEPT, DESIGN, DEVELOP**, and **TEST**. After each cycle, iterations are made based on the users' feedback, thus improving the final product.

- **Research**: Conduct in-depth research that includes competitor benchmarking, field studies, focus groups, contextual, and individual interviews, just to name a few of the research techniques available, and collect sufficient data and insight into the user's needs to develop useful personas that will guide the rest of the UCD process.

- **Concept**: The data collected in the research phase will define the scope and requirements of the project, while the personas will guide the usability goals and user scenarios for the user testing that will be performed using paper prototypes. Challenges will quickly be highlighted by the user's interaction with the prototype and solutions can be proposed to streamline the concept.
- **Design**: At the design stage of the UCD process, the concept will be pretty solid with user-testing to support the project requirements and direction. The technical and functional requirements can be fleshed out in more detail with task flows, user journeys, wireframes, and prototypes together with visual designs of what the concept will look like after implementation.
- **Develop**: The concept can be rock solid and the visual designs breathtakingly beautiful, but if the implementation does not focus on meeting the best practice guidelines and accessibility standards, the usability of the product will be highly affected.
- **Test**: After implementation, the final product is tested using focus groups, field studies, customer surveys, performance analysis, and so on, to highlight any usability issues to improve the product during the next cycle. The UCD process is an iterative cycle that measures and evaluates the initial scope and requirements, and ensures the product is on track and improved with each cycle.

UCD, also called **user-driven development** (**UDD**), incorporates lean startup principles with the methodologies of agile development. The focus of UDD is to make the user part of the development cycle and not treat the user as an external factor. With this approach, the UX strategy will also need to adjust to the development cycle, depending on which software development methodology is being used, when creating a product.

Software development methodologies

Understanding the two main software development methodologies, waterfall and agile, will give more context to how the two main UX approaches, **Lean UX** and **Agile UX**, are related to each other, and the benefits of each.

- The waterfall methodology, a traditional project management approach to the process, focuses on sequential phases within software development. One step must be done before the next step can be started, hence the waterfall reference. This approach focuses on software developers first collecting the entire project's requirements before building the architecture, after which the design is done, followed by the development step and, finally, testing for deployment. With the waterfall approach, there is no room for iteration or improvement. When a step has passed, you cannot go back to make changes. This methodology that has been used for years is very rigid and does not allow for improvement, which contradicts the core essence of UX, which is iteration, testing, and improvement.

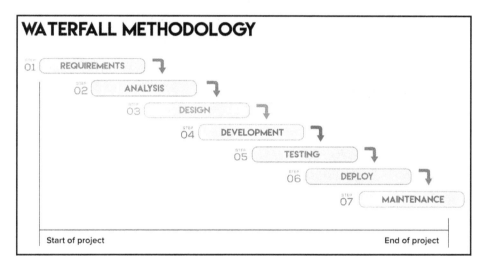

- The agile methodology is the modern software development approach that combines several iterative-focused practices to create a repetitive development cycle within the project life cycle. The development cycle consists of the same steps as the waterfall approach; the difference is that this development cycle will start from the first step as soon as the last step is done. This allows the different teams involved in the creation of the website to work on specific features (smaller parts within the bigger picture) and release it live for users to access. These features can be tested, and improvements can be made in future development cycles. In this context, the development cycle is done within a set period of time called a sprint. Depending on the company and project, this period of time can vary from one week to up to three weeks, in which a cross-functional team of specialists have to finish a specific set of development tasks for release. After the completion of these developments tasks, the **quality assurance** (**QA**) team will test and sign off for deployment.

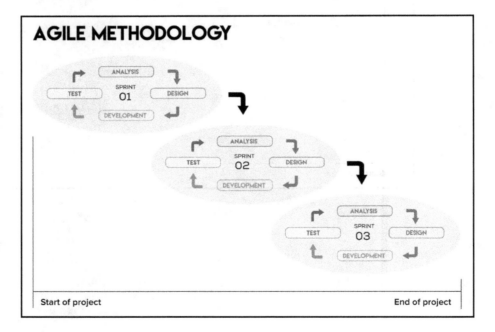

Lean UX versus Agile UX

The basic concept of Lean UX is an inexpensive, analytics-driven approach to create a **Minimum Viable Product** (**MVP**), and drive the development of the MVP with creating a demand in the market using user feedback.

A Minimum Viable Product (MVP) can be any product, not necessarily a digital product, but in this case, we refer to a digital product, which can be a software application, website, or mobile app, that only has the bare minimum features to make it usable by the user.

From the user's feedback interacting with this MVP, improvements are made in the development phase and then released again. Thus, the user's response is only measured after release and using the product. This approach unites product development and business through constant measurement and ensures a digital product can be created in a short period of time. The testing and validation of the product are done through three basic steps--build, measure, and learn.

Agile UX is derived from the agile methodology and incorporates short status meetings in regular intervals with cross-functional teams to improve communication. It's all about the collaboration of teams and the delivery of the product by uniting designers and developers during the product development cycle. What makes Agile UX effective is the fact that you're testing against fixed outcomes. You have full control over the amount of sprints needed to create a specific feature, and with each sprint you analyze, test, and reiterate every change made in the previous sprint. This ensures a continuous improvement of quality and refinement of the product.

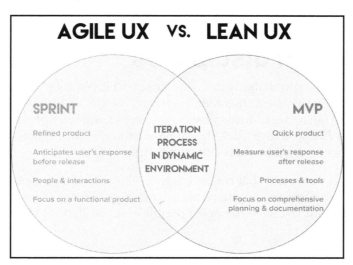

It's natural to assume that if you adopt a Lean UX or Agile UX approach, it will replace traditional UX. On the contrary, these approaches complement the tradition UX and make it more flexible to fit into the dynamic environments we find ourselves in when developing digital products. To put this statement in context, let's briefly look at what tradition UX is. Tradition UX relies on the core principles of design and usability; first do all the research and groundwork, and then go into development.

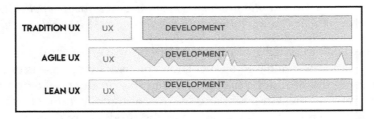

Agile UX produces a more refined, high-quality product, while Lean UX produces several products that are less refined but refinement increases with each released. It seems that Agile UX is perfect, so why bother with Lean UX? The original agile methodology focuses on an improved smooth process for software development and, unfortunately, design was never included in this process. Agile UX is about building a product faster with less risk, despite what it looks like. So, Agile UX is not so perfect after all. A lot of companies use both interchangeably, depending on the project. Agile UX fits naturally into the agile culture of software development, and Lean UX brings in the inexpensive data-driven approach to improvements. There is no right or wrong way. Use the methodologies that work within your environment and your project to deliver the best product for the user.

UX and design disciplines

The UX field of study is exponentially growing at such a rapid rate, and with this expansion comes a variety of different specialties that branch out of UX and into other design disciplines. Even though some of these disciplines seem similar (especially because most of them have the word *Design* in the title), they have distinctive focal points that differentiate one from the other and contribute to the bigger picture of HCD.

- **UCD**: Also called UDD, it is the design philosophy that provides the guidelines within a software development cycle to always focus on the user's wants, needs, and limitations to create the best possible end product for the user.

- **Iterative design**: It follows these UCD guidelines within a development cycle of a digital product that includes research, concept, design, develop, and test. After each cycle, iterations are made based on feedback results, thus improving the final product.
- **Product design**: It is the practice of creating an innovative new product for the user.
- **Interaction design (IxD)**: It looks at the way users interact with the product through different types of interaction, such as multitouch and gesture-based interfaces.
- **UX research**: It is also called user research or design research, and is the specialty of researching and analyzing the user's needs, behaviors, and motivations to interact with a product.
- **UX design**: It focuses on creating an overall satisfactory experience for the user when interacting with a product by improving the usability and accessibility.
- **UI design**: It ensures that all the touch points of the digital product are not just visually appealing but also support the user journeys and end goals of the user.
- **Visual design**: It is the practice of using color, typography, illustrations, and photography to communicate a message.
- **Industrial design**: It is the practice of designing concepts for manufactured products.
- **Service design**: It is the practice of aligning a company's infrastructure, employees, and services in such a way as to improve the quality of interaction between the company and the user.

From the list of UX and design disciplines here, it's clear that each specialty plays a significant role in the user's experience and interaction with any product (not just a digital product, such as a website or a mobile app). The two fields of study that are interlinked and sometimes mistakenly seen as the same discipline are UX and UI. In the next section, we'll discuss these two roles and the unique roles they play in the user's experience with a digital product.

The unique attributes of UX and UI

The misconception that UX and UI are the same disciplines creates some frustration with UX and UI designers, who are expected to perform tasks they're not always specialized in nor passionate about. Of course, there's always the exception of those who enjoy both UX and UI design and can effortlessly shift between the two. Both UX and UI designers focus on usability and improving the user experience, one more analytical and the other more visual. Here is a more detailed breakdown of each and how they complement each other:

- **UX designers** are strategic thinkers who have a conceptual approach to solving problems. They enjoy the challenge of diving into data and taking it apart by analyzing every possible element. UX designers understand the importance of every piece of information, even if it seems insignificant to others, it may have an impact on the bigger picture. No stone is left unturned during the research phase. They know that the UX strategy is just as strong as the data and research done. While UX designers are digging in the dirt, UI designers usually prefer not to get mud on their shoes. They usually wait for the UX designers to finish the digging and give guidance on how to convert the findings into an aesthetically pleasing and user-friendly website.
- **UI designers** are creative thinkers. They're skilled artisans with a visionary approach to taking data and using interaction design principles to create a website that's not just aesthetically pleasing but user-friendly as well. While a UI designer's focus is mainly on functional presentation of a website by crafting a smooth user interface, a UX designer's focus is on the interaction of the user with the website.

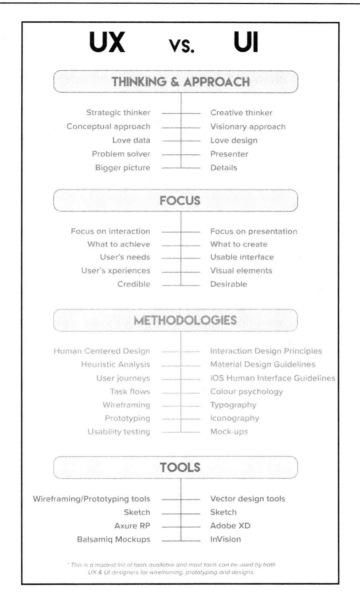

This preceding visual comparison is only an example to explain the main (not limited to) differences between the two specialties. There are many designers who enjoy both UX and UI design and can execute the tasks from both fields successfully. Also, keep in mind that the tools of the trade change often and the tools you use are purely personal preference or project-specific.

The list provided is merely a guideline of established applications and it's advised to try all the tools available. This will not just improve your overall skill set but give you a broader understanding of executing UX tasks within different environments.

Summary

Hopefully, you now have a better understanding of user experience as a discipline and the many facets of UX that contribute to creating high-quality digital products that tick all the usability boxes. Basic UX principles, such as HCI, design thinking, and UCD, are only a handful of the methodologies that contribute to UX as a whole. These methodologies have a never-ending cycle, which means the UX of a product is never done; it's an ongoing iterative process by choosing a suitable methodology for your product, for example, a cross-functional team collaboration with Agile UX or an analytical-driven approach, such as Lean UX. It's all about what is right for the project you're working on. In the first chapter, we mostly referred to *digital products*, as the concepts and methodologies discussed are usually applied to any digital product, but from this point forward, we'll focus on UX for websites only. In the next chapter, we'll look at best practices for creating user interfaces, including *Google Material Design and iOS Human Interface Guidelines*.

2
Stand Out from Your Competitors

Branding has been around since the time people first started trading goods. Originally, a brand was the representation of the person or company selling the goods such as a striking logo and a catchy tagline. But just as the trading industry has evolved more modern methods of trading, so have the brands to support them. Branding has evolved from being mainly a visual representation to a comprehensive sum of components that build a satisfying customer experience with the brand. It's within this sum of components that UX plays an integral role in the success of the brand. In this chapter, we'll explore the context of UX within these components, and how to utilize both to differentiate a brand from its competitors. Let's have a quick look at the topics covered in this chapter:

- Brand identity versus brand image
- Branding visuals, personality, and relationships
- The role UX plays to improve a brand's identity
- How to stand out from competitors
- Differences between B2B and B2C

Branding in modern times

Traditional branding is rooted in the perfect balance between *brand identity* and *brand image*. The brand identity is the visible visual elements of the brand, such as the brand's name and logo, typography, colors, and design elements that distinguish the brand from other brands in the user's mind, while the brand image is a combination of the perception and experience the user has with the brand, as well as how they view the brand's personality and values.

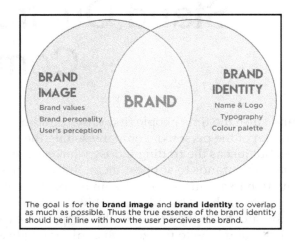

The goal is for the **brand image** and **brand identity** to overlap as much as possible. Thus the true essence of the brand identity should be in line with how the user perceives the brand.

In the new digital age, people's interaction with universally available brands has increased due to limitless access to the digital information available. For the first time, users can access vast amounts of information on the brand. Everything from advertisements, blog articles, product reviews, and so on is available for the user to access from their personal computer or mobile phone. This extensive link between the user and brand has given the user the power to help mold and shape the brands they interact with. Based on this brand evolution, the definition of a brand also needs to evolve to include the entire customer experience that's become more and more part of the brand today. The following is the definition of a brand by the *Nielsen and Norman Group*:

> *"A brand is a subjective perception of value based on the sum of a person's experiences with a product or company that ultimately influences that person's sentiment and decisions in the marketplace."*

Looking at this mature way the user interacts with the brand, the conclusion is that the brand does not just consist of the perfect balance between the brand image and brand identity as traditional standards expect, but also includes all the elements that make up the customer experience. The user observes the brand though *visuals* such as logos, typography, and more. Secondly, the user relates to the brand based on the brand's *personality*, the way the brand interacts with the user such as the tone of communication and lastly, through the *relationship* between the user and the brand. How does the brand treat the user when the user walks into the store or when the user calls the customer center?

Case study - brand identity versus brand image - Jeep

All brands have (or should have) brand guidelines that includes the basic rules of the brand's *identity* and *personality*. Such a brand guide includes guidelines on usage of colors, typography specifications, iconography, look and feel of imagery, the voice of the brand (the way copy and tag lines are written), and brand values (what the brand stands for), to name the most essential guidelines that are usually included. These set guidelines will not only guarantee that the brand is always represented in a consistent and professional manner, but will also ensure that the way the user perceives the brand is in line with the brand's identity. The following are a couple of examples from Jeep's brand guidelines:

- **Color guidelines**:
    - The logo will only be displayed in either *Jeep green* or *Jeep black;* each of these colors are predefined with a set Pantone, hex, and RGB value
    - The logo may be used as an inverted logo, thus white on *Jeep green* or white on *Jeep black*

- **Logo guidelines**:
    - The logo can never be displayed without the registered trademark symbol ®

- The logo may not be displayed with a drop shadow, with an opacity, or as a repeated pattern

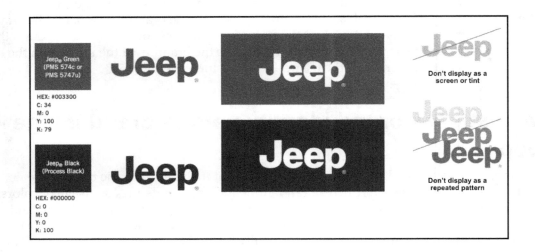

The following is the brand value taken from Jeep's website

"Our core values are embodied in every Jeep vehicle's DNA. Jeep vehicle owners have long known that **Go Anywhere. Do Anything.**® *is a way of life, not just a slogan."*

The slogan "Go anywhere. Do anything" empowers the user to challenge themselves, to believe that there are no boundaries and anything is possible with Jeep. The imagery used is illustrating just that. Jeep vehicles are photographed in rugged terrains that give the feeling that there are no boundaries when it comes to driving a Jeep. The terrain might be challenging, but that won't limit the adventure.

It's clear that the visual guidelines must reinforce the brand values, but it does not stop there. The brand's activity in the media and in society must also be in line. For example, Jeep's of road adventure experiences offered to users and their outstanding customer service also reinforces the brand image and the user's perception of the brand.

Branding - visuals

When creating the brand guidelines, it's important to ensure all aspects of the guide--logo, typography, color palette, iconography, and so on-- are created for all possible mediums the brand will channel to. In the digital age that we find ourselves in the brand guidelines must be flexible and cater for the dynamic ever-changing digital environments in which the brand will live. Within the visual context UX is making the brand visually adaptable to any possible scenario and platform it might find itself in:

- **Logo**: The basic guidelines for designing a logo look at the medium it will be used on such as print or digital. The next factor is color. Should the logo be full color or only use a spot color? Should the logo be flat design or have gradients? All these factors are important, but let's throw some UX factors into the mix:

  Is the logo simple enough, or can it be simplified to use as a favicon? A **favicon** is the small logo in the top of your browser tab when you open a website. The formatting of a favicon is 16x16 pixels or 32x32 pixels, which is pretty small. If you have a logo with too much detail, the logo will look blurry and sometimes unrecognizable on such a small scale.
  The following is an example of four well-known brands and their original logos:

  And, how they incorporated their logo to favicons for their websites:

  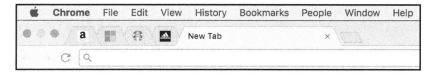

Let's take a detailed look at the favicons:

- *Amazon* did an amazing job of combining all elements, the black typography and orange arrow from the original logo into the favicon without making it busy and difficult to recognize the brand. Putting the elements in a white container reinforces the brand's look and feel.

- *Microsoft's* logo is simple enough to use as is in the favicon. It's ideal to have an icon or typography in the brand logo that can be used as a single recognizable visual element like the four squares of the Microsoft logo.

- *Starbucks'* logo is interesting and unique, but too detailed to simplify for smaller ratios. The favicon is blurry and barely recognizable as seen in the preceding screenshot. It is possible to create a new simplified version of the current logo to use for smaller ratios like favicons, app logos, and more by using, for example, just the star in a green circle as illustrated in the following screenshot.

- *Adidas'* original logo is designed well to be utilized for smaller ratios, but is just not implemented correctly for the web. By using just the three stripes, which is iconic of the Adidas brand, the favicon will be clear and easily recognizable, as illustrated in the following screenshot:

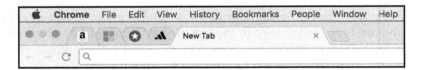

Can the logo fit into a square dimension? If your brand has an app or there's potential that there might be an app in the future, the logo must be scalable to be used on different devices such as iOS or Android. All apps have icons displayed as entry points to access the app. This point can be illustrated clearly through the previous favicon example, which is also a square dimension.

- **Typography**: The origin of typography is deeply rooted in print where the letters lived on a physical surface, which larger letters which are more easily readable than in the current digital era, where we have to cater for smaller letters, that live within an environment of light glaring from computer and mobile screens. Due to the amount of hours we spend on these devices, typography online has become a lot more important to reduce strain on the eyes and improve readability of the copy.

Keep the typeface simple. People work on personal computers, students study on their laptops, and most people stare at a computer or phone screen between 3-10 hours a day. Thus reading on screen can put unnecessary strain on a person's eyes if the typeface is too detailed or too small for the device. Typography is divided into two main types of typefaces, namely **Serif typefaces** and **Sans typefaces**. The following is a clear example of the difference between the two typefaces and a short explanation of which typeface works better for print and digital:

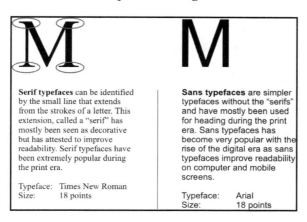

Serif typefaces can be identified by the small line that extends from the strokes of a letter. This extension, called a "serif" has mostly been seen as decorative but has attested to improve readability. Serif typefaces have been extremely popular during the print era.

Typeface: Times New Roman
Size: 18 points

Sans typefaces are simpler typefaces without the "serifs" and have mostly been used for heading during the print era. Sans typefaces has become very popular with the rise of the digital era as sans typefaces improve readability on computer and mobile screens.

Typeface: Arial
Size: 18 points

It's also good practice to have a webfont version of the font you're using for the website. A webfont is a font that's not pre-installed on the user's computer when browsing a website, but instead the webfont reference is coded in the backend and is downloaded when the user opens the website in a browser. This will allow you to use a wide variety of fonts outside of the basic Arial and Verdana fonts that usually come standard when a personal computer is purchased. You can find an endless source of webfonts online on Google Fonts: `https://fonts.google.com/`

- **Color palette**: The color palette within the brand guidelines is probably the most tricky to create. Based on the mediums in which the brand will be represented, the colors used will have a great impact on the messages conveyed to the user.

Does your color palette include colors used for *system notifications and warnings* such as error messages when the user fills in a form incorrectly? It's easy right, error messages are red, but what if one of your brand's primary colors is red like *Virgin Atlantic*? In the following screenshot, the **Check in** form lives within a container with shades of red as the background:

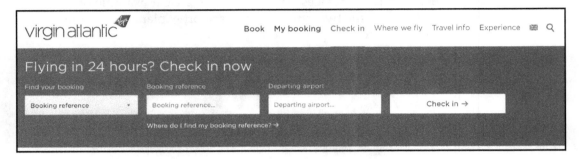

- The error message iconography and copy is also red, which does not allow the error message to stand out within the form elements.

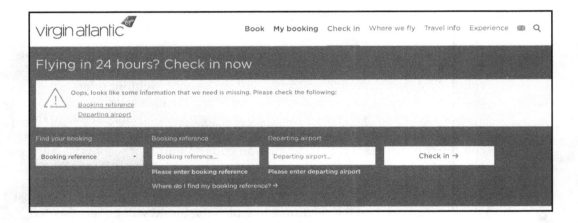

Another example is if your color palette consists of many colors such as red, green, blue, orange, and yellow, would notification messages stand out within the UI? Will the user easily notice the notification or is there a chance that the notification can get lost with all the colors present on the UI? The following is an example of Taco Bell's login form, which consists of black, blue, gray, turquoise, pink, and red. As you can see, it's really hard to notice the error messages within the form:

Is the color palette accessible? Do the colors comply with the **Web Content Accessibility Guidelines** (**WCAG**) standards? At a later stage in this book we'll discuss accessibility in design in more detail.

- **Iconography**: When iconography is used, will it be clear to all users using the website, despite cultural and technical backgrounds? We won't go into detail again as we already discussed this topic in the previous chapter.

These are just a couple of visual touch points to highlight how UX is an integral part of the brand. The presentation layer of a brand is important, it's the experience the user has with the brand that can make or break the relationship between the user and the brand.

Branding - personality

The *brand essence* is the heart of the brand, the core values and vision, who the brand is and what the brand is promising its customers. These attributes of the brand essence are in fact the same attributes that are included in the *value proposition* of a digital product. Where the brand essence is high level and focuses on the core values of the brand as a person, a *value proposition* can be crafted for specific parts of the brand, for example, the promise of value the product (your website or mobile application) is giving to the user, or the promise of value the customer call center of your brand is giving to the user. Thus there can be several value propositions with core values and ways in which these sections, be it the website, the mobile app, or the customer call center will satisfy the users needs. Later in the book we'll go into detail of how to create a value proposition and the benefits of creating one. For now it's important to know that the brand essence and the value proposition of a digital product such as a website are essential to one another. These two should overlap as much as possible to ensure the brand is true to itself and all teams within the company are working towards the same goal.

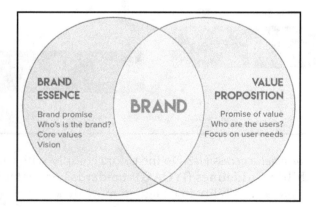

The brand is a personality with core values and vision, it has promises of value and is available to interact with the user on different levels. The same way a human interacts with another human depending on the circumstances, so too does the brand have unique behavior patterns to interact with the user depending on context.

Branding - relationship

The relationship between the brand and the user stretches from the digital world all the way across to real-life interactions. The array of touch points, which are any possible contact points the user will have with the brand such as the website or the store where the product can be bought, all contribute to the overall **customer experience** (**CX**) and invoke an emotional connection and build a loyal relationship. In the next chapter, we'll look at building emotional connections with users in more detail. A brand's behavior in the digital world includes interactions with users through the website, email communication, or social media. The way the website communicates information through imagery, brand guidelines, and UI animations to the personalization of emails, tone of email copy, and the frequency of emails being sent all add to the relationship dynamic between the brand and the user. Behavior on social media is a very powerful channel for building brand-user relationships. Not only is it public, but the user can directly interact with the brand on a more person level, the same way the user interacts with family and friends. The brands behavior in real life has to support the brand's personality online and its core values throughout every possible contact point the user will have with the brand.

Apple is by far one of the best examples of a brand that strongly pursues customer experience and takes building a relationship with the user very seriously. Apple understands that the smallest detail can contribute to a memorable customer experience and leaving the user with a willingness to go through that customer experience, again and again. Let's look at the cycle of buying an Apple product and the little details that promote the "Apple experience":

1. The *Apple iStore* naturally draws attention. The interior is light, futuristic, and if you look closely, the color palette used consists mainly of neutral colors such as white and silver, White is known to symbolize perfection and purity, subconsciously a person is drawn to it. A small percentage of the palette consists of blue, known to have a relaxing effect on the human psyche, or purple, that is known to be a luxurious color. Blue and purple are usually seen on the wallpapers of devices. It is an enjoyable user experience being in the iStore.

2. Other than the brick and mortar presence of Apple, the *iStore staff* are friendly and helpful. The staff don't have to convince the customers to buy an Apple product, the product already has an exceptional reputation, the staff are merely there to assist in the user experience.

3. After the purchase, you take the experience home. The *package design* of an Apple product is not just aesthetically pleasing, but also absolutely practical. Every cable, connector, or instruction manual is neatly packaged with a custom-wrapper. The experience of opening the product is delightful.

4. When you interact with the actual *product*, the quality is tangible. The casing is beautiful to look at, the material is durable, and the touch of the product almost feels like velvet. The experience of handling the product is pleasurable.

5. Lastly, the *functionality* of the product easy to use. When you start your new MacBook for the first time, the wizard seamlessly takes you through all the steps. There are no additional installations and the full process takes you less than 15 minutes to get up and running. The experience of interacting with the operating system is effortless.

It's clear that every touch point contributes to the overall experience and relationship of the brand, but, within a highly competitive digital and e-commerce space, the brand will need to differentiate itself from its competitors in a more in-depth way than just products. This is where UX gives a brand the edge to really stand out against competitors. The way a user feels and experiences the brand is more valuable than just having a great product. From the high-level touch points we've touched on during the cycle of buying an Apple product, it's clear that each point focuses on enticing a specific sense or emotion to reinforce the user's experience with the brand. Thus, good UX (the user's experience during interaction with the product) promotes great CX (the customer's experience with all the touch points while purchasing a product) and collaboratively manifests a solid **brand experience** (**BX**) that can push a brand to new heights and great profits.

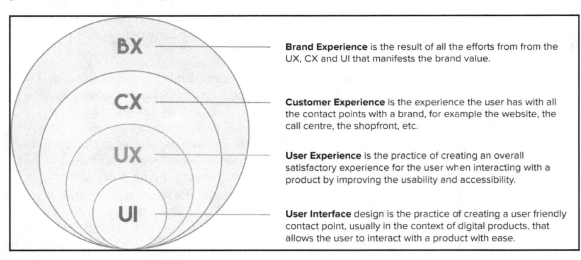

Brand Experience is the result of all the efforts from from the UX, CX and UI that manifests the brand value.

Customer Experience is the experience the user has with all the contact points with a brand, for example the website, the call centre, the shopfront, etc.

User Experience is the practice of creating an overall satisfactory experience for the user when interacting with a product by improving the usability and accessibility.

User Interface design is the practice of creating a user friendly contact point, usually in the context of digital products, that allows the user to interact with a product with ease.

Although in this book we'll only focus on digital products, specifically *UX for Web*, it's important to never lose sight that UX is in everything you do for a user.

How UX differentiates a brand from competitors

SWOT analysis is a traditional marketing methodology used in strategic business planning to identify internal and external factors that can influence the company's goals; these factors can be divided into **STRENGTHS, WEAKNESSES, OPPORTUNITIES,** and **THREATS.** The first two factors are based on the internal resources, such as financial resources, employees, patents, and copyrights, that are available to the company to utilize company strengths and improve weaknesses. The last two factors are based on external influences, such as market trends, demographics, environmental and economic regulations, which affect all companies.

For a UX SWOT analysis, the traditional SWOT analysis is used as the foundation, and UX components are analyzed accordingly. From the preceding diagram, the **STRENGTHS** and **WEAKNESSES** are of your own website, for example, the search functionality is easy to use and provides accurate search results, while the fact that your website is not responsive will have a negative impact on the overall experience.

Your competitor's weakness is an opportunity for you to stand out and provide a better experience, for example, if your website complies with accessibility standards and allows a wider variety of people to access it. In the same way your competitor's strengths can be real threats, for example, if your website's page loads are not optimized, users would much rather go to your competitor's website.

Conducting a competitor UX analysis

Traditional competitor analysis in marketing terms focuses on aligning the marketing strategy with the business vision by defining the scope and nature of the industry, who are the direct and indirect competitors, and what are the key components to compare with these competitors. Comparisons can include location (where the retail stores are based), price, quality of product or service, and convenience, to just name a few. A competitive UX analysis differs from the traditional competitor analysis in the sense that the focus is not just on internal and external sources, but rather on how the competitors compare in *overall user experience* and *usability standards*.

It's more than just comparing websites and weighing up the design effectiveness and differentiation, but rather evaluating the way the site is used and if the user enjoys interacting with it. Don't forget that a website has deeper user interactions that also need to be evaluated, such as the feedback loop from filling in an online form, subscribing to newsletters, chat bots, and so on. All these interactive components contribute to the overall experience and usability of the website. An easy trap to fall into when doing a competitor analysis is copying the competition's website, functionality, or strategy. Imitation seems harmless, but it's important to always stay true to offering a unique experience. What works for another brand's website might not be the best solution for your website.

A typical competitor UX analysis is between 2-4 competitors; the more you add into the equation the more complicated the process, which can skew results. Competitors can be divided into two categories:

- **Direct competitors**: Who have the same product, service, or users
- **Indirect competitors**: Who have similar products and services, but different users

The criteria for a competitor UX analysis is dependent on the brand and outcomes needed, sometimes a high level analysis is sufficient and other times an in-depth analysis that focuses on the smallest interaction of a specific component is needed.

Either way the following list of criteria is a basic list that should be used as a foundation for any competitor UX analysis:

1. **Content**: The content on the website needs to be useful and structured in such a way that the user can easily find what they're looking for. For example, the way pages are structured within the site, the way the menus are laid out for navigation, and the naming of headings and labels for links and form elements.

2. **Creative**: The aesthetic look of the website needs to be in line with the brand identity and at the same time be innovative and trendy.

3. **Heuristic principles**: The 10 heuristic principles for UI design from the *Norman and Nielsen Group* include crucial usability points to be incorporated in the analysis such as consistency, visible system notifications, error prevention, and the freedom for the user to be in control. The full list of 10 principles will be discussed in greater detail later in the book and can be found on the *Norman and Nielsen Group*'s website: `https://www.nngroup.com/articles/ten-usability-heuristics/`

4. **Micro-interactions**: Micro-interactions do not refer to tacky animations with no real purpose, but rather the way the website responds when the user interacts with it. For example, does the navigation slide out smoothly? Or does it just appear?

5. **Customer service**: When filling in a "request a quote" form, how quickly does a customer service agent respond? Sometimes websites have a chat component in the bottom right of the website screen. When using this service, how helpful is the person on the other side?

One of the factors that can skew results of the competitor UX analysis is if the person conducting the analysis has limited insights into the competitive market or the brand. Having more than one person doing the evaluation will ensure that there's different perspectives and no biased insights. Another factor to keep in mind is that the industry is constantly evolving. Brands are constantly revising their products and services, coming up with new ways on how to promote them, launching new campaigns, and so on. Thus a competitor UX analysis needs to be done on a regular basis to stay relevant.

Case study - competitor UX analysis of fast food brands

This case study focuses on the fast food industry. You have just been employed by McDonald's to relook the user experience of the McDonald's website. Within the UX process one of the things you'll look at is if the McDonald's website is standing its own against the competitors:

1. **Identify competitors**: The following are screenshots of the home page from each of the competitors included in the competitor analysis. Please keep in mind that at the time of publishing this book, these visuals might have changed.

Even though there are many competitors that can be used for this case study, we settled on Burger King as the direct competitor and KFC for the indirect competitor. Burger King is a direct competitor because the products sold at Burger King and McDonald's are mostly the same. Chicken and beef burgers with chips and drinks.

KFC is an indirect competitor because KFC is also a fast food chain, but it only sells chicken and no beef, as the direct competitor to the same user.

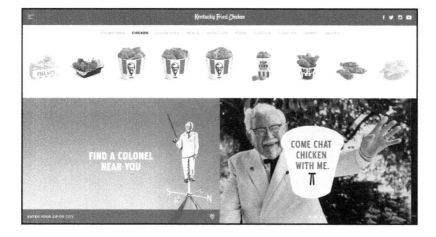

2. **Content and navigation**: The labels of McDonald's main navigation have quite a lot of links and are quite small, which might confuse the user. With the white on black text it's also hard to read and distinguish between the different links. When a link is selected the entire page jumps as it's loading the images, which makes it hard to browse the website.

Burger King's main navigation page is clear and easy to read. The typography supports the brand identity and the site is easy to navigate.

KFC's content is clearly structured in categories and each product has its own page with the relevant information. The active and inactive states of the link color (grey versus black), as well as the fade out images, make it clear where the user is in the navigation.

3. **Aesthetics and style**: McDonald's use of color is not reinforcing the brand. The home page looks a bit bland with only the logo in color. Also, the main image when the user enters the site is of soft drinks and not a juicy burger. The hero image can be more enticing. The presentation of the product looks appetizing.

The deals are clear with a creative touch to keep it interesting.

Burger King's use of color is excellent. The brand is well represented and the hero image is clear and enticing. They use a different angle to display the burger with separate ingredients, rather than just a burger as used in most burger adverts. The products are clear on a white background, which makes them stand out more.

The deal's design style follows the traditional "sale look" of a big bold price and *call to action* on an image.

KFC is using all visual elements to support the brand identity. The color palette is spot on and amplifies the product range beautifully.

KFC follows the same clear product on white background approach, but the promotions are not as clearly marked as the other competitors; it disappears within the main navigation.

KFC promotions

4. **Heuristic analysis**: McDonald's form validation has clear notification messages to explain to the user what's gone wrong and what's expected. However, the design is not simplistic and the overwhelming visuals can be distract the user from finding what they're looking for.

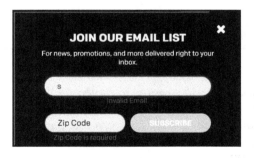

Burger King's website is simplistic and mostly consistent, thus the user knows at all times where they are on the website and what they're looking at. There are no areas within the website where the user can move outside the bounds of what's available for interaction, and thus no system notifications are present.

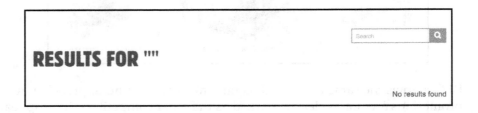

KFC's browsing experience is mostly consistent, though where the user does interact with system notifications such as error messages in the form validation, the styling could be more clear and the message, more descriptive, for example, by using "*Please add your first name*" instead of "**This is a mandatory field**", which sounds very impersonal.

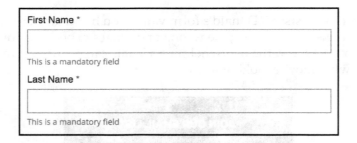

5. **UI animations**: McDonald's seems to have no UI animation, except when the main navigation expands. Moving through the website pages has a jerky effect and there are not smooth traditions from one page to another.
Burger King also seems to have no UI animation, except for the slider on the home page. The transition between pages when navigating through the website is abrupt and the pages jump from one to another.
KFC is utilizing the UI animation the best from all the brands. The burger menu opens in a sequence and also KFC uses a loader if images take too long to load.

From the high-level categories we briefly discussed, the following comparison table can be drawn up. Please keep in mind that each of these categories can be discussed in a lot more detail and this case study is just a guide to get you started on your own competitor analysis. The following matrix was used to calculate the scores within the table; you can draw up your own matrix and set your own guidelines for the evaluators to score:

- **Score 1-3**:
    - **1**: If the competitor has none of the elements present
    - **2**: If the competitor has 20% of the required elements present, but they've been executed poorly
    - **3**: If the competitor has 20% of the required elements present and they are executed well
- **Score 4-7**:
    - **4**: If the competitor has 30-45% of the required elements present and the execution is evenly balanced between excellent but could have been better
    - **5**: If the competitor has 45-60% of the required elements present and the execution is evenly balanced between excellent but could have been better
    - **6**: If the competitor has 60-70% of the required elements present, the execution is evenly balanced between excellent but could have been better
    - **7**: If the competitor has 70-80% of the required elements present, the execution is evenly balanced between excellent but could have been better
- **Score 8-10**:
    - **8**: If the competitor has 80% of the required elements present, but the execution could've been done better
    - **9**: If the competitor has 90% of the required elements present, but they've been executed well

- **10**: If the competitor has all the required elements present and they've been executed well

	McDonalds	Burger king	KFC
Content & Navigation	5	9	9
Aesthetics & style	6	9	9
Heuristic Analysis	5	5	5
UI Animation	3	2	8
	4.7	6.2	7.7

As you can see from the score matrix in the case study we scored well-executed elements higher than having more elements present but executed poorly. **Quality over quantity** goes a long way with user experience. It is better to have less features and implement them correctly than have features that are not working as well as they should and impact the enjoyment of the user.

B2B versus B2C

When designing an e-commerce website, one of the first things to determine is, who you're designing for? Are you selling to other businesses or are you selling to consumers? Designing for **B2B** (**business-to-business**) is quite different than designing for **B2C** (**business-to-consumer**). Both parties are still human at the end of the day, thus the basic UX principles apply for both approaches. It's certain aspects of the user experience that need be tweaked to cater for the user's needs, which is different if the user is actually a group of individuals (B2B) versus an individual (B2C):

- **B2C characteristics**:
    - With B2C there is just *one decision maker* and the time it takes to make a decision is normally quick.
    - The B2C purchase is usually *strongly motivated by emotion* as the user is buying a product or service for themselves or someone they know. Thus the brand image plays a crucial role in influencing the emotion of the user, and as a result the decision making.
    - The product is usually straightforward and *easily available*.

- With accessible products, the *pricing structure is mostly basic*. Pricing is transparent and the user knows upfront what the product or service will cost. Additional costs such as shipping are always visible on an e-commerce website and in most cases the user has the option to up-sell their product by adding additional extras such as a laptop bag when buying a laptop. With additional costs there are also discount vouchers and loyalty programs. The user knows in advance what the total price of the item is when making the decision.
- The purchasing *flow is uncomplicated*. The user chooses the product or service, adds personal details such as delivery address, and makes the payment.

Because the B2C user can choose from a variety of websites, their decision to buy from a specific website is heavily influenced by brand, the price, and of course the user experience of the website. Users will not return to a website with a lengthy checkout process that is confusing, neither will they pay more for a product that they can get from another website if the brand image is not solid. Brand loyalty plays an important role in a B2C user's decision-making process and typically goes hand in hand with user experience.

- **B2B characteristics**:
    - With B2B there is a *group of individuals* that stands behind the final decision, and the time to make a decision is much longer than with B2C as the decision will have to follow the correct channels within a company and be approved by more than one person. This group of individuals is divided into *choosers* and *users; users* are the individuals that will use the product or service within the organization, while choosers are the individuals that will make the final decision if it's really needed and make the purchase. Often the user will need to justify the need for the product or service, thus ensure the content on the website supports both the needs of the users and choosers.
    - The B2B purchase is *not emotional* in the sense of personal motivations or impulse buying, but rather an emotion of responsibility such as considering the impact the decision will have on a team.

- The *product or service is typically complex*. One of the factors that makes these types of products complex is the number of people that will use the product, for example, buying software licenses. The price for one licenses usually differs to an option for 5-10 people using the licenses, or more than 30 people and then there's an unlimited licenses. Another factor is time. How long is this licenses valid? Is it only for 30 days, a year, or an unlimited period? With most products or services the B2B user can choose additional support or maintenance for the purchase, which complicates it even more.
- The pricing structure thus needs to accommodate all these different components of a product and service, which makes the *pricing structure quite complicated* and also the price of a B2B product a lot higher.
- With the complex pricing tiers, the checkout flow needs to cater for all the possible combinations for the B2B user to build their own custom product or service. Also, the company details require additional information such as business billing information, tax numbers, and so on, which makes the *checkout flow more comprehensive* than B2C.

The B2B user is mainly focused on cost-effective pricing structures and quality of the product or service, which means the option for the user to build their own custom product to fit their team's needs within their budget is the main decision driver. No company will agree to pay for a service they'll not utilize 100%. Brand loyalty also plays an important role within the decision-making progress, but taps into a different angle than the B2C user. For the B2B user it's important to do business with a brand that has a flexible product or service and excellent customer support. There are some key points to consider when adding content to your website to support the B2B customer through the purchasing process:

- **Supportive content**: For the user who is in the early research phase, content to explain what solutions the product or service is offering, together with supporting content such as case studies, technical white papers, and buying guides will be very helpful to a user to consider the product or service.
- **Analytical content**: Provide concrete data and analytics to the user and choose to allow them to compare the solutions of your product or service with your competitors.

- **Sharing of content**: Because the purchase decision is a collaborative group effort, the user will most likely need to share relevant information to convince the chooser of the benefits of the product or service. Allow sharing options of products, reviews, and shopping carts for the user to share the necessary information.

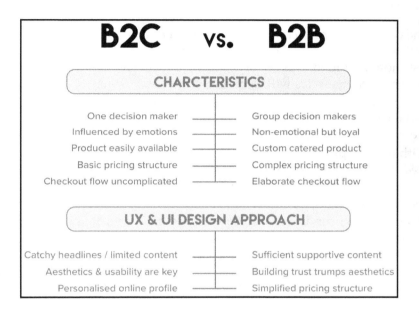

Now that we've identified the main characteristics that influence the B2C and B2B user, let's look at the approaches to design for these users' needs.

B2C design approach:

- The content strategy should ideally focus on *catchy headlines and no excessive content*. The user doesn't want too much to read about the products. If there is a need to provide large amounts of content then this should be cleverly managed within the UI with accordions.
- Due to the fact that the product for the B2C user is most likely available on several other websites, the *aesthetics and usability* of the website is critical for decision making.

- Although the B2C checkout flow is naturally uncomplicated, it's easy to lose focus and complicate the flow with too many unnecessary fields, or not supplying the B2C user with the information they need to finalize the purchase. Offer the user with easy checkouts by creating an *online profile* where future checkouts can be done with one click.

B2B design approach:

- The cost of the product or services is higher, thus the B2B user needs *as much content as possible* to make an informed decision. Supportive content such as testimonials, videos, FAQs, or blogs are beneficial to convince the B2B user that the product or service will cater to their needs.
- An aesthetically pleasing website is always valuable to influence users, but in the B2B user's case *building trust* and providing the sufficient content to encourage the decision-making process is crucial.
- With the complex buying cycle of the B2B product or service the *pricing structure needs to be simplified* and easy to understand. If the pricing structure is too complex or confusing the B2B user will rather go to a competitor with a more user-friendly layout.
- Offer the B2B user different *communication options* such as a telephone number to a support center or emergency contact, online queries forms, and online demo requests.

Case study - B2C and UX

In this B2C case study we'll look at a South African online kitchen and homeware store, *Yuppiechef*. Yuppiechef is well known in South Africa for their quality products, aesthetically pleasing UI, and personalized user experience. The online store offers a wide variety of products, from low-priced sale goods to exclusive appliances in higher price ranges.

Even though similar type products can be bought from several other websites online, Yuppiechef's products are always high quality and have a certain level of exclusivity to them such as unique colors and product design.

The UI of the website is minimalistic with no excess colors, visual elements, or content to distract the user from the products. The color palette consists of different shades of gray and white and this palette functions as a blank canvas to allow the products to be clearly and stylishly presented.

There is no complicated pricing structure, but the use of red as a positive reinforcement to make a purchase is debatable. Although red can be associated with danger, it's also an active color that promotes movement. Subtle visual elements to promote valuable content, such as the four colors available for the kettle and the case of six bottles of beer, assist the B2C user in their decision-making progress by giving the information up front and letting the user search for the additional information.

The main banner on the home page gives the user the option to browse all products by high-level categories based on the user's interests, instead of just displaying a list of the product categories as most websites do.

When the user views the full details of a product, a **call to action** (**CTA**) block is displayed with all the available options the user has for this particular product in one place. The user can change the product's color or the quantity in one click. The **Add to Cart** button is clear, but not overwhelming. At the bottom of the CTA block there's a security promise to reinforce the trust and credibility of the website; this message is visible in the footer at all times as well as during the checkout flow.

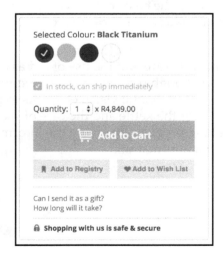

During the checkout there's a step indicator at the top of the page to show the user where they are in the process; this helps improve the perception of the user when checking out on an e-commerce website. If the user it not aware of the amount of steps or information required to reach the end goal it might have a negative impact. Imagine walking in a dark tunnel blindfolded, if you just have to take one step at a time and concentrate on not falling over obstacles, the distance will feel a lot further than if you were not blindfolded and could see the light at the end of the tunnel. The knowledge of knowing where you're going and what's expected makes the journey easier. It's the same with a checkout flow. Making the step indicators clickable is another way of allowing the user to manage their own journey so they'll be able to go back and edit each step.

Also notice that at the top of the page the user has the option to require help through the customer service or check on shipping information. The user is not expected to leave the checkout flow for this content as it's easily accessible.

Case study - B2B and UX

The B2B case study analyzes the *Adobe's Creative Cloud* website. This is an excellent example of combining B2C and B2B users, which makes it more complicated as each user has a different set of needs that will motivate the decision-making process. Other than combining both B2C and B2B users, the product on offer is not just for individuals or companies, but both B2C and B2B can choose selected software applications within the collection of the Adobe Creative Cloud.

For example, a company is working on an in-house magazine project. They need 1x unlimited Adobe Photoshop licenses, 3x Adobe InDesign licenses for three months only, and 20x Adobe Acrobat licenses valid for six months. The combination of individuals, teams, timeframes and support can become very complicated, but Adobe has created an easy-to-understand layout to deal with the complexity.

They cleverly added four tabs at the top to allow the user to navigate to the section that would apply to their situation and needs:

- **B2C** : **Individuals** and **Students and Teachers**
- **B2B** : **Business** and **Schools and Universities**

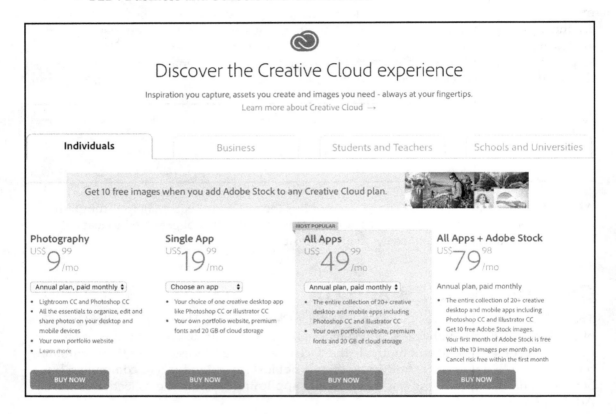

For individuals (B2C) the products are listed in column format to give a clear comparison between the options available. The headings for each option are simple with one-word explanations of what needs will be addressed below each heading, for example, under **Photography** the user will know that the list will contain photography-related items. Within the dropdown underneath the price, the user can choose which package they would like to sign up for. The compact presentation of all the necessary information the user will need to make a decision is in one place. The user is not expected to go looking for any information elsewhere.

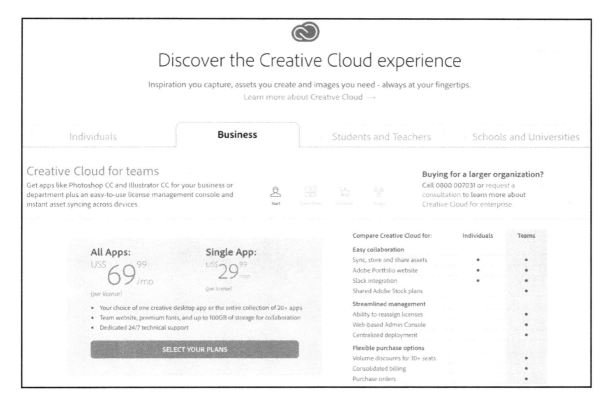

The plans for *business* (B2B) are a bit more complex than B2C as other than the option to choose a single product opposed to a combination of products, the B2C packages offer collaboration between team members, integration with third-party applications, management of licenses, and discounts for large volumes. This all depends on the company's available budget, and which applications will be necessary for which team members over different timeframes. It's clear that these types of purchases take time and an audit will have to be done in-house to establish what the exact needs are, and then for these needs to be signed off from the different team managers. To reduce the complexity of the decision making, Adobe skillfully adds a step indicator at the top to show how "easy" it is to purchase and adds contact details to assist with the decision making.

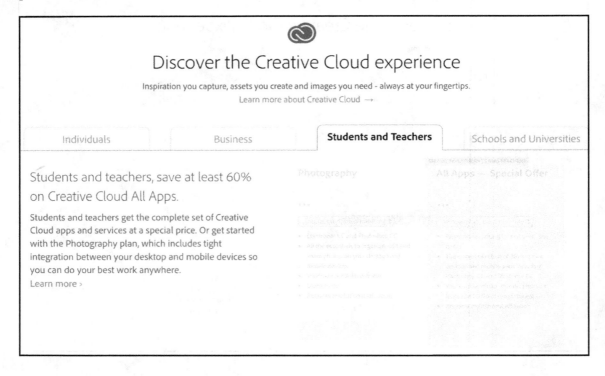

Students and Teachers and **Schools and Universities** fall into a unique B2C and B2C category as they are both related to the education industry and qualify for discounts. This is a manual process that needs to be driven by human interaction.

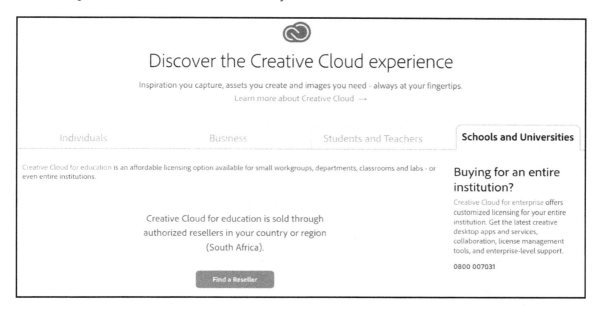

Summary

From the content in this chapter we can clearly see that branding and UX are inseparable, and methodologies used for both overlaps in some instances and combining these methodologies just strengthens the brand. The brand essence and brand guidelines should never be developed without the input of the UX team to assist with contextual input of platforms used, such as websites or mobile apps. In the next chapter, we'll use the knowledge we've gained from understanding brands better, their interaction with the user and direct and indirect competitors, to build a stronger emotional connection with the user.

3
Creating an Emotional Connection with the User

UX designers, UI designers, and Product Managers are all constantly looking for new and innovative ways to create unforgettable user experiences through cutting edge technology, usability standards and innovative aesthetics in the UI design. In the previous chapters we looked at the use of color, UI design, and brand elements that help build a relationship between user and brand. Just like any relationship between humans, these theoretical attempts at building a lasting relationship between user and brand are pointless without emotion. So how do you create an emotional connection with the user? More importantly, how do you keep that emotional relationship alive in an online world with excessive marketing campaigns and an endless list of products and services to choose from? The following topics, discussed in this chapter, will help create and keep that emotional connection with the user:

- Creating a digital personality the user can relate to
- Familiar tone of voice when communicating with the user
- Micro-interactions as rewards in the UI
- Give guidance through anticipation design
- Establish trust and credibility

Creating a digital personality the user can relate to

For the user, a human, to step into an emotional relationship with another human, brand, or technology the user must relate to the other party on the same level. People are mostly attracted to other people based on their values and personality. Someone with a good sense of humor makes people laugh and tends to be a popular person to be around. In the same way, someone with a nurturing personality that always makes sure the people in their presence are well fed and comfortable reinforces trust. Personality traits express emotions and fortify meaningful interactions with other people.

Just like some personality traits that you have control over and others you don't, in the same way you don't always have control over how your design's personality might be accepted by a user. For example, if the website design's main color is yellow (because this is the brand's color), there's nothing you can do when a user who is not fond of yellow perceives the design negatively. In another instance the user may not like horses, but the brand has a horse element incorporated in the logo and this element is thus reinforced throughout the website design. The use of this visual element might have a negative impact on building an emotional connection with the user, but again this is out of the designer's power.

Even though you cannot control every emotional cue with the user, you can focus on the elements that you can control. In his book, *Emotional Design: Why we love (or hate) everyday things*, Don Norman explains the three levels of visual design and how they can be incorporated with emotional cues to build products that are not just beautiful and functional, but that interact with the user on an emotional level:

- **Visceral design**: Relates to the user's intuitive reaction to a design based on basic biological preferences. This reaction is an inborn notion that comes from spontaneous human decision-making with an immediate emotional response. Visceral design impacts the way the user reacts and feels when looking at a design for the first time.
- **Behavioral design**: Relates to the user's functional approach to a design based on usability. The way the user uses a piece of functionality on a website, effortlessly or with frustration, taps into the the behavior design. Functionality comes first.
- **Reflective design**: Relates to the user's referential connection to a design based on association, be it cultural or through personal experience. The user's background and personal perception of concepts will influence the way a design is perceived and how the user feels afterwards.

The success of a website can be awarded to the perfect balance of these three levels of design; one is not superior to the other and they cannot function independently. Every website triggers a visceral reaction through first impressions of the design, the behavioral interaction supports the usability and functional use of the website, and the reflective attribute reinforces the entire experience with the user's personal emotional connection with the website.

Maslow's Hierarchy of Human Needs is a motivational theory in psychology invented by Abraham Maslow in 1943 to explain the way humans are motivated by their needs. Maslow theorized that the most basic physiological needs, such as physical requirements for human survival like food and water, must be satisfied first before a person can go onto fulfilling the next level of need, which is safety and security. The fulfillment of needs build up from the bottom of the 5-tier model as shown in the following figure. The same principle of Maslow's Hierarchy of Human Needs is applied to Aaron Walter's Hierarchy of Emotional Design. According to Walter, a digital product's design must be functional first, before it can be reliable or usable, and most products are missing the top tier of pleasure because the user's basic needs are not satisfied.

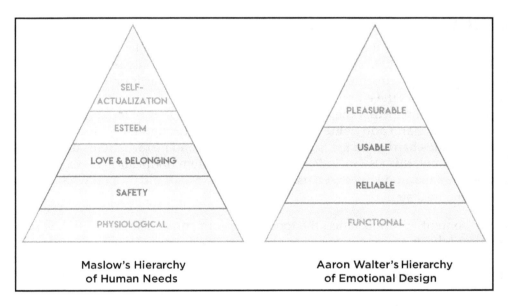

Humans build trust and emotional connection through feedback, the interaction of one person doing or saying something and the second person responding to it in a positive manner. This back-and-forth interaction creates trust; a negative feedback loop will break down trust and ultimately the emotional connection too.

In the same way, the user interacts with a website, by browsing and reading or filling in an online form and if the website responds with positive stimuli such as easy navigation to access all of the content or a user-friendly online form with clear fields, the emotional connection is strengthened. By repeating this process, a strong emotional connection can be built with the user.

Speaking a clear language

A good start to creating a digital personality the user can relate to on a personal level is by mimicking a real person's traits digitally. Speaking to the user in a tone of voice they can relate to and using appropriate cultural references will make the user feel comfortable and help build the emotional connection. All people want to feel appreciated and loved. It's natural human behavior, and incorporating the user's name within the website's UI or email communication will build upon that urge to connect.

Keeping the tone relevant

Content is usually one of the elements that is overlooked, which leaves the user bored or frustrated when trying to interact with the website. It is commonly seen as a placeholder in the design, a secondary feature to the overall look and feel. This is one of the main factors that negatively impact the emotional connection with the user. The content must be structured in such a way that the user can easily find what they're looking for and it must also have substance and add value to the user's journey through the website. Having really good content that's hard to access is counterproductive and just frustrates the user. When referring to content, this also includes instructions, system notification messages, transactional emails, and labels. The user should have clear guidance on what's expected to continue to the next step.

Other than content with substance, the tone of the copy must resonate with the user. If the targeted user falls in a younger age group between 18-25 years, the tone should be informal with some sense of humor to keep the emotional connection relevant. However, be careful of inappropriate slang or words that might not have the same meaning across different countries or cultures. The way the content is written adds to the personality and gives the website human attributes, thus enforcing an emotional connection.

Being as human as possible

When writing copy for email communication that is sent out when the user interacts with the website, the sentence structure is sometimes very formal, instructive, and impersonal. Emails with no personality are seen as an annoyance; instead these system emails (sometimes called transactional emails) should be seen as a perfect opportunity to have a conversation with the user and build on the emotional connection. Personalization is non-negotiable when talking to the user. A simple reference to the user's name in an email will make the user feel unique.

Another useful communication tool is a **live messenger**, in which an actual person is available to chat to via a messenger widget on the website, or a **chatbot**, which is a piece of functionality with pre-defined messengers programmed to have a conversation with a user based on specific questions. The latter is very popular, but can be tricky to build an emotional connection with if not implemented correctly. The user might feel frustrated if the chatbot cannot guide or answer the user's questions, or comes across as *a machine* with no personality and just frustrates the user, which breaks the emotional connection down throughout the experience.

Giving visual rewards

An important factor in building an emotional connection between humans is to give visual cues, such as body language. When a person winks at another person, the visual indicator of winking is confirmation that the one person likes or approves of the other person. Through this visual cue the emotional connection between these two humans is strengthened, and in the same way visual cues such as micro-interactions and anticipation design can improve the emotional connection between the user and the website.

Incorporating micro-interactions in the UI

Micro-interactions are simple UI animations that convey a message to the user while they are interacting with the website. These micro-interactions can be functional by guiding the user through a series of steps to complete a task, or can be for purely entertainment value. A functional micro-interaction is a real-time visual validation when a user enters a new password, or a grayed out submit button for an online form, that only activates when the user has completed all the fields.

Probably some of the best known micro-interactions are Facebook reactions, which have replaced the static like button on posts. This little feature offers the user instant gratification as the UI responds with a simple animation and also reinforces the emotional connection with the user.

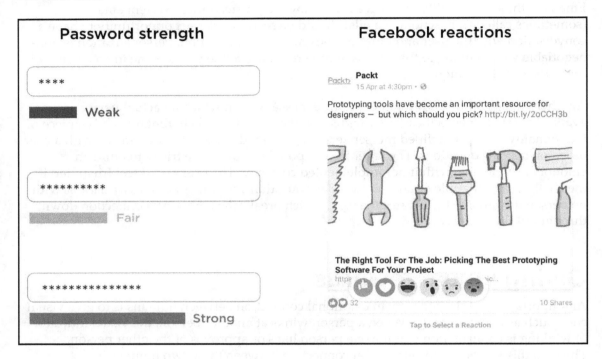

Making the UI discoverable and giving incentives

It's human nature to be curious and the pleasure of accidentally stumbling upon something you didn't know was there is very satisfying. Incorporating little UI rewards or interactions to surprise the user throughout the user's journey will not only keep the user entertained, but intrigued enough to continue interacting with the website to find more UI gems. Several social media platforms, such as LinkedIn, have a visual profile strength or profile-completed indicator that rewards the user for completing sections of their online profile. *Asana*, a well-known task management tool for product development teams, has a cute unicorn animation when a task has been completed before the deadline.

These little visual incentives create a subconscious yearning for the user to continue interacting with the platform to receive more positive stimuli.

Giving guidance through anticipation design

This design approach focuses on guiding the user through the user journey by eliminating as many steps as possible, and by utilizing business logic together with the user's past behavior on the website. **Cognitive load** is a psychological term used to describe the amount of mental effort it takes a person to perform a specific task. If a website's functionality and UI design does not reduce the cognitive load then UX has failed in creating a light and enjoyable user experience for the user.

The **autosuggest** functionality when doing a search uses business logic to serve the user with available options within the relevant context, and also uses previous searches to create a prediction of potential searches the user might include in the future. **Geolocation** is a feature to track the user's location through an IP address or GPS on a mobile device and serve the user with relevant content based on their location, such as suggesting nearby restaurants, events, or music festivals.

Entertaining by providing useful information

It's getting harder to entertain users with the excessive amount of content online, but nonetheless, subconsciously the user is always looking for some kind of entertainment value. Entertainment does not necessarily mean playing a game or watching a funny video, but rather offering a rewarding value to the user. For a businessman browsing articles related to his profession, these articles can offer interesting facts that are categorized as entertainment. Another useful example of entertainment is an interactive map on a travel website: the user can search for holiday destinations and check different routes available to a destination. Entertainment can thus be categorized as any available interaction on the website that offers the user an enjoyable and satisfying experience.

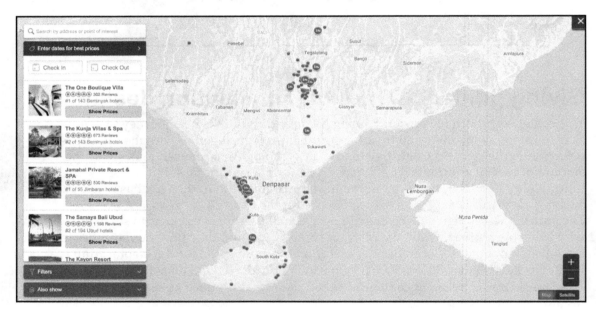

Establishing trust and credibility

As much as humans enjoy the company of entertaining personalities who make people laugh and feel good, the most important factor of an emotional connection is trust. Without trust the laughter is fake and interaction not really enjoyable. In the first two points we looked at different ways of engaging with the user to trigger an emotional connection, but trust is the foundation on which these triggers can truly take root. Trust goes deeper than the aesthetics of a website, so how do you build trust?

Do the brand values and value proposition come through the content of the website? The tone is the way the content is presented, but it's the substance that will build trust. Is the website safe for online payments? Does the user feel that they can trust the website with confidential information? Copy and visuals to give the user sufficient information about security measures taken on the site can be supported by visuals of a security icon and well known financial institutions. Is the website often offline? This will also make the user feel that the website cannot be trusted. Testimonials and star ratings from real people give credibility that the content is indeed real and not skewed for marketing purposes. Travel websites such as TripAdvisor (`https://www.tripadvisor.com/`) and Booking.com (`https://www.booking.com/`) make use of this kind of trust building.

Summary

By attempting to create an emotional connection with the user through technology, there's always a risk, as with human relationships, that it will fail. The proposed emotional connection might not resonate with some users; they might not understand the context or they just might not like it due to personal reasons. As long as the brand stays true to itself and the design is thought through, the majority of users will interact with the website, enjoy the tone of the personality, and love the little UI gems hidden in the user journey. In the next chapter, we'll explore the importance of UI design for the user and the product, and how the elements in the user interface improve usability.

4
Best Practices for Usability Within the User Interface (UI)

As covered in Chapter 1, *The Fundamentals of UX,* within the UCD process, each of the steps plays a significant role in creating a quality product that users enjoy to use. The research and concept phases are essential for laying the foundation, but the visual design brings the concept to life. Websites can be beautiful, but they also need to be easy to use, by using industry standard user interface best practices such as Google's Material Design and iOS Human Interface Guidelines the UI will not just be aesthetically pleasing, but will also tick all the usability requirements. The following topics in this chapter will lead the journey through best practices for UI design:

- Origin of UI and the birth of the Graphic User Interface (GUI)
- Color theory and the impact color psychology has on the user
- The relation between color and web accessibility
- Best design practices such as Google Material Design and iOS Human Interface Guidelines
- Best practices for effective iconography

Introduction to UI

Before we look at the history of the user interface and where it derived from, let's first clarify what the term UI means and the different aspects of it.

A **user interface** (**UI**) is an interactive layer between the person (user) and technology (device).

This interactive layer can be manipulated with features and functionality that are driven by development and visual elements rooted in established design guidelines. By finding the perfect balance between these two pillars, the UI of a digital product will not just increase the usability and accessibility, but also enhance the overall UX of the product.

UI design is thus the practice of creating the GUI of a digital product. In this book, we will be looking at websites specifically, by using visual elements that combine an accessible color palette, style elements such as borders, backgrounds, and icons. All visual elements have a color, and the color of an element can greatly impact the interaction of the user has with the UI of a website.

In the previous chapter, we looked at the history of UX and how a basic interaction between a person and a physical tool has evolved into a complex interaction between a person and a device. In between the Toyota production system in the 1940s and the Xerox PARC experimental project in the 1970s, the first touch screen was conceptualized by Eric Arthur Johnson, an engineer from England between 1965 and 1969. Johnson wanted to create a touch screen for air traffic control and wrote *Touch Displays: A Programmed Man-Machine Interface, Ergonomics,* in which he explained the working of the touch screen with diagrams and photos of a prototype. In 1969 he was granted a US patent for his invention:

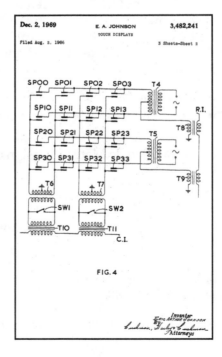

Although Johnson conceptualized the first touchscreen, it was a Danish engineer, Bent Stumpe, who actually built the first touchscreen device, called **PLATO (Programmed Logic for Automated Teaching Operations)**.

An ergonomic man-machine interface incorporating an adaptive pattern recognition-based control system, US 8046313 B2
PLATO IV (1972)

Around the same time, the Xerox PARC experimental project developed the first GUI, called *Xerox Alto,* which was built for non-commercial use in 1973. The Xerox Alto offered **WYSIWIG (What you see is what you get)** editing with a mouse. Remember, during that time the mouse was also the first of its kind! The Xerox Alto GUI was quite unconventional, and Xerox didn't commit to drive this invention as they didn't have the vision for this technology.

In 1979, Steve Jobs saw potential in the GUI and traded $1 million of Apple's stock for the Xerox GUI technology:

The Xerox Alto, the first GUI   1985 - Steve Jobs

Steve Jobs has taken the GUI technology from Xerox and created technology we cannot fathom our lives without. Mobile phones, laptops, smart TV's electronics, microwaves, and more, are all devices we wouldn't be able to interact with without a GUI. Now that we know what a UI is and how it came into existence, let's look at the different aspects of UI we can use to create a great user experience.

Color psychology

Color psychology is the study of hues as a cognitive influence on emotions and ultimately human behavior. Color does not affect each person the same. Age, gender, and culture are all factors that affect how people perceive a color. Even something as unique as a sensory connotation between a person and past experience can have an impact.

The retina in your eye is covered with millions of light-sensitive cells. When you look at a color, these little light receptors, some shaped as rods and others as cones, within your eye translate the light reflected from the object in the form of color by sending nerve impulses to the part of your brain called the hypothalamus. The hypothalamus then sends signals to the pituitary gland, which in return transmits signals onto the thyroid gland.

The latter then prompts the release of hormones. This is the reason why we have specific emotions that relate to a specific color. We'll dig deeper into color and emotions a bit later. Let's first look at the color theory and how colors are created through the light:

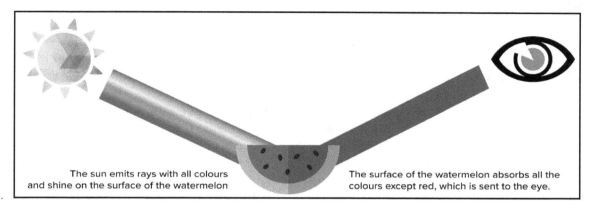

The sun emits rays with all colours and shine on the surface of the watermelon

The surface of the watermelon absorbs all the colours except red, which is sent to the eye.

Each color in the color spectrum represents a different light wavelength, and every object absorbs different wavelengths of color depending on the object. In the preceding figure, the red watermelon absorbs all the light wavelengths except the wavelength, which is the color of the object, which is in this case is red. When we say the watermelon absorbs the colors, we mean they disappear and are not visible to the eye. In another example, we can take a pair of purple sunglasses. The sunglasses will absorb all the light wavelengths, making them invisible to the eye and just reflects the light wavelength that represents the color purple to the eye. If an object does not absorb any of the light wavelengths, but instead reflects them all, the object will appear white. If an object absorbs all the light wavelengths it will make all the colors vanish and appear black.

A broad guideline for which light wavelengths represent which colors is as follows:

- Longer light wavelengths are usually reds, oranges, and yellows
- Short light wavelengths are for blues and greens

Within the human eye, two-thirds of the cone-shaped reflectors process the longer light wavelengths, while the other third process the shorter wavelengths. Thus, the human eye can perceive a wider spectrum of warmer colors than cooler colors. The color theory of light is slightly different than basic color theory and there's no need to know the science behind this theory in depth. It will be helpful to understand how color and light work as the color you'll be working with is on a device screen, which is in fact light.

A Swiss psychiatrist, Carl Gustav Jung, was a highly influential individual who worked in the fields of psychology, anthropology, and philosophy, to name just a few. He pursued an intense study of colors' properties and meanings across cultures to see if there's a potential use of color in art as a tool in psychotherapy, which eventually transformed into the modern field of color psychology.

The six basic principles of color psychology according to Jung are as follows:

1. **Color has a specific meaning**: A color can have a positive meaning to one person and a negative meaning to another person.
2. **The meaning of a color is learned in either of the two following ways**:
   - **Contextually learned**: A person can learn that the purple cup with tea doesn't taste sweet and thus associate any purple cup, despite what's in it, as not appealing
   - **Biologically learned**: As a person born into a Chinese family, it's natural to associate white with death and mourning as used in the Chinese culture
3. **A person automatically perceives and evaluates a color**: It's natural to look at a color and evaluate it without a conscious evaluation process. For example, if a person sees red liquid on their skin they will not consciously go through a process of deciding what it might be, automatically the color will be evaluated as perceived as blood. It's a subconscious action.
4. **The evaluation process causes behavior**: A specific behavior is motivated by the color perceived by the person. If the person sees a red light and perceived it as a danger, the person will take action to avoid the situation.
5. **Color influences automatically**: A person's decisions are automatically influenced by color. Color can sway a person to buy one product over another.
6. **Color meaning lives in context**: A color can have different meanings based on where the color is perceived. This can be in different countries, cultures, textures, food, or devices.

As you can see, color is not just color. It is a very powerful and influential tool when designing the UI of a website. We'll discuss the different aspects of color in more detail in the following sections.

The color wheel

The foundation of the color theory is based on the color wheel, a circular diagram of colors developed by a well known English scientist, Sir Isaac Newton, in 1666. There are various versions of the color wheel, but the basics stay the same. The most common version of the color wheel is the RYB (red-yellow-blue) model and it consists of 12 colors. Primary colors are red, yellow, and blue, as shown in the following figure:

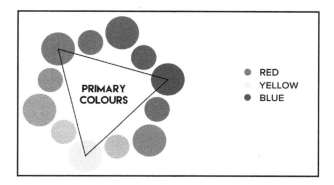

The secondary colors are a mix of two primary colors and they create green, orange, and purple, as shown in the following figure:

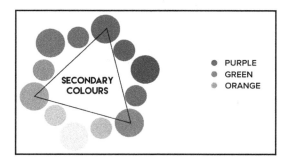

The tertiary colors are created by mixing primary and secondary colors.

Warm and cool colors

The color wheel can be divided into two main sections, namely warm and cool colors. Warm colors are energetic and consist of red, yellow, orange, or a mixture of these colors, and make objects look like they're closer than they really are, while cool colors are calm and made up of blue, green, and purple, or a mixture of these colors. Cool colors make objects look farther away or smaller:

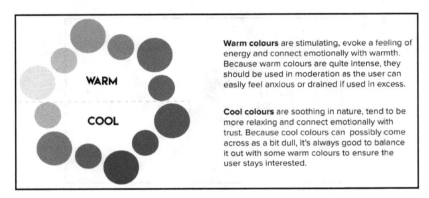

Warm **colours** are stimulating, evoke a feeling of energy and connect emotionally with warmth. Because warm colours are quite intense, they should be used in moderation as the user can easily feel anxious or drained if used in excess.

Cool **colours** are soothing in nature, tend to be more relaxing and connect emotionally with trust. Because cool colours can possibly come across as a bit dull, it's always good to balance it out with some warm colours to ensure the user stays interested.

When designing the UI of a website, it's important to use a good balance of warm and cool colors in your design. If you use only warm colors, the design can become too intense and the user might feel anxious and leave; with only cool colors, the design can become boring and lose the interest of the user. White, black, and gray are considered to be neutral colors and they don't fall into either the warm or cool category.

Color symbolism

Colors can have vastly contradictory meanings in different contexts, sometimes even within cultures or the same culture over separate time periods. When working with a specific target market, do some research on the users that will be using your website. Which country or culture are they from?

The following is a very basic list of colors and their meanings. Each color can be researched in more depth depending on the target market and project:

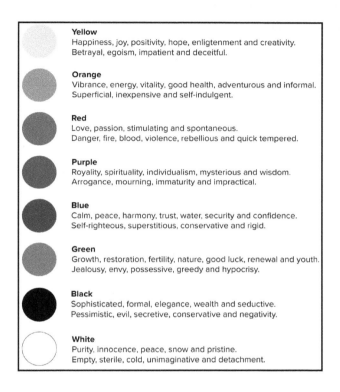

Yellow
Happiness, joy, positivity, hope, enligtenment and creativity.
Betrayal, egoism, impatient and deceitful.

Orange
Vibrance, energy, vitality, good health, adventurous and informal.
Superficial, inexpensive and self-indulgent.

Red
Love, passion, stimulating and spontaneous.
Danger, fire, blood, violence, rebellious and quick tempered.

Purple
Royality, spirituality, individualism, mysterious and wisdom.
Arrogance, mourning, immaturity and impractical.

Blue
Calm, peace, harmony, trust, water, security and confidence.
Self-righteous, superstitious, conservative and rigid.

Green
Growth, restoration, fertility, nature, good luck, renewal and youth.
Jealousy, envy, possessive, greedy and hypocrisy.

Black
Sophisticated, formal, elegance, wealth and seductive.
Pessimistic, evil, secretive, conservative and negativity.

White
Purity, innocence, peace, snow and pristine.
Empty, sterile, cold, unimaginative and detachment.

There are several interesting case studies done with color and the impact the different colors have on people and society; however, keep in mind that the results of these case studies have not been recognized as obsolete, but it is still worth a look at how color can be used to influence and how people can perceive color based on context.

Case study 1 - blue street lighting in Glasgow, Scotland

During 1999, blue street lights were were installed on Buchanan Street in Glasgow, Scotland to improve the appearance of the city. This cosmetic change of lighting has surprisingly reduced the crime rate significantly.

The following statistics on a public website :(https://www.whatdotheyknow.com), has been provided by Sergeant Susan McGinlay from the Force Disclosure Unit, Strathclyde Police:

Table 2

Detected crime data[1] for selected area in Glasgow City Centre[2]

By calendar year, 1998 to 2004

Crime category	January to December						
	1998	1999	2000	2001	2002	2003	2004
SVC - Serious Assault	4	1	3	1	1	0	1
SVC - Robbery	5	3	3	3	3	0	4
SVC - Other Violence Crimes	0	1	1	1	0	1	0
SVC - Indecency Crimes	1	3	8	1	0	1	0
Housebreaking (Domestic)	0	0	0	0	0	0	0
Housebreaking (Other)	3	9	10	1	3	5	10
Motor Vehicle Crime	3	2	3	0	0	0	0
Theft	4	14	8	10	8	5	22
Shoplifting	52	127	163	99	28	31	50
Other Dishonesty	25	37	51	29	22	69	28
Vandalism/Fireraising etc.	2	3	1	5	4	4	6
Offensive Weapons/Knives	3	11	10	6	4	5	15
Drug - Supply	6	8	7	4	15	6	3
Drug - Possession	8	23	7	8	19	10	32
Other Misc. Crimes	9	10	9	5	13	7	19
Common Assault	9	17	34	14	19	14	34
Breach of the Peace	48	47	69	36	43	40	59
Racially Aggravated Conduct/Harassment	0	0	0	0	0	1	2
Anti-social Behaviour (Scotland) Act 2004	0	0	0	0	0	0	0
Drunk and Incapable	1	1	3	3	4	5	7
Consumption of alcohol in designated places	15	9	16	7	4	7	17
Other Misc. Offences	18	5	9	4	19	6	13
Dangerous driving offences	0	0	1	0	0	0	0
Driving Carelessly	1	0	0	1	0	0	1
Drink, Drug driving offences incl. Failure to provide a specimen	1	0	1	0	0	0	3
Speeding offences	0	0	0	0	0	0	0
Seat belt offences	2	0	0	0	0	0	0
Mobile phone (whilst driving) offences	0	0	0	0	0	0	0
Other Driving Offences	6	4	8	7	6	10	9

[1] *Data was sourced from the Corporate Crime Database and is based on the date that the crime report was raised. Only records recorded on the Crime Management System are included, no conditional offer of fixed penalty data is included.*

[2] *Data was selected if the x and y co-ordinates recorded on the crime report were mapped along Buchanan Street (including one premise deep either side) between Bath Street and Argyle Street. Please note that approx. 32 percent of crimes have no x & y co-ordinates recorded and are therefore excluded from the data provided.*

Source: Corporate Crime Database

From the statistics, it's apparent that not all crimes were reduced, but theft, vandalism, possession of knives, and drug related crimes were all reduced. Let's look at potential reasons why these crimes might have been reduced by the change of color in street lighting:

- Blue is a calming color, and subconsciously, the blue reduced the urge to commit a crime
- Blue lighting subconsciously represents the police and thus gave the feeling of authority watching

These statistics cover a variety of crimes and should thus be read in this context as these results are not conclusive results to support the theory that the blue lighting did indeed reduce crime. The purpose of this case study is to broaden your perception of the potential of color.

Case study 2 - blue lighting in railway stations in Japan

The second case study also focuses on blue lighting, but in a different context. Japan has the highest suicide rate in the world, and it can be blamed on stressful urban living. There are several preferred suicidal spots, but railway stations are at the top of the list. The authorities are constantly busy looking at ways to reduce the number of suicides. In Katsushika, Tokyo, the Shin-Koiwa train station is infamously known as a suicide hotspot. The following changes have been installed at the station based on the following assumption:

- Blue plastic panels have been installed on the roof to give blue lighting.
- Three big television screens are constantly showing underwater footage of dolphins and sea creatures as well as landscape with mountains and oceans. The color spectrum of these scenes is mainly blue and green, which are calming colors.

Also, in Yokohama, at Gumyoji station, blue lighting has been installed and it was confirmed by Keihin Electric Express Railway Co. that since the new lighting was installed suicides has reduced significantly. Regarding the colors and their different meanings in different countries, in Japan the color of the police is red, not blue. Thus, the idea that blue lighting subconsciously represents authority will not work in Japan.

As mentioned previously, these case studies are not formal research and solid outcomes. It is likely that the change of color in lighting is unusual and people feel uncomfortable to commit crimes under these circumstances. However, you will greatly benefit from reading such case studies and broaden your perspective of the power of color and how color can influence the users that browse the websites that you design.

Color and web accessibility

Web accessibility is an integral part of UX and it refers to the practice of inclusive design, which focuses on creating digital products that can be accessed by all people, including people with special needs, thus removing barriers that would prevent a user from interacting with a website. In the chapter that covers web accessibility that is still to come, we'll discuss this topic in detail and see how to create websites that users who need assertive technology can access.

Now we're just going to touch on the different people that would be impacted by a UI design that's not designed with accessibility in mind. There are several different types of color blindness:

- **Red-green confusion**:
    - Protanopia
    - Protanomaly
    - Deuteranopia
    - Deuteranomaly
- **Yellow-blue confusion**:
    - Tritanopia
    - Tritanomaly
- **Monochromacy**

When designing a website, there are several free tools you can use to assist with the design. These tools will simulate a specific color blindness and you'll have an idea of how your design will look to someone who can't see the whole spectrum of colors. This becomes quite important if you have call to action (CTA) buttons prompting the user to sign in or to buy a product. If the color of this button fades into the background, the impact will be lost.

The following is an example of a button design using the Sim Daltonism tool:

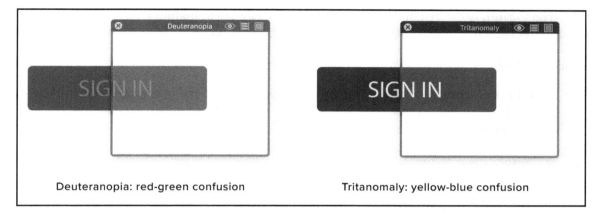

The two most important factors to keep in mind while doing UI design are as follows:

- **Sufficient contrast**: The contrast ratio between the text and background should be at least 3:1 and 4.5:1 for AA standard. Don't worry too much about the ratios now, we'll cover this in the Web Accessibility chapter. The key is to design with high contrast.
- **Use color as support**: Don't indicate important information with colors only. Use text, icons, and visual elements to reinforce it.

Best design practices

There is no set guideline for best design practices because technology and the industry standard change constantly. Design trends evolve constantly. Every year you'll find articles and blog posts on the designed trends of the following year. One year, flat design is in and all design elements and icons are design according to this style; in a couple of months, skeuomorphism is the next big thing and designers are designing according to this new trend, so when we speak of classic and timeless design in the following sections we're referring to not incorporating every new design fad, but rather finding a happy medium between keeping the design fresh and timeless.

Skeuomorphism is the design concept of making items represented resemble their real-world counterparts.

Google's Material Design guidelines

Material Design is the visual style guide created by Google to maintain the consistency of UI design elements across different platforms, with full scalability. They took the 10 Classic Rules of Design and added a technology spin on it to advance innovation in the digital space. Let's have a quick look at these design rules Google expanded on:

- **Less is more**: A simple design is not boring, instead the visual elements are used strategically to create a holistic design that's pleasing and easy to use.
- **Neutral trumps eccentric**: Supporting the first rule, neutral does not mean boring, but rather stripping away unnecessary elements that will distract the user from the main goal of the design.
- **Transparency**: Users can easily pick up dishonest tendencies, so leave the gimmicks and trickery and present the user with the honest truth. You'll win more users like this.
- **Classic and timeless approach**: Don't get caught up in current design fads, use design approaches that have been working for years. Follow the color wheel and keep it simple.
- **Don't overdesign**: Try to take visual elements away for your design to still have impact, rather that adding more visual elements that have no real purpose.
- **Remember the details**: Make sure your i's have dots and t's have crosses, no pixelation, no misalignment of lines or borders.
- **Be conservative**: Don't use all energetic colors, but balance colors out with warm and cool colors. Constant visual elements that are very detailed will make the design cluttered and busy.
- **Don't rush**: Take your time and think your design through. Design is strategy.
- **No explanation needed**: Design in such a way that no explanation is needed; iconography must be clear and buttons must look clickable.
- **Aesthetically pleasing**: Overall, the design must be easy on the eye, it must be pleasing to look at.

From these basic rules of design, Google created a living (continually updated) design guide that includes several UI element styles based on these three key principles:

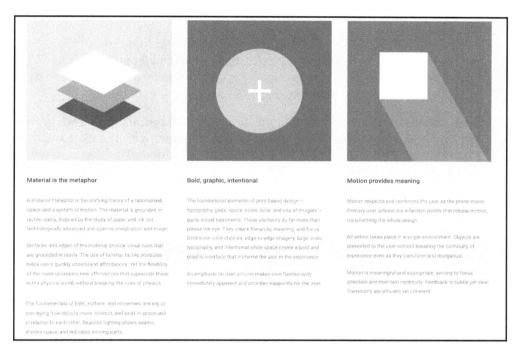

Material is the metaphor

A material metaphor is the unifying theory of a rationalized space and a system of motion. The material is grounded in tactile reality, inspired by the study of paper and ink, yet technologically advanced and open to imagination and magic.

Surfaces and edges of the material provide visual cues that are grounded in reality. The use of familiar tactile attributes helps users quickly understand affordances. Yet the flexibility of the material creates new affordances that supercede those in the physical world, without breaking the rules of physics.

The fundamentals of light, surface, and movement are key to conveying how objects move, interact, and exist in space and in relation to each other. Realistic lighting shows seams, divides space, and indicates moving parts.

Bold, graphic, intentional

The foundational elements of print-based design – typography, grids, space, scale, color, and use of imagery – guide visual treatments. These elements do far more than please the eye. They create hierarchy, meaning, and focus. Deliberate color choices, edge-to-edge imagery, large-scale typography, and intentional white space create a bold and graphic interface that immerse the user in the experience.

An emphasis on user actions makes core functionality immediately apparent and provides waypoints for the user.

Motion provides meaning

Motion respects and reinforces the user as the prime mover. Primary user actions are inflection points that initiate motion, transforming the whole design.

All action takes place in a single environment. Objects are presented to the user without breaking the continuity of experience even as they transform and reorganize.

Motion is meaningful and appropriate, serving to focus attention and maintain continuity. Feedback is subtle yet clear. Transitions are efficient yet coherent.

Google's Material Design Guidelines: three principles

The key UI element styles can be put into the following categories:

- **Motion** : Motion as defined by Google, in the world of material design is used to describe spatial relationships, functionality, and intention with beauty and fluidity. How do features move from one position to another? If a navigation side panel expands from the side of the screen, how will it move? Will it slide in from left to right in 0.5 seconds? Will it slightly jump when closed? These are subtle animations to refine the UI's interaction with the user.

- **Style**: The purpose and use of color with bold hues, deep shadows, and bright highlight, together with icons and imagery. Typography provides set typefaces (Roboto and Noto) for native operating systems and applications. This is not compulsory to follow, but it is good to know the backup font family you're working with.

- **Layout**: The layout guidelines are driven by baseline grids and structural templates used in print design. Keeping to these systematic guidelines consistency comes naturally and allows layout to fit all screen sizes, thus the design is responsive and scalable.

 Google's definition of the use of layout in Material Design: Material Design is guided by print-based design elements such as typography, grids, space, scale, color, and imagery to create hierarchy, meaning, and focus that immerse the user in the experience.

- **Components**: The list of components within the Material Guidelines gives clear specifications of how the components would interact with the user and what exactly it will look like. These UI components include buttons, lists, menus, form fields, tabs and tooltips .

- **Patterns**: The patterns guideline includes the broader aspects of the UI, for example, launch screens. What will a screen look like when it's opened for the first time? What elements will be visible to guide the user to interact with the UI? Another example is error messaging. How do the error messages interact with the user? How are messages conveyed to the user and how is the user guided to proceed past the error state of the UI?

- **Growth and communication** (Google's definition of growth and communication): The growth and communications guidelines contain best practices and components to help users quickly and intuitively understand what they can do with your app, including on-boarding, feature discovery, and gesture education.

- **Usability**: The usability category covers guidelines that focus on accessibility and bidirectionally. Accessibility focuses on making the UI as usable as possible despite any limitations the user may have, be they temporary or permanent. Bidirectionally offers guidelines on mirroring the UI for RTL (right to left) languages such as Arabic and Hebrew.

Each of the preceding categories has detailed sub-categories, and gives clear guidelines to what best practices are when dealing with a specific element. Google's Material Design Guidelines is a living document that is continually updated as the design aspects within the documents are refined to be more impactful.

Google's Material Design guidelines are available at `https://material.io/guidelines/` .

iOS Human Interface Guidelines

The iOS Human Interface Guidelines are the basic UI guidelines Apple has provided for designing iOS apps. These guidelines are mainly focused on iOS apps, but they can be applied to all digital products, including websites.

The following are the three essential themes that run through the iOS platform, taken from Apple:

1. **Clarity:** Throughout the system, text is legible at every size, icons are precise and lucid, adornments are subtle and appropriate, and a sharpened focus on functionality motivates the design. Negative space, color, fonts, graphics, and interface elements subtly highlight important content and convey interactivity.

2. **Deference:** Fluid motion and a crisp, beautiful interface help people understand and interact with content while never competing with it. Content typically fills the entire screen, while translucency and blurring often hint at more. Minimal use of bezels, gradients, and drop shadows keep the interface light and airy, while ensuring that content is paramount.

3. **Depth:** Distinct visual layers and realistic motion convey hierarchy, impart vitality, and facilitate understanding. Touch and discoverability heighten delight and enable access to functionality and additional content without losing context. Transitions provide a sense of depth as you navigate through content.

iOS Human Interface Guidelines: https://developer.apple.com/ios/human-interface-guidelines/

It's highly recommended to always keep up to date with market leaders such as Google and Apple when it comes to technology and design, as these companies build the operating systems (OSes) as well as the applications that run on these OSes in which your website will be viewed. For example, on an Android device the browser the user will use to view your website is created by Google, and on the other hand, on an iPhone the browser the user will use to view your website is created by Apple. Keep to these guidelines as much as possible.

Case Study - UI design for websites

We've covered color psychology, best practices for UI design, and how to build an emotional connection with the user. This case study is based on a tattoo studio called *More Than Hype*, in the heart of Cape Town, South Africa. The look and feel of the website represents the classic 18th century architecture of the building and the personality of the More Than Hype brand :

Brief for the MTH website

Create a modern, yet classic design for the More Than Hype website. The brand's mission statement highlights not being part of any hype, thus the classic and timeless approach to the look and feel of the website. The website structure must be simplistic, no gimmicks, no over the top designs elements, and no complicated features. The color palette must be timeless, the imagery will be provided from a local photographer from *Work at play Photography and Design*. The needs of both the tattoo studio and users should be aligned and simplistically executed.

The studio's needs are as follows:

- Represent the More Than Hype brand (brand image and identity).
- Receive accurate information from potential clients regarding their tattoo enquiries
- Display a variety of tattoo styles to showcase the studio's diversity in artwork offered
- Sell More Than Hype merchandise online

The users needs are as follows:

- Effortlessly browse through the available services, that is, tattoo styles
- Easily make online bookings with a specific artist
- Easily find the location of the tattoo studio

UI design

For the More than Hype website, the **10 Classic Rules of Design** have been applied:

- **Less is more:** The layout of the pages is well constructed with a static header, body of content, and a footer across the website.
- **Neutral trumps eccentric:** There are no unnecessary elements that will distract the user from their main goal of the website, which is browsing the available services and making an online booking with their chosen artist.

- **Transparency :** The content is honest and factual. The mission and vision of the brand is clearly conveyed in one central place and the biographies of the artists are not boasting and straight to the point:

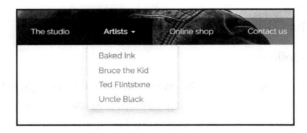

- **Classic and timeless approach:** The black and white color palette is consistent throughout the design and reinforces the classic look and feel.

- **Don't over design:** All visual elements have a purpose. There are no decorative UI elements or gimmicky animations that will take away from the classic look and feel of the website. All icons are flat with a solid color. 3D icons can make a design look cluttered and because we're focusing on timelessness, flat, single color icons are the best fit for the design. White icons on a dark background and dark gray icons on a white background:

- **Remember the details:** All imagery is of the highest quality and from the same photographer to ensure a consistent classy feel. Category elements have circular holding shapes while artwork have rectangular holding shapes.
- **Be conservative:** Ties in with no. 4. The black and white color palette is consistent throughout the design and reinforces the classic look and feel:

- **Don't rush:** This is a personal virtue of the designer. Even though as a designer, you always work against a deadline, take a moment to stand back and observe your design objectively.

- **No explanation needed:** The overall design is simplistic, all CTAs are clear. The contact details are visible on every page for easy access.
- **Aesthetically pleasing:** The design is aesthetically pleasing to look at:

Language and semiotics

Creating a successful UI solely rests on the presentation and effective relaying of the message to the user. The message can be conveyed through language (labels, content, and so on) or visual elements such as **iconography**. You can create the most aesthetically pleasing website, but if the language and visual elements of the UI do not support the message, it can be horribly misinterpreted and have a negative impact on the website.

Semiotics is the study of signs and symbols and their meanings.

Semiotics is timeless, and having a good understanding of this subject is priceless in the long run. Web design trends change monthly, but semiotics is an established field of study with tremendous insights into the user's understanding of visuals. With a good understanding of semiotics, you can create effective iconography that conveys a message that will not confuse the user. The biggest challenge with iconography is not size, but that the visual element, which is the icon, conveys the same message to all users that interact with it.

Best practices for effective iconography

Iconography is the use of visual elements and symbols to convey a specific message to the user when interacting with a device. It's a basic practice that's used in UI design and can greatly improve the user experience when used correctly. Some research studies have found that iconography is not as effective as we would like to think; apparently the user doesn't find it easy to memorize. Both of these arguments are debatable and have merit. Unfortunately, the impact of icons has been corrupted by designers using icons for decorative purposes only and not to support a message.

The bottom line is, as a designer you should make conservative decisions when using iconography in your design and when you do use it, make sure the design follows the following guidelines:

- **Keep it simple:**
  Because an icon's size can be anything from 48 x 48, 32 x 32, or as small as 16 x 16 pixels depending on the device size, the design for an icon must be extremely simple so it stays clear and visible when it's resized. If the icon design has too much detail, the icon can become blurry and the user will not know what it looks like.

- **Keep it in context:**
  There are universal icons used across all digital products, such as websites, mobile apps, and system UIs, such as the search magnifying glass. Never take universal icons for granted, always test your final icons with real people. Two universal icons that have blurry meanings are the heart icon and the star icon. Both of these are icons that are used for different purposes across different platforms. Sometimes it's used to bookmark sites and other times it's used to favorite items. The checkmark is also a great example of how icons change meaning in different context. The checkmark means correct in Britain, but incorrect in Sweden and Finland. In America a red checkmark is wrong, while a green or black checkmark is neutral.

- **Include a label (if possible):**
  Well-known icons are frequently manipulated and changed aesthetically to fit in with a specific brand image or UI design. In this case it's safer to accompany the icon with a label.

- **Always test:**
  It doesn't matter how simple your design or concept is, always ask someone not working on the project with you, preferably a real user, to interact with your icon designs. It's an eye-opening experience to see how people perceive icons you think are simple and straightforward.

According to the UX leaders, the Nielsen Normal Group, it should not take you longer than five seconds to think of an icon to represent a concept.

 Use the five-second rule: if it takes you more than five seconds to think of an appropriate icon for something, it is unlikely that an icon can effectively communicate that meaning.

Grid examples are available from Google's Material Design guidelines and iOS Human Interface Guidelines. Use these templates, available for free to download, when designing icons:

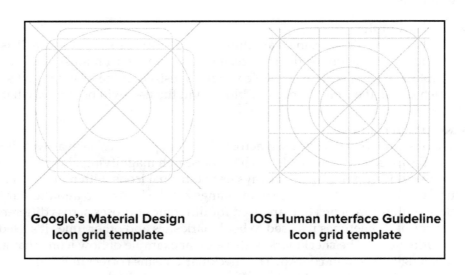

Google's Material Design
Icon grid template

IOS Human Interface Guideline
Icon grid template

Case study: languages versus flags

In this case study, we'll look at the possible misinterpretation of icons based on the user's country of birth versus country of residence. You've probably browsed an international website with flag icons in the top right corner. Have you ever given it real thought what exactly the intention of the flag icons are?

- Is it to choose your country from where you're browsing?
- Is it to choose the language that you want to read the website in?
- Is it to choose the currency you would like to pay when buying a product?

Let's first define what a language and a flag represent: a **flag** is a visual symbol that represents nations or countries. A **language** is the method of communication between groups of people either spoken or written. Flags are thus unique to a nation or country while a language is spoken by a group of people that can stretch across borders of countries. Using a flag of a country to represent a language is not just confusing, but can also offend users:

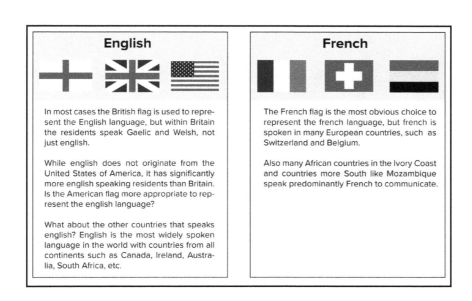

English

In most cases the British flag is used to represent the English language, but within Britain the residents speak Gaelic and Welsh, not just english.

While english does not originate from the United States of America, it has significantly more english speaking residents than Britain. Is the American flag more appropriate to represent the english language?

What about the other countries that speaks english? English is the most widely spoken language in the world with countries from all continents such as Canada, Ireland, Australia, South Africa, etc.

French

The French flag is the most obvious choice to represent the french language, but french is spoken in many European countries, such as Switzerland and Belgium.

Also many African countries in the Ivory Coast and countries more South like Mozambique speak predominantly French to communicate.

Summary

Now that we've looked at some of the most important aspects of UI design for digital products, hopefully, it's more clear that UI design is not just about designing an aesthetically appealing website, but a combination of factors that make up an enjoyable UI. By choosing a color palette to reinforce the brand image and aligning the overall design with industry best practices such as Google's Material Design and iOS Human Interface Guidelines, your website will be set apart from the thousands of other websites online. In the next couple of chapters, we'll look at the practical UX methodologies to improve the content and usability of your website.

5
Set a Solid Foundation - Research and Analyze

When creating a website, as with any product, you could just start by designing and building it. However, unless you are very lucky, this strategy is unlikely to end with a great website. Without knowledge about things such as your potential users, the business requirements, and the competitors in the market, you will create an inferior product that your target market does not want. Research provides the data that gives you the required knowledge.

As a UX practitioner, you first need to think of your users: who will be using the website; why they want to use it; and when they will use it. You cannot create a product that will really work for people without exploring who those people are. This is user research.

In this chapter, we will describe research, with our examples focusing on studies typically conducted during the discovery phase of a project. We will examine studies used to evaluate or test website designs, such as usability tests, in Chapter 9, *Optimize your UX Strategy with Iterative User Testing*. In this chapter, we will begin by categorizing and defining different types of research. Then we will describe the UX research process. Part of research is using the UX practitioner's expertise to evaluate interfaces and content. The next section discusses this, using *heuristic analysis* and *content audits* as examples. Finally, we will describe qualitative and quantitative techniques available to a UX researcher.

The topics covered in this chapter are:

- Defining and categorizing research
- Setting up a research plan
- Doing expert analysis

- Using qualitative techniques
- Using quantitative techniques

Before beginning, it is important to state that research methodology is a subject about which there is a lot of theory and discussion. We are not delving into this subject deeply: we aim to provide you with a basic understanding about the issues involved, with a strong practical focus, so that you can make informed decisions about conducting research. This chapter should be the starting point of your studies into research methods if you aim to do a large amount of user research.

Defining and categorizing research

We conduct research to gain data about a problem or area of interest. There are many different methods for gaining data, such as interviews, questionnaires, experiments, observations, and content analysis. Deciding which methods to use depends on your resources, the problem that you are researching, your audience, and your preferences.

No matter which methods you choose, it is important to plan and organize research carefully, so you can be sure that you are getting the right data and interpreting it in the right way. The research that we conduct as UX practitioners typically does not need the rigor that more formal research requires. However, we must aim for quality in our research so that our time is not wasted and we gain results that help us create effective designs. Two criteria are often used to judge the quality of research:

- **Validity**: This is the extent to which the research measures what you want, and not something else. For example, if you ask someone if they like your website, perhaps you are actually measuring how much they want to please you, rather than how much they like your website. Are the users that you are testing with a good example of your target audience? Can you generalize these results to your target audience?
- **Reliability**: This defines the extent to which the research can be repeated with the same results. It tests the measurement instruments that you are using. Will these same questions or tasks generate similar enough results if we apply them again to the same people?

There are various types of validity and reliability, and many formal methods of testing research for validity and reliability. We do not have to conduct formal tests. However, these concepts are useful for us to judge our research plans. The reason we carefully set up research plans and control our research is to make sure that it is reliable and valid.

Another concept to keep in mind while conducting research is that of triangulation.

Triangulation is a social science technique for ensuring the validity and quality of research by combining multiple methods in a research plan. If multiple methods and researchers are used, weaknesses and biases in each have less influence and the data produced is more rich, detailed, accurate and reliable.

Therefore, we ideally try to include multiple researchers when any subjective method is used, and we try to use multiple methods during website development to ensure the best results.

UX research can be categorized in various ways. Perhaps the most apt categorization is whether you research with users or without users. Any UX research plan must include users. You cannot design a product as a UX practitioner without interacting with your users in some way. This is at the core of the discipline. However, we don't only need user data to design a product effectively for our users. It is also important to have data about all the following elements:

- **Users**: The people who will be using your product. If you are an e-commerce site like Amazon, you may consider most of the world's population to potentially be your target users. In this case, you should include a good cross-section in your studies, including people who may have more trouble on your website, such as older people who are not technologically informed. Your website may have a more niche audience, for example financial managers, in which case you will need to select users for your studies more precisely. We will discuss recruiting users in more detail later.
- **Business**: The business for which you are building the website. There will be business requirements that must be weighed against user needs, including corporate identity and values, infrastructure, KPIs, and stakeholder expectations. Some of this information will be gathered through reviewing documents; some will require stakeholder interviews.
- **Technologies**: These are the technologies you may potentially be using in building your websites, and the constraints on design that they introduce. This knowledge is likely to exist within the team already, but may require some research.
- **Standards**: Frameworks, guidelines, and rules for designing and building websites. These are existing worldwide or company standards that should be followed to deliver a usable, consistent website. For example, Google's *material design* and the *Web Content Accessibility Guidelines*.

- **Domain**: This relates to the subject matter of your website content. If you are redesigning a website, you will need to look at the content of the existing website. If it is a company website, this will be closely related to business; you will gather the subject matter by understanding the business. If the website is about a subject, such as flowering plants or games, then you will probably need to research the domain.
- **Competitors**: It is important to look at competitors in your market so that you can learn from them. This can involve users, but is more likely to involve a review of competitor websites, and other sites discussing competitor brands.

As can be seen, there are many things that it is useful to research when building a website. Many of them do not involve interacting with people at all. Some of this data will already be available; we will not have to gather it through research, but we will have to spend time examining it and working with it. This is also part of a research plan--*reviewing* and *analyzing* existing knowledge.

There are several other ways of categorizing UX research, besides whether it involves users or not. We focus on two useful dimensions here:

- **Quantitative versus qualitative**: These categories are about the nature of the data and how you gather it.
- **Discovery versus evaluation**: These are about when you conduct the research, in terms of the phases of product development. Different terms and divisions may be used, such as *formative versus summative*, or *strategize, execute, assess* (Nielsen Norman Group).

We will now describe quantitative versus qualitative research, and when to conduct research as shown here. Other potential categories include:

- **Context of use**: This defines whether the data is gathered in the user's context (in the field), or whether users are brought into the controlled conditions of a testing laboratory. This also relates to moderation, which is whether the research is conducted without a facilitator present, or facilitated by a UX researcher. Most remote research is unmoderated, although technological advances mean we can increasingly moderate remote tests.
- **Focus**: There are different areas of focus within UX research, such as usability and user experience, information architecture, content and tasks, competitors, and stakeholder interests. Multiple methods can be used to gather data in each area. For example, competitor analysis can involve usability testing, expert cognitive walkthrough, or doing a content audit of competitor websites.

The following diagram shows common UX research methods, and where they typically fall on the qualitative/quantitative and discovery/evaluation dimensions. The discovery/evaluation dimension has been sub-divided into typical phases of product development to show more accurately where these methods are typically used. Most methods can be used at other places on both sets of dimensions, by modifying their processes slightly.

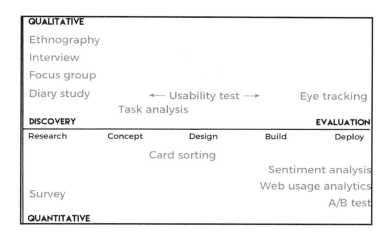

User research methods

A few things are useful to note by examining the diagram:

- Quantitative methods tend to cluster where a website is deployed. This is because they involve larger numbers of participants, which are easier and cheaper to obtain when your website is deployed. With quantitative methods, we typically want to ask how many people did something or had a problem.
- Qualitative methods tend to cluster during the research and concept phases. This is because they are usually used to answer questions about why and how things happen. These are very important questions to ask when researching and doing concept design.

- The methods that are closer to the *discovery* side do not require a website to work with. They are used to find out about participants' context, for example ethnography and diary studies, and their attitudes and thoughts about the market and competitors, for example surveys. The methods closer to the *evaluation* side require a website, or a prototype, as they measure participants' behavior with the product or attitudes about the product, for example A/B tests and sentiment analysis.

- Usability tests are shown with arrows because they are the core UX practitioner's method, and flexible--they can be conducted with varying degrees of quantitative and qualitative focus, and can be used in different ways anywhere in the project timeline. They also combine well with other methods. For example, a remote usability test with carefully chosen metrics can be delivered remotely to 20 participants with a survey to gather quantitative data; or conducted in a lab with five participants and an interview to gather qualitative data. During research, usability tests can be conducted on competitor websites or on your own site to inform a redesign; during deployment, usability tests can be conducted to set benchmarks for creating usability standards for your website. We describe usability tests in detail in `Chapter 9`, *Optimize your UX Strategy with Iterative User Testing*.

Understanding qualitative versus quantitative research

Qualitative and quantitative research refer to the type of data that is gathered. As the names suggest, quantitative data is about quantities and qualitative data is about qualities. Quantitative methods typically deliver lots of numbers that show how big an effect is or how many people experience it, whereas qualitative methods deliver fewer detailed findings in the form of words, videos, and images that show why and how an effect is happening.

These distinctions have various effects. The following diagram indicates some of these differences. Later in this chapter, we will describe the techniques of each approach, with examples.

Here, we briefly focus on some of the more important differences in comparison.

QUALITATIVE	vs.	QUANTITATIVE
APPROACH		
Descriptive		Defined
Exploratory		Experimental
Insight-driven		Statistical
Flexible		Structured and rigid
Contextual		Universal
Detailed and rich		Cause and effect
METHODS & DATA		
Observation		Measurement
Interpretation		Tabulation
Patterns and groupings		Ranking
Reasons, opinion, feelings, motivation		Time, errors, success rates
ANALYSIS & PRESENTATION		
Understand trends		Find universal law
Provide insights		Generalise results
Quotes, stories, images, video, diagrams		Numbers, statistics, tables, graphs
USERS & TIMELINE		
Small numbers		Large numbers
Individual selection		Random sample selection
Typically early		Typically late

Quantitative versus qualitative methods

Let's take a look at some of the ways in which quantitative and qualitative methods differ:

- **Data**: Quantitative methods deliver numbers about things such as task times and error rates. These numbers can be coded and analyzed mathematically using statistical techniques. Researchers can show things such as how many of your users will prefer different design options (for example, A/B tests) or how many think your website is easy to use (for example, surveys). This is usually presented with tables, graphs, and calculated results. Qualitative methods deliver insights about things such as why users probably do not find what they are looking for in your menu, or how they typically use their phones during the day. They provide us with ideas about how to design effectively for people. We typically present qualitative results using words and diagrams, with examples of real user experiences from our studies using quotes, images, and video segments.

- **Sample size**: Statistics work by claiming that an effect experienced by your study participants, or sample, can be generalized to all your users. To do this, your sample must be carefully selected to be representative of your users, and large enough that the statistics are accurate. This is why quantitative methods require so many participants. Qualitative methods do not claim to be generalizable in the same way. However, for insights about a population to be credible, the sample must also be very carefully selected. Because qualitative methods require fewer participants, they can be individually selected. *Probability sampling* should be used if you want to apply statistics most effectively. This means that every possible user has a chance of being selected. There are various probability sampling methods, but they all require random selection. Qualitative research usually uses *non-probability sampling*, which means participants are not chosen randomly. They can be chosen by convenience, which is the least reliable method. More often, they are chosen according to criteria or quotas, which define characteristics of the overall user population.

- **Methods**: Because they need so many participants to gain results, quantitative methods rarely involve direct interaction by a UX researcher. Data is more often collected remotely, via surveys or tools such as Google Analytics. Qualitative methods rely on the experience and understanding of the researcher, therefore they usually involve direct interaction, for example interviews and usability tests. Where these are used remotely, tools such as Skype are used so the researcher can still interact with and observe the user.

- **Analysis**: Analysis of quantitative results is quick and relatively simple if you have been rigorous about your study design and know your statistical methods (or know a good statistical software package). Since you are collecting and analyzing numbers, the process is relatively automated. In qualitative analysis, researchers look for patterns and create structure in the data. Qualitative analysis is time-consuming, as it requires reviewing hours of detailed data carefully, and cannot easily be automated. Qualitative data can be coded; in fact, analysis should be guided by a metric to help researchers keep their focus during analysis and reduce subjectivity.

- **Combination**: Because they answer the same questions in different ways, it is often best to use qualitative and quantitative methods in combination. For example, you may notice an effect in a usability test or ethnographic study, and then set up analytics on your website or set up an A/B test to find out the extent to which that effect was found in the target population.

Deciding when to conduct research

We indicated the phases of the product development cycle when specific UX methods are typically used in the preceding *User research methods* diagram. We also indicated that the methods you choose can be used at any point during product development. It depends on the knowledge that you need and want to gain, and the resources available to you.

Although these phases are often not linear and will be repeated iteratively during product development, we will discuss them linearly.

During *discovery*, which roughly equates to *research* and *concept* in the diagram, the team is working out what kind of website to create and conducting formative research. You will be finding out about business stakeholder requirements, and the needs and goals of users. At this point, there will be open questions about content, style, focus, and so on. You may also be considering various technological options for your website, such as whether you want a dedicated mobile site and whether you want to employ innovative technologies. If you are redesigning an existing website, you may want to conduct usability tests or focus groups on the website to find out which areas are most problematic for current users. You could also do more quantitative research by looking at web analytics about the existing website or creating a survey and sending it to current users. If you are creating a new website, you may want to know more about your potential users, so conduct an ethnographic study to find out more about their lives. You may conduct competitor analysis quantitatively or qualitatively to find out what competitors are doing in the market.

During *evaluation*, which roughly equates to *build* and *deploy* in the diagram, the team is exploring how well the website works and conducting summative research. You probably want to measure how well the website performs against benchmarks or business KPIs. For this you could conduct usability tests or use web usage analytics, or ideally both, so you get detailed qualitative data and quantitative statistics. You may also want to fine-tune your design. For this you could use rapid iterative usability tests, which are valuable for making small changes to a relatively mature design. You could also conduct A/B tests if you are uncertain about which changes to make, or sentiment analysis to find out what users are saying about your website.

Between *discovery* and *evaluation*, and part of both, is *design*. This is where you apply the data from your research and discover more questions to ask, or want to evaluate your designs with prototypes before building in code. Again, usability tests and interviews are useful here. You may also want to conduct research on parts of the design, such as card sorting or tree testing (inverse card sorting) for information architecture, and task analysis to design the task flow of the website.

Describing UX research methods

In this section, we will briefly describe common UX methods as they would be applied in a website development project. They are listed here alphabetically. We include methods that require testing with users and methods that rely on the UX practitioner's expertise. These expert methods should ideally be carried out by at least three to four experts to check for consistency of findings. The following table shows these methods organized by **FOCUS**, and shows the typical *context of use*. Some methods are repeated in different areas of focus because they apply equally in both.

FOCUS	METHODS	CONTEXT
USABILITY & EXPERIENCE	A/B test	Field
	Cognitive walkthrough	Lab
	Diary study	Field
	Ethnography	Field
	Eye tracking	Lab
	Focus group	Lab
	Heuristic analysis	Lab
	Interview	Lab / Field
	Sentiment analysis	Field
	Survey	Field
	Usability test	Lab / Field
	Web usage analytics	Field
INFORMATION ARCHITECTURE, CONTENT & TASKS	Card sorting and tree testing	Lab / Field
	Cognitive walkthrough	Lab
	Content audit	Lab
	Ethnography	Field
	Heuristic analysis	Lab
	Interview	Lab / Field
	Survey	Field
	Task analysis	Lab
	Web usage analytics	Field
STAKEHOLDERS	Content audit	Lab
	Ethnography	Field
	Interview	Field / Lab
	Survey	Field
COMPETITORS	Competitor analysis	Lab
	Cognitive walkthrough	Lab
	Heuristic analysis	Lab
	Usability test	Lab / Field

Table of UX methods by focus and context

Let's have a look at each method in the table:

- **A/B test**: A quantitative method where a single design change is made for a website. Two versions are created and compared by dividing participants into two groups and giving one version to each group. This is called **multivariate testing** if there are more than two versions. You need the same number of user groups as you have design variations. We discuss A/B tests in more detail in Chapter 9, *Optimize your UX Strategy with Iterative User Testing*.

- **Card sorting**: A quantitative method for creating or adjusting a *website's information architecture* and *terminology*, which informs site navigation design. Participants are asked to group concepts into categories so the designer can understand how they think about the information. *Inverse card sorting*, or *tree testing*, tests findability by asking participants to find items in an existing navigation structure. Card sorting is discussed in detail in Chapter 6, *Create a UX Strategy - Users and Content*.

- **Cognitive walkthrough**: An expert method where the UX researcher completes tasks on the website or prototype, using their knowledge of usability guidelines and standards to review it from a user perspective and find problems.

- **Competitor analysis**: An analysis of competitor websites to find out what they do well and badly, learn more about the domain, and discover best practices in the market. It is a meta-method, as different methods can be used to analyze the competition, for example content audits, heuristic analyses, cognitive walkthroughs, and usability tests. We described competitor analyses in Chapter 2, *Stand Out from Your Competitors*.

- **Content audit**: An expert analysis of the content that will be on the website. If you are redesigning an existing website, then this will list every piece of content on the website, including downloadable content and webpages, and assess whether it should be included in the new website. If there is no existing website, then the content audit is used to understand the content that will be on the website. We describe content audits in this chapter in the *Doing expert analyses* section.

- **Diary study**: A qualitative method where participants are given a diary to record regular aspects of their lives, such as when they do certain behaviors, for example, when they do a Google search, or when they interact with your website. Typically, participants keep the diaries for some time and are often interviewed at the beginning and end of the study. Other objects besides diaries can be used, for example, disposable cameras or apps with reminders.

- **Ethnography**: A qualitative method where the researcher studies people in the contexts in which they will be using the website, such as their homes, work, or social environments. It is used to understand the culture, beliefs, motivations, and behavior of a group of people, from their own perspective. We discuss ethnography in this chapter in the *Using qualitative techniques* section.

- **Eye tracking**: A method that can be used both qualitatively and quantitatively, depending on the number of people you test with. Participants' eye movements are tracked as they look at a web page. The results are shown in heat maps, which show where participants looked and for how long, and gaze plots, which show the sequence of eye movements. This gives information about what features are examined, which are ignored and how quickly the user scans each page. Specialist equipment and analysis software is needed for this method.

- **Focus group**: A qualitative method where a group of 5-10 participants are guided in an open discussion about an idea or product. This could be the concept for a website or the website itself. The method is typically used to understand people's attitudes and feelings about the concept or product.

- **Heuristic analysis**: An expert method, where an existing website is reviewed by the UX practitioner using heuristics, based with the practitioner's expertise, for example, usability guidelines and psychological or perceptual theories. We discuss heuristic analysis in this chapter in the *Doing expert analyses* section.

- **Interview**: A core qualitative method where the UX researcher asks participants questions about themselves and their experiences with a website. They can be structured or flexible. Contextual interviews are conducted in the participant's context or in the context of product usage. They are often used with usability tests. We discuss interviews as a core qualitative technique later in this chapter, and as part of a usability test session in Chapter 9, *Optimize your UX Strategy with Iterative User Testing*.

- **Sentiment analysis**: A quantitative method where social media sites are monitored for specific mentions, to understand how people are reacting to the website or brand. These mentions are usually automatically coded as positive, negative, or neutral.

- **Survey**: A quantitative method where a questionnaire is designed and shared with many users, usually by email or online. The questions must be designed carefully so as not to introduce bias.

- **Task analysis**: A qualitative method used to plan and understand the tasks on a website from the user's perspective. Once the UX researcher has researched the website's potential users and the tasks that they can perform on the website, task analysis is used to design the task and interaction flow of the website. For each task, researchers map out what triggers the task, what users already know, what they need to be told, how they will finish the task, and the processes and tools they will use to finish it.

- **Usability test**: A qualitative method where a user is observed performing tasks using a website, or prototype. These test the ease of use and learnability of the interface, where problems happen, and how the user feels about the experience. Usability tests are often paired with contextual interviews to gather more information about the experience. We discuss usability tests in detail in `Chapter 9`, *Optimize your UX Strategy with Iterative User Testing*.

- **Web usage analytics**: While not strictly a method, we have added web usage analytics here, as they have become a cornerstone of UX web research. Free services such as Google Analytics are simple to add to a website, and provide quantitative results on how people are using it, for example, reports on which page users leave the site from, and typical paths through the website. We discuss how to plan and incorporate web usage analytics effectively into your research in `Chapter 9`, *Optimize your UX Strategy with Iterative User Testing*.

Setting up a research plan

Research takes time and resources. It underpins the whole project, as design decisions are made based on the outcomes of research. Therefore, it makes sense to plan it carefully so you create a solid foundation for your website. Just like projects need project management to ensure that they meet their goals successfully and timeously, research benefits from creating and following a structured research plan.

Research plans should be documented and shared with the team and stakeholders. They help you to ensure that everyone is aware of the research and involved in it. It is always a good idea to have as many team members involved in the research as possible. If everyone involved in the web project is aware of the reasons for and results from the research, there are less likely to be conflicts over user needs and design decisions in the future.

Although UX research does not aspire to the rigor of scientific enquiry, the components of a research plan are based on the scientific method. The scientific method is the process that guides scientific research, and has been used for centuries to plan and conduct research successfully.

At its simplest, it can be described as principles guiding a process of making predictions based on hypotheses or theories, and then testing those predictions to find out if the hypotheses were correct. The following diagram shows typical steps of the scientific method, alongside a UX research plan:

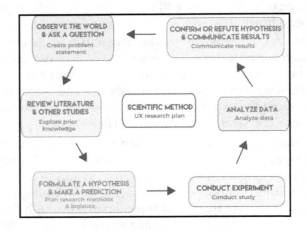

The scientific method and UX research

The steps of a research plan are:

1. Deciding on a problem statement or research question.
2. Exploring prior knowledge and literature.
3. Planning research methods and logistics.
4. Conducting the study.
5. Analyzing data.
6. Communicating results.

We describe the research plan as a series of steps, which map to how it will be documented. However, like the UCD process, it is more of an iterative cycle, with some steps being revisited. For example, you will probably return to *step 1* and refine your problem statement after having explored prior knowledge in *step 2*. We will examine each of these steps in turn, using the example of *a redesign project for an e-commerce site selling clothing*.

Deciding on a problem statement

When you begin a web design project, you should first work out what the problem is that you want to solve. This is based on why you are creating the website. It is one of the more difficult parts of creating a research plan.

 Your problem statement should indicate the goal of the project in enough detail that it communicates the reason for the research and the high-level conditions for success.

For example, if you are redesigning an existing website, then your web presence is not satisfactory or sufficient. However, this is not enough information for the problem statement.

The problem statement for re-designing a clothing e-commerce site might be: *Redesign the site to display the product range more clearly and enhance the company brand. This should improve retention of existing customers and increase online sales.*

If you are part of a business where research is conducted regularly as part of continually improving the website, it can be difficult to decide what to research. In this case, a framework might help you decide on the most important user experience issues for your business to investigate. For example, Google's research team developed the **HEART framework** for thinking about which web analytics to examine. The components of the HEART framework are:

- **Happiness**: User attitudes, such as satisfaction and perceived ease-of-use
- **Engagement**: Level of user involvement in your website
- **Adoption**: New users for the product or features of the product
- **Retention**: Returning existing users
- **Task success**: Efficiency, effectiveness, and error rate

There are various sources that can inform your problem statement or selection of framework, such as the business' or website's value propositions or **key performance indicators (KPIs)**. Like the HEART framework, KPIs can guide ongoing research in an organization as they relate back to business goals. KPIs are measures used to evaluate the progress and success of business goals. The KPIs for different departments of a business, such as marketing or accounting, will be different as each department has its own goals. UX KPIs focus on goals related to customer behavior and experiences. These should be based on your organization's specific customer experiences to be most effective, although general UX goals such as maximizing task success rate are a good way to begin.

If you are developing UX KPIs within an organization, it is also important to align them to key business goals to gain internal traction for your research. Examples of typical business goals are increasing revenue or market share, or decreasing costs.

KPIs and other information to inform your problem statement may be immediately available to you, or you may have to do some initial reading and interviewing to discover them. This is *step 2* of the research plan, which we will discuss next.

Exploring prior knowledge and literature

Once you have defined your problem statement, you can take stock of the knowledge that already exists in the design and development team, in the business, in the market, and in other literature. Questions to ask include:

- Has any research already been conducted about the target users of the website?
- What are the business requirements for this project? Are there key performance indicators (KPIs) that should be considered as conditions for success?
- What is the value proposition of the brand? Are there value propositions specific to this project?
- Who is the competition, how successful are they, what are they good at, and what are their value propositions?
- What technological constraints are there? What are the probable technological requirements?
- What is the domain of the website? Is there any knowledge within the business about this?

Gaining some of this information will mean reading documents and articles, or reminding yourself about UX principles. Some of this information may require more research to find information, patterns or apply guidelines, for example, interviewing stakeholders about business requirements or domain knowledge, or conducting an expert analysis of an existing site to find problems before a redesign.

 In our clothing e-commerce example, the business KPIs for this project are mentioned in the problem statement, "retention of existing customers" and "increase online sales". A good start in exploring prior knowledge would be to interview key stakeholders about these KPIs for more detail.

If you do not have access to these details, then you probably need to conduct a separate research project to discover them. For example, consider the value proposition(s) of a business. A **value proposition** describes in one or two short sentences why the brand, product or service is different from competitors and why the user should interact with or commit to the brand, product, or service. Examples of values are affordable pricing, high quality unique products, or exceptional experience when interacting with the brand. As we stated in Chapter 2, *Stand Out from Your Competitors*, the way people perceive brands influences where they spend their time and money. Therefore, it is important to ensure that the website messaging matches the value propositions of the business. If the UX researcher does not have value propositions to work with in designing the website, they might need to conduct studies to find out what potential users respond to and define values for the website.

 In our clothing e-commerce example, the problem statement indicates that the project aims to "enhance the brand". The design team needs to know the value proposition of the brand to enhance it. If you found out that the business brand was not well defined internally, you would need to conduct studies with potential and existing customers of the business to find out what value they perceived in the brand, or how they responded to possible values. This could be done through a range of methods, for example, ethnography, contextual interviews, or sentiment analysis.

The output of this step should be a summary of patterns and ideas from prior knowledge that will feed into the design of this study. At this point, you should be able to plan your research practically. The previous two steps must have provided the necessary information, or more preliminary research may be necessary.

Planning research methods and logistics

Once you have decided on a problem statement and explored the prior knowledge available to you, you have enough information to plan the research for what you do not know. There are several steps here:

1. Plan how to test your problem statement practically. Choose metrics to answer it.
2. Choose one or more research methods that will allow you to gather the data and measure the metrics.
3. Plan research logistics and create checklists.
4. Do a pilot test if appropriate.

We will discuss each of these following steps, using our clothing e-commerce example. The problem statement from our example is:

Redesign the site to display the product range more clearly and enhance the company brand. This should improve retention of existing customers and increase online sales.

Turning your problem statement into measurable metrics

The first step is to turn your problem statement into testable questions or metrics. A good testable metric has three qualities:

- **Time**: It is measured over a specified time, so you know when to stop measuring.
- **Benchmark**: It is measured against a benchmark, so you know what good and bad values are. This benchmark can be an industry standard or a value that has been calculated within your company.
- **Distinct**: It is based on distinct actions or reactions by the user. This can be measured directly by analytics or coded from more qualitative data.

Some qualitative methods do not deliver data that can be turned into a testable metric. In these cases, we define the questions that we want to answer to provide rich context for our designs. These can be useful for creating scenarios and stories about people to educate the design team and stakeholders about their users.

The Google HEART framework provides a useful method for turning your problem statement into testable metrics--The **Goals-Signals-Metrics** formalism. The value of this formalism is that it helps you to turn your abstract goals into specific, measurable metrics. If you are missing information, this becomes obvious as you work through the process.

 In our example, it would become clear that "enhance the company brand" is too vague to be measured practically and needs more information, leading to a separate study to test customer engagement with business values.

he following diagram shows a possible Goals-Signals-Metrics table for our e-commerce example:

GOALS	SIGNALS	METRICS
Enhance company brand	Positive social media comments about the brand values of "comfort while exercising" and "wide range to fit all sizes"	Positive mentions of brand with value keywords on Twitter and Facebook
Display product range more clearly	Customers find products more easily	Number of clicks to find product
Improve retention	Increase numbers of returning customers	Increased proportion of return visitors
Increase online sales	Increased conversion from visits to sales	Increased proportion of sales to visits

Goals-Signals-Metrics example

There are four goals in this problem statement. The first two, *display product range more clearly* and *enhance company brand* are more implicit, as they look like design actions. However, if we examine the statement carefully, within the Goals-Signals-Metrics formalism, it should be clear that the success outcomes are business goals and not UX goals. We need interim UX goals, with related signals and metrics, to be able to check validity of the research. For instance, if we build the designs, but they do not lead to increased online sales or improved retention, we cannot be sure whether the problem is:

- that our designs displayed the product range more clearly and enhanced the company brand, but this did not lead to increased sales and retention
- that our designs did not display the product range more clearly or enhance the company brand

To test where the problem is, we need to know whether we designed according to the specification. To do this, we need to test our designs with users. This example highlights the need for UX KPIs related to specific UX goals within an organization, which are distinct from the business's goals and KPIs.

Signals and metrics in the Goals-Signals-Metrics formalism match to the UX KPIs. They share the same requirements for being effective and measurable--time based, benchmarked, and related to distinct requirements. Some examples of typical UX KPIs that can easily be tracked with analytics or surveys are task success rate, time on task, error rate, net promoter rates (likelihood of recommending the website to others), and level of customer satisfaction.

Choosing a research method

Once you know what you want to research and the metrics that you want to use, you can decide which research method(s) to implement. While specifying the metrics, you have probably already narrowed this down, as certain metrics can more easily be gathered using specific methods, for example analytics, usability tests or questionnaires.

The method will have implications for the kind of data that is produced, the number of participants, and how the data can be analyzed. We have already discussed these issues, and we will be discussing some specific examples in later sections, so we focus on high level concerns here. Some considerations to guide your decision are:

- *Do you want statistically significant results, which is useful for persuading stakeholders or benchmarking?* You need many participants, so choose a quantitative method where this is easy to achieve, such as leveraging web usage analytics, A/B tests or remote unmoderated usability tests.
- *Do you want details about what problems people are experiencing on your website?* You need a qualitative method where you can observe people interacting and possibly ask about it. For example, moderated usability tests, or contextual interviews.
- *Do you want to know more about people's feelings, attitudes, and experiences in their lives or around the domain?* You need a method that tracks feelings, asks questions, and/or allows observation of people in context. For example, ethnography, surveys, interviews, or sentiment analysis.

When you choose the method at this level, you also choose the data analysis. You can start gathering, preparing, or researching:

- **Statistics**: Review the statistics package or the specific tests that you will use to analyze the numbers in a large study.
- **Codes**: Create the codes and keywords that you will use to guide your qualitative analysis. These will be based on the metrics that you identified previously.
- **Task criteria**: Define the tasks that you will ask participants to perform, and the criteria that you will measure their performance against.

In our e-commerce example, we might decide to conduct a usability study to determine whether users find products more easily; sentiment analysis to find out if customers are responding to our refined brand values; and analytics to check if we've improved retention and increased online sales.

Planning research logistics and creating checklists

There are many logistics that need to be organized for a research project to be completed successfully. It is a good idea to create checklists that you can check items off against as they are handled. The nature of these checklists will depend on the project and the method. We will provide example checklists for the methods we describe in detail later in this chapter and in Chapter 9, *Optimize your UX Strategy with Iterative User Testing*. Here are some of the practical details that you will need to consider when creating checklists:

- *How will you recruit participants for your research?* Will your team recruit participants themselves, use an external recruiter, use analytics of customers who visit your website, email from your customer list, use social media, or some other method?
    - If recruiting, you will need to create a *recruitment brief and screening questions* to describe the type of participants that you want, in terms of their demographics, interests, and capabilities.
- *What will participants need during the session?* What, if any, incentives will you need to collect beforehand? Will they need refreshments? What information do you need to tell them before the test session? Will they use paper, a computer, a phone, or other supplies during the session? Are you testing a prototype? How will that be presented?
- *Where will the research happen?* Will it happen in the field, in a lab, remotely with a moderator, or remotely unmoderated?
    - If the research happens in the field, you will need to carry everything you need with you. See the ethnography example in the *Using qualitative techniques* section for more details.
    - If the research is happening at a lab, you will need to book it, either internally or externally.
    - What support do you need at the venue? For example, someone to greet participants as they arrive, or IT support.
- *What equipment is needed for the research?* You may need computer equipment, cables, cameras, microphones, portable Wi-Fi hotspots, USB storage and sticky notes.

- *When will the research happen?* The dates and times of test sessions, or the dates when surveys will be sent out, or the cut-off for analytics.
    - If recruiting, participants will need to be reminded closer to the time to lessen no-shows.
- *Who will be attending research sessions?* It is very useful for stakeholders and team members to attend research sessions, in person or remotely. This is the only contact with real users that many of them will have. Seeing people trying to use the product is one of the best ways to persuade stakeholders and team members about user experience problems:
    - If team members will be attending the sessions, they need to be invited and provided with guidelines on how to behave.
    - For both observers and participants, you will need refreshments.
- *What research documentation do you need?* For example, consent forms for participants, scripts for researchers, guidelines for observers, directions or maps to the facility, participant and observer lists with their contact details.
- *What is the structure of the research session?* How each session will be structured, for example, how participants will be welcomed, and the tasks that they will be given.
- *What could go wrong?* Have plans for things that might go wrong. For example, if you do not have Wi-Fi or your equipment breaks, have a local copy of your website, or some paper print outs that you can use to get some data from participants.

Conducting a pilot test

Once you have prepared your research study, conduct a pilot test with at least one, but ideally a few, representative users to check that it works the way you expect it to. This will help you in a number of ways, depending on the research:

- Make sure the instructions are understandable to participants
- Test the difficulty and timing of your tasks to ensure that you have created them at the correct level and they do not take too long
- Practice your script and facilitation before the real test
- Make sure that you have remembered everything that you will need, and that it all works properly

Schedule pilot tests for some time before the real study, so that you have time to fix problems with tasks, scripts, or equipment. Make sure that the pilot testers are similar to the participants of the real study. If you do not have time or resources to accomplish this, then at least make sure that they are unfamiliar with the research.

Conducting the study

If you have done all of the preparation described in this chapter, conducting the study itself should be fairly straightforward. The reason for the preparation is to make the study run as smoothly as possible, so you can focus on interacting with participants and gaining valid and reliable results.

As the preceding sections indicate, a lot of preparation goes into a research study. However, if you have created checklists and checked them off as you prepare, and conducted a pilot test, you can be reasonably sure that you are ready.

If you are conducting moderated research:

- Pay attention to everything during the study. Take photos if possible to document the sessions for later.
- Take notes as you will likely not remember to write down all observations later.
- Meet with observers between sessions to discuss observations, and any questions or suggestions they may have.
- Save recordings after each session, or record to the cloud if possible, so that you do not lose anything.
- Organize each participant's documents, so that they are not mixed up later.

If you are monitoring unmoderated research, such as surveys or web usage analytics, check in regularly and organize the results. Then you can adjust the research if necessary.

Analyzing data

We will not describe data analysis in much detail here, as it varies considerably depending on the study:

- A web analytics study or A/B test will provide many numbers that you will enter into specific statistical tests, depending on what you want to find out. For example, a comparison of average task times and success rates between two groups who experienced different designs; or an idea of whether significantly more people are visiting certain areas of your site after a design change.

- An ethnography will provide artifacts in the form of photos, videos, original documents, or copies, and so on, which need to be examined according to metrics that you have defined. There will also be extensive observations that need to be coded and their content analyzed.

There are many other types of results. You may not even perform your own analysis. Companies such as Optimal Workshop and UserTesting are research platforms that help you with remote studies and perform initial analysis for you.

We will discuss various forms of analysis in detail as we describe specific research methods later in this chapter and Chapter 9, *Optimize your UX Strategy with Iterative User Testing*.

Presenting results

Once you have conducted the research, various things need to happen with the results:

- **Design input**: Research informs design, so the results should be communicated to the design team, so they can make decisions on how to act on the research results.
- **Bugs and code fine-tuning**: If bugs occurred in the software during the study, or obvious improvements to the code, communicate this to developers in a list or the software management tool being used.
- **Report or presentation**: Prepare a report for stakeholders and team members who were not able to attend the research sessions. This should include many of the details from the research plan to provide context for the results and describe the participants.
- **Research plan**: Save the research plan in a project repository so it can be used or referred to for future research.
- **Next research**: Ideas for future or follow-on research may have emerged from the study. Record these and potentially start planning them.
- **Raw data**: Save the raw data from the study in a project or company repository where it can be referred to again. This includes spreadsheets of numbers, photos, videos, recordings, notes, prototypes, and so on.

Doing expert analyses

As a UX practitioner, you must conduct research with real people and users of your products. However, when you first approach any research problem it should be examined and analyzed using your expertise.

This will provide you with a solid foundation for the rest of the research and design. All through a project, you should continue to review the work in this way.

In this section, we will examine two methods that rely on UX practitioners' expertise-- heuristic analyses and content audits.

Heuristic analysis

Heuristic analysis is an expert UX research method, where the practitioner evaluates an interface using selected heuristics. Heuristics are practical guidelines for doing work, based on established principles. Heuristic analysis should never replace testing an interface with users; it has been shown that one expert will only find about a third of the usability problems that will occur in a usability test. However, it is very useful to enhance your research. The heuristics are also guidelines that are useful to be aware of during usability tests, so they are worth knowing.

Heuristic analyses can be conducted on a live website, or on a prototype. Therefore, they can be used very early in a web design project to evaluate early designs. Ideally, a heuristic analysis should be performed by at least three to five people independently, to find a good number of the probable usability problems. It is likely that you will not have time or resources to fix all of the problems, so it is a good idea to assign severity and frequency ratings to the findings, to guide designers in fixing the problems. For each problem, each evaluator should indicate:

- **Severity**: This can be a number or a color code indicating whether the problem is minor, major, or disastrous. A *minor* problem is one that is unlikely to cause the user more than a little irritation. Too many of these will cause dissatisfaction with an interface. A *major* problem is one that is likely to cause the user some concern or difficulty, but they will overcome it. A *disastrous* problem is one that the user is unable to recover from. These must be fixed or the interface will be unusable.
- **Frequency**: How often the problem occurs. If a minor problem occurs many times on the website, it could become a major problem because of users' increasing dissatisfaction.
- **Related heuristic**: The evaluator should specify the heuristic(s) that relate to the problem, and describe how they are related.

Some heuristic analyses also indicate positive findings: parts of the interface that are delightful or likely to work very well for the user.

The heuristics that are used in a heuristic evaluation can vary greatly. They should be stated at the beginning of the evaluation report, with a description of each heuristic, so that readers can fully understand the evaluator's decisions.

- You should begin by considering project-specific heuristics, as these will be most applicable to your website. These might relate to your business' or website's value propositions, or other visual and interaction guidelines provided by your organization.
- The heuristics that are most often used were developed by Jakob Nielsen, of the Nielsen-Norman group, and Rolf Molich. These 10 principles are broad guidelines for finding typical usability issues within a user interface. We will describe these next, and you can find them at www.nngroup.com/articles/ten-usability-heuristics/
- There are many other heuristics that can be used. One of the more comprehensive lists that is worth following comes from another member of the Nielsen-Norman group, Bruce Tognazzi. His list is titled *First Principles of Interaction Design* and contains 19 major guidelines, each with several sub-principles. They can be found at asktog.com/atc/principles-of-interaction-design/

If you are unsure of where to begin, Nielsen and Molich's 10 Usability Heuristics are a useful and concise place to begin. The heuristics are:

1. **Visibility of system status**: Users should always know where they are on a website, and how they got there. The website should provide feedback about what is going on so that the user notices it in time. This can include animations, micro-interactions, website notifications, and explanatory copy. For example, *showing a loading indicator or progress bar when a page takes longer than half a second to load*.

2. **Match between system and real world**: The website should use language that is easily understandable to its users, not technical terms or jargon. Interactions should feel natural and information should be laid out logically, using familiar conventions. For example, *design the reading level of your website to be appropriate for your audience, especially if your users are likely to include second-language speakers*.

3. **User control and freedom**: Users should feel in control of their experiences while interacting with a website. Allow users to easily undo actions or cancel processes that they have started. While browsing a website the user must at all times have the opportunity to correct information or reverse actions if they feel they've made a wrong turn. Users will be encouraged to explore and interact with your website, thereby becoming more engaged. For example, *on an e-commerce site allows users to easily remove items from the checkout basket. They will likely be happier to put items in the basket and may end up buying more from you.*

4. **Consistency and standards**: Follow standards and be consistent in how you present different services on your website and respond to user actions in similar circumstances. This will help ensure that users do not become confused about correct actions to take or the meaning of images or words. Using platform standards such as iOS Human Interface Guidelines and Google's material design helps to create this consistency. Users form expectations for how things will look and behave, often based on conventions that they have experienced elsewhere. For example, *the shopping cart icon clearly signifies the checkout on e-commerce sites. If you use a different icon or term, it is likely that users will not easily find the checkout. Or they will find it because it is in the upper right corner of your website, which is another standard.*

5. **Error prevention**: A good design should try to prevent users from making mistakes by ensuring that problematic situations do not occur or are well communicated. This usually requires designing according to your users' mental models about how things work. You can also introduce confirmation messages when users are deleting things, but be careful about relying on them too frequently as users will learn to click through and ignore them. *An example of error prevention is form fields such as telephone numbers, which allow users to enter their numbers in a variety of ways: with or without spaces, brackets, and dashes. The fields are designed to operate according to users' mental models, not constrain them into a specific form.*

6. **Recognition rather than recall**: People recognize objects, phrases, and actions much more easily than they recall them. A website should reduce users' cognitive load by making all interactive objects and options as visible as possible. Users working through a process on the website should not have to remember information from step to step; it should be visible or obvious where to retrieve it. For example, *search facilities that offer suggestions when users start typing help those who misremember or misspell search terms by offering options for recognition.*

7. **Flexibility and efficiency of use**: Allow users to customize their experiences on your website, especially actions they perform frequently. Offer experienced users expert ways of doing things, while making things simpler and easier for novice users. For example, *image search facilities that offer a simple search box, but also provide the ability to open more advanced options, which constrain the search further.*

8. **Aesthetic and minimalistic design**: Every element and piece of information in the UI should have a specific purpose. The interface should be uncluttered, so that elements do not fight for attention. For example, *background images and flamboyant typography can make content difficult to read and distract from images that you want users to focus on.*

9. **Help users recognize, diagnose, and recover from errors**: Error messages should use simple, plain, non-technical language to explain to users what went wrong and how to recover. They should be in context and be visible. For example, *if a user makes an error on a form field, place the error message close to the field, use multiple means such as color and font weight to highlight it, and direct the user's attention to it.*

10. **Help and documentation**: Even though the ideal is that websites do not need documentation, there are often cases where useful hints can reduce user frustrations and make their experiences more enjoyable. If you offer help, make sure it is clear, easy to find, and lists practical steps for action. For example, *if an e-commerce website offers to deliver purchases, there should be a link to information about deliveries easily visible in the checkout process.*

Content audit

Whether starting a project from scratch or redesigning an existing website, a content audit is useful as it creates a consolidated list of content items that should be included on your website. This provides an easy reference when planning your information architecture, where you design or redesign the structure in which content items relate to one another. It will help you visualize how much content you have and its quality, both of which influence the scope of the project. It will also provide an artifact for everyone working on the project to refer to, which helps to ensure that everyone is communicating effectively.

If you are redesigning an existing website, then evaluating its content will help you decide which content should not be included in the redesign, because it is not valid anymore, or it duplicates other content. It will also help you decide which content to promote more because it is popular.

If you are creating a new website, perform a content audit by listing all the resources that you will be using to create the website. These could be spreadsheets, forms, white papers, paper documents, manuals, images, videos, and so on. In this section, we will describe how to inventory the contents of an existing website, but you can easily modify the process to consider project and business resources instead.

To create a simple content audit, create a spreadsheet with columns for each piece of information you want to record about each content item. Content items can be recorded hierarchically, beginning with each webpage, and drilling down to each piece of text, image, and download. You might want to place different types of content, such as pages versus downloads, on different sheets, depending on the size of the website. Typical columns include:

- **ID or reference code**: This is a unique value to identify the content item.
- **Navigation**: Shows the position of the content item within the website hierarchy.
- **Page title**: This is the title used within the page's HTML metadata. This is the same title that will be displayed on the browser tab.
- **URL**: The path to the page where the content item exists.
- **Content type/page type**: Different content types on your website, such as blog posts, forum pages, main content pages, pages with interactive elements like a map, images, PDF downloads, and so on.
- **Description**: A brief description of the page contents.
- **Last updated**: Date of when the content item was last updated.
- **Owner**: The person responsible for the content. This is often the author.
- **Action**: What should be done with the content. Should it be deleted, kept, modified? This could potentially be a couple.
- **Analytics**: Number and title of columns depends on the analytics that you want to collect. For example, visits, bounce rate, conversions, links, shares, and so on.
- **Comments**: Can be useful to record observations about the content item such as missing elements, or comments on quality.

A full content audit can be very time consuming. If you do not have the time to inventory every page, you can gain insight by auditing a sub-section of the website. Choose what you audit carefully, so you have a good overview of the site. Use analytics to select pages that are popular, and low traffic pages. You may want to concentrate on more recently modified items for items such as blogs and forum posts, if you have content stretching back a few years.

As you perform the content audit, you can evaluate the content. For example:

- **Age**: Divide content into latest, stale, or expired, and timeless items.
- **Relevance**: What content is rarely used and perhaps should be removed; what content is popular and perhaps should be extended or access to it improved.
- **Missing**: Where are there holes? What new content do you need?
- **File types and formats**: Are they still valid? Do they need to be updated?
- **Tone and quality of content**: Is the tone and quality of the content consistent throughout the site? Is the terminology used the same?
- **Metadata**: Are page titles descriptive and accurate to the page content? Do the page descriptions reinforce the key page messaging?
- **Messaging**: Do you have pages supporting the purposes of the site? Do they do this effectively? For example, do you have effective pages for brand awareness, searching for products or articles, choosing between products or articles, converting to buy or download?
- **File sizes**: Are your image and download sizes optimized for the web?

Using qualitative techniques

The two primary techniques for qualitative data gathering are *interviews* and *observation*. Most qualitative methods use one or both of these techniques. Content analysis is the primary technique for data analysis. We will discuss all these techniques in `Chapter 9,` *Optimize your UX Strategy with Iterative User Testing* when we describe usability testing. Here, we will briefly describe them and give tips. Then we will describe an example ethnography, which is a qualitative method that uses both observation and interview techniques.

Interviews

Interviews can be structured, unstructured, or semi-structured. A structured interview consists of a set of questions, which are followed without deviation. An unstructured interview consists of a conversation that is loosely guided by topics. Semi-structured interviews combine a set of questions with the flexibility to deviate or ask further questions during the interview. Semi-structured interviews are the best form for UX--the questions provide structure and ensure that the interviewer gains the information that is required; the flexibility allows unforeseen insights to be gained.

UX practitioners must be careful how they use interviews. A common adage in UX is *Watch users act, don't listen to what they say*. This is a valid point. If asked what they would do in specific circumstances, people generally speculate incorrectly about their actions. It is always best to watch someone try to perform an action, rather than asking them how they would do it. However, if we want to find out about people's typical daily activities, their attitudes about something, or their knowledge about a domain, interviews are very useful.

Tips for interviewing

- Have a script for the interview, with the questions that you want to ask. You can use this to guide your notes. However, do not be too tied to the script. If it makes sense during the interview, be open to deviation.

- Arrange questions in a logical conversational order that also prioritizes them. If you run out of time in an interview, you want to be sure that you've addressed the most important items in your script.

- Spend a few minutes at the beginning of the interview explaining the process to the person you are interviewing, and making them feel comfortable with you and the process. Ask a few ice-breaking questions, such as general questions about their work and interests.

- Always ask for real examples to anchor people's answers. If you ask about opinions or feelings, ask about the last time they felt these things and why. Ask for details about the situation, people and objects involved and other contextual details. These will trigger accurate memories about critical moments.

- If you want to ask about people's actions, ask specific retrospective questions to anchor people's memories, rather than general activities. If necessary, you can ask add-on questions to probe further. For example, *tell me when you first looked at Twitter yesterday?* rather than *when do you typically look at Twitter during a day?* A possible follow on question here is *so, you didn't look at your phone before breakfast yesterday?*

- Ask closed-ended questions leading to open-ended questions. You do not want only yes and no answers. However, these can lead usefully to more open answers in an interview. For example, *do you have a Twitter account?* followed by *why is that?*, *when do you use it?*, or *can you tell me about the last time you posted?*

- Do not ask leading questions. For example, ask *what do you think about Twitter?* rather than *do you like Twitter?*

- To record the interview, ideally either have another researcher with you who will take detailed notes, or record the interview. If you do not have a notetaker present and cannot record the interview, take brief notes that will spark your memory later. Use the questions as a guiding structure for your notes. In all cases, make sure that you set aside time after the interview to reflect on the interview and fill in the details in your notes. If you have a notetaker, you can compare important findings. If you have a recording, your notes will help you find crucial parts of the recording.
- Since interviews are not a quantitative technique, you can change details without affecting the results negatively. This means that your questions can and should evolve as you interview more people and discover questions that do not work, or new questions that should be asked.

Observation

Observation involves watching people either performing specific tasks, or doing their normal activities without any directed actions. Observation can also involve participation, where you take part in people's activities and reflect on the experience. You can either watch people in a lab setting, such as on-site usability tests, or in the field in their own contexts. Observation in the field provides rich data about people's lives and the contexts in which they will use your website. In the lab, it provides details about how they approach tasks.

Tips for observation

- Prepare a guide for the kind of things you want to observe, so you know where to focus your attention.
- As with interviews, spend some time at the beginning telling participants about yourself and the research so they feel comfortable with you there.
- Take notes about the context in which people are acting. For example, the spaces, the documents, the people, daily schedules, equipment, software, and furniture. Draw diagrams or sketches.
- Take notes about processes that people follow, and workarounds they use for when processes or software does not work the way they need it to.

- If possible, take photos and videos of the context, objects, and documents that people use. Ask people to give you copies of important documents for your analysis.
- Think of the kinds of design deliverables that you want to create from the research and let this guide your observations. For example, user journey maps, personas, scenarios, and stories.
- Look for the triggers for actions, and the typical results of actions to understand user needs and expectations.
- Observe how the people interact: how they communicate, interrupt each other, and support each other.

Content analysis

Whether you observe or interview people, you will generate a large amount of semi-structured or unstructured data in the form of words, images, videos, photos, and so on. Analyzing qualitative data takes a long time and can be overwhelming. Here are some hints for how to begin the analysis:

- Use your questions or observation guidelines to help structure the content. These are based on reasons you wanted to conduct the research and will help you deliver meaningful results.
- Extract user scenarios of action, journeys, and descriptions of people for your deliverables as you work through the content.
- Begin by using mind mapping as you review the data, to identify trends and patterns that you can use to structure it.
- Look for unexpected findings and surprises. These are valuable indicators of user needs or conditions that you have not considered yet.
- Gather quotes, video segments, and photos to support your design arguments and create background information for reporting to stakeholders.

Ethnography example - a financial services broker portal

Ethnography involves going into the field into people's real-world contexts and observing them without interference. You can ask questions about things you observe, but never direct people's actions.

As an anthropological technique, it often involves spending months or years with a group of people. As UX practitioners, we do not have that luxury. However, spending some time with user groups can deliver a lot of the value that traditional ethnography does. Even if you only spend a few hours in someone's context, you will gain a much richer, more accurate understanding of how your website can fit into their lives.

In the example we consider here, a team is redesigning the website for a financial investment institution. They want to improve their online portal for brokers to manage client portfolios. Before beginning design, you want to understand how brokers accomplish the task now and in what context, so you can design a portal that they will want to use.

You would set up observation of brokers associated with the financial institutions. Stakeholders here would be required to introduce your team to the brokers and secure access. Ideally, you would want to visit 3-5 different broker offices of different sizes or types, to gain a rounded picture. Conduct stakeholder interviews first and domain research, to gain background information that will inform the questions you ask and the observations you make.

Some questions to consider:

- Who does what work in the broker's offices? What roles are there that will have to be catered for on the portal? What rights and permissions do those roles need? Are there overlaps?
- How do broker's currently work with clients? What are the steps involved? What are the associated documents?
- What is difficult for brokers with the current system? What workarounds do they use?
- Are there particular time periods that are more or less important, and why? For example, times of day, days of the week, or weeks and months of the year, such as the financial year end?
- How do brokers store client details? How do they retrieve them when they want to talk to them?
- How important is face-to-face interaction with clients? To what extent can these be replaced with remote contact?

As you observe, more questions will emerge and some of the initial questions will fall away as they are not interesting when the context is appreciated.

Using quantitative techniques

In many ways, it is easier to use quantitative techniques for research, as long as you follow the structures and guidelines for setting them up. The difficulty with quantitative techniques is that the results do not have context. The context provided with qualitative research provides some insight into its validity. With quantitative techniques, numbers are often shown for how big an effect is, or how often something happens without describing how they were gathered or calculated. These numbers rely on careful data gathering and use of the correct statistical techniques for the size and shape of the population.

If you have analytics based on actual usage of a website, this provides some reliability, as the numbers come from people who are actually using your product. However, if you gather quantitative values through usability testing or surveys, the metrics that you use to gather the data and the sample of people that you test with is often hidden. This information must be included in any report so that the validity and reliability of the research can be examined. We discuss these details in `Chapter 9`, *Optimize your UX Strategy with Iterative User Testing* when we discuss using metrics for usability tests, analytics, surveys, and A/B tests. Here, we briefly describe statistics used for analysis, and how to choose a statistical test.

Using statistics

Statistical analysis is the method of analyzing quantitative results. The topic is too extensive to cover properly here. Many concepts such as power, population distribution, standard deviations, and so on, are important to consider. However, they are highly mathematical and difficult to grasp. Here, we will highlight a few concepts to be aware of before using any statistical tools or packages. They will provide you with a starting point for continued reading:

- **Statistical significance**: This is whether the value that you found in your test sample of users is due to chance or represents an actual value in all your users. If a result is significant, it means that it likely occurs in the larger population. Significance is reported with a particular confidence level (see the third point). Most statistical tests aim to calculate that likelihood (descriptive statistics, such as averages and ranges, aim to describe a sample and do not necessarily have to extrapolate to a population).

- **Sample size**: Sample size matters a lot in quantitative studies, as the statistics are only valid predictors of real values if your sample is a good size. To be completely rigorous, you should calculate the required sample size for the power and confidence interval you want to achieve in your research. However, as a general rule of thumb, you need 15-20 people per group to find reasonably large effects in the data. So, for an A/B test where you are testing two versions of the software, you need about 40 people. For card sorting, you need about 15 people.
- **Confidence level or p-value**: This refers to how confident you are that the results that you find in your sample can be applied to all users. Usually, statistics are considered good enough with a 95% confidence level, or a p-value of 0.05. This means that there is a 5% chance that the result you found does not actually exist in all users.
- **Confidence interval**: This is the range of values around a statistic where your confidence level applies. For example, if you found the average error rate in a set of tasks to be 1.5 with users you tested, a 95% confidence level will give you a range of values around 1.5, say 1.3 to 1.7, where you can be 95% certain that individual values from users you have not tested will occur.

Deciding which statistical test to use

To decide which statistical test to use to calculate your result, first work out whether your data is discrete or continuous:

- Discrete data consists of specific options, for example yes/no, pass/fail
- Continuous data is information that is measured on a scale and can have any value along that scale

For discrete data, we are often trying to work out whether the number of people who chose an option or passed/failed is significantly different to a benchmark or another group's value. A chi-squared test would usually be used for comparing groups and a binomial test for comparing against a benchmark.

For continuous data, we are often trying to work out whether two sets of values are significantly different to each other. For example, if two groups are given questionnaires about their experiences with two versions of a website, are these values significantly different, which means that one website is preferable to the other, or is the difference in questionnaire scores just due to chance? For two groups, a paired t-test is often used to calculate the values, while for more than two groups ANOVAs are used.

Summary

In this chapter, we have described how to conduct research as a foundation for your web design project, and to ensure its success throughout the project.

We began by defining and characterizing research, considering validity and reliability, quantitative and qualitative research, when to conduct research and common UX research methods.

Thereafter, we described how to set up and manage a research process from creating the research question to analyzing the results.

We discussed how to bring your own expertise into the research, and then delved into qualitative and quantitative techniques.

In the next few chapters, we will describe some of the deliverables that you can create to describe your research and define your UX strategy (Chapter 6, *Create a UX Strategy - Users and Content*), and how to design and create prototypes for your website based on the research and deliverables (Chapter 7, *Bring Your UX Strategy to Life with Wireframes and Prototypes*).

In Chapter 9, *Optimize your UX Strategy with Iterative User Testing*, we will return to research to describe how to test your designs, such as through usability tests and A/B tests. We will take many of the aspects that we have discussed here in theory and put them into practice then.

6
Create a UX Strategy - Users and Content

After laying the groundwork by analyzing the available information and doing some market research for your brand and website, you can start working on the actual UX strategy to achieve your goals and create a successful website. In this chapter, we'll look at the second layer of building blocks for a successful UX strategy by creating useful personas to give your strategy direction, building a solid **Information Architecture (IA)**, and creating a supporting sitemap with task flows to provide smooth user journeys. To get started with a UX strategy, the following components will be discussed in detail:

- Create functional personas
- Build a solid IA
- Card sorting as an IA tool
- Construct a site map
- Create task flows and user journeys

Creating personas to guide your UX strategy

When talking about personas, one assumes it refers to the *target market* or *segmentation* of a campaign or brand, the terms often used in marketing to describe the groups of users a brand or product is marketed to. The traditional target market is usually a collection of users created from data sourced from analytics or market research. Target markets tend to be treated as a clinical entity, like a set of numbers, whereby user research together with analytics and market research make the target market more personal and relatable to all the teams within an organization.

What is a persona? In the UX context a **persona** is a fictional character with human characteristics, behaviors, and needs based on a segmentation of the target market collected from actual data through field research.

It's a common misperception that personas are created from gut feel, and isolated from actual data, by marketing and UX teams. Actually, personas are more than just a dataset sourced from analytics; the personality traits and behaviors of personas make them more human and give designers, developers, and marketers the insight to relate to the users they're creating a website for.

Characteristics of a useful persona

Now that you know what a persona is, how do you create a useful persona for your UX strategy? Always remember that the UX industry evolves rapidly, and new and better ways of doing things surface weekly, thus the guidance for personas is not set in stone and is only a basic guide to get started. Create personas that are unique and useful to your UX strategy. The example we'll use in this book will follow the following structure:

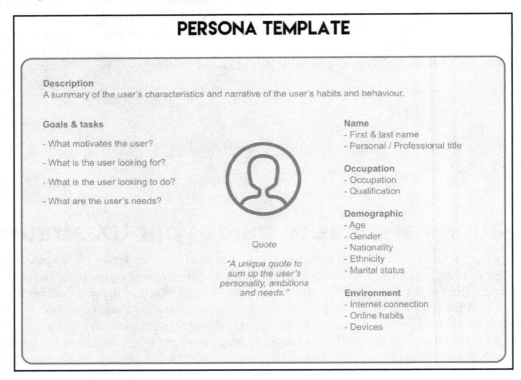

From the preceding basic template, a high fidelity example has been crafted of a typical persona used in a UX strategy based on the fundamental market research available for a specific brand. The target market consists of the following data:

- **Age**: 18-31 years
- **Gender**: Female
- **Education**: Tertiary education (diploma or degree)

PERSONA EXMAPLE

THE INNOVATOR

Amara Faye, is a young African American woman in her early twenties who lives in the vibrant city of Los Angeles. The city fits her personality perfectly as she lives for creative input from her environment. She knew from a young age that she wants to go into a creative field and being an Art Director comes naturally to her. She studied Visual Communication at the Los Angeles Creative School and landed her first job right after at an ad agency. She owns a Macbook Pro, iPad & iPhone and is connected to the internet 24/7. She spends on average between 5-8 hours a day online for both work and personal purposes.

What motivates Amara?
With her creative nature, Amara is motivated by anything visually stimulating, from taking art classes to exploring upper class deep house clubs in the CBD of Los Angeles.

What is she looking for?
Amara is looking for new creative ways to express herself.

What is she looking to do?
Amara is looking for inspiration to keep her up to date with new creative trends.

What are Amara's needs?
She wants to explore inspirational and creative platforms online.

"Find that creative spark and look for ways to make it a fire"

Name
Amara Faye (Miss)

Occupation
Art Director
BA in Visual Communication

Demographic
24, Female
African American
Single

Environment
10MB Fibre & 3G
5 - 8 hours a day
Desktop, tablet & mobile

Building a solid information architecture

One of the fundamental components of a successful website is the navigation. How does the user navigate through a website to find what they're looking for? If the menu items are not labeled correctly and clearly, or the information is not categorized accurately under the associated sections, the user will find it difficult to find what they're looking for and leave the site with no intention of coming back because they'll be under the impression that the website does not have the particular information they were looking for. In most cases this is not true, the information is indeed on the website, but it's not always easily accessible to the user.

Thus the IA, the way information is structured on a website, is an important component that's often overlooked because it's seen as an easy thing to create. How hard can it be to create a menu for a website, right? Creating a solid IA for a website has a couple of facets that need to be considered such as where the content lives within the broader picture based on the user's perception, how many flows are there to reach this content, and will the users be able to find these flows. In this section, we'll look at site maps of a website and use card sorting methodology to group content into understandable chunks for the user.

Card sorting

Card sorting is a research technique that makes it easy and affordable to find patterns in the way users organize content. These patterns are called the **mental model** of the user and they help UX designers to evaluate the IA of a website. Card sorting is not the ultimate technique to find the perfect IA of a website, it's merely a tool to understand the existing content and its flaws, or the potential strengths of future content on a website.

A card sorting technique is conducted with a set number of participants who are asked to sort and categorize content in groups that makes sense to them. This is an insightful exercise to shape the user-centered taxonomy of a website. There are two basic types of card sorting techniques and a third hybrid approach:

- **Open card sorting technique**: In open card sorting the user is given a number of content sections and is asked to group the content as they see fit. The user is asked to create categories and give the categories names of how they see makes sense to them. This approach is most useful when creating a new website; the outcome will give a good indication of how the user sees the content and what makes sense overall to all the participants.

- **Closed card sorting technique**: In closed card sorting the user is provided with a pre-selected set number of topics or labels into which the user can categorize the content. This approach will force the user to take existing content and add it to a label. This approach is most useful for an existing website to evaluate if topics and labels makes sense to the user, and which sections will need adjustment to improve usability. Other than structure, closed card sorting can also help prioritize content.
- **Combination of open and closed card sorting**: In some cases it's possible to combine the open and closed card sorting technique by giving the user a pre-selected number of topics into which they can sort content, and also allow the user to create their own topics if they feel the content given does not fall into any of the pre-selected topics. This approach allows for more creativity and freedom to generate ideas.

How to conduct a card sorting exercise

Let's take a look at the following steps mentioned to understand how to conduct a card sorting exercise:

- **Choose content to be sorted**: Decide on the outcome of the card sorting exercise. Is it to organize existing content on the website or is it to find guidance with content sorting on a new site? It can also be a combination of evaluating the existing content and adding the freedom to create new topics and explore new expansions within the website.

  Content to be sorted can be single pages or sections (a collection of pages). Whatever the granularity of content, keep it consistent. Thus if the user must do a card sorting exercise with single pages, do not include a section, or vice versa. For example, if a user is expected to sort product categories, do not include low level content such as questions from the FAQs section.

  Don't use too many cards in your card sorting, it might become too overwhelming or take too much time and hinder the user from making quality choices. Limit the amount of cards used to no more than 40 cards.

- **Choose participants**: Participants should include actual users and not colleagues, as fellow colleagues, perception is skewed as they will mostly likely have a preconception as to why the exercise is being done and for what purpose. The exercise can be done in person, one-on-one, or in small groups with a facilitator. Groups not exceeding 12 are a good size, manageable, and will give a good sampling of feedback. The facilitator will guide the exercise much like a focus group with objective guidance. Groups tend to discuss the topics and thus provide richer feedback than individuals. Individuals have to think internally and depending on personality don't dig deep into the topics as an open discussion might do.
- **Execute card sorting**: Ideally a card sorting exercise should be done multiple times with good sampling to ensure all of the feedback is reliable and useful. Card sorting can be done online through any of the many online card sorting tools available. This is beneficial if the users are not able to come in to a personal card sorting exercise, and it is also less intimidating as the user can just do the exercise in the comfort of their own home on their personal computer.

Case study - Leadtrekker footer evaluation

Leadtrekker is a South African based **Lead Management System** that helps agencies and businesses convert more sales leads. The website is a basic informative website for users to gather information. The request was to re-look the structure of the footer as a main source of information for the user, to be able to guide them to any page on the website:

- **Type of card sorting**: Open, the user can create their own groups from the content presented.
- **Selected content**: All existing footer links, as well as useful links that can be found throughout the site.
- **Number of participants**: 10 potential (not existing) users.
- **Execution**: Online through an online card sorting with a user-researched platform called **Optimal Workshop**. Optimal Workshop offers several easy-to-use tools for teams to conduct user research. You can have a look at their platform here, `https://www.optimalworkshop.com/`.

The following is the first sight the user will have of the card sorting exercise. The cards are all listed on the left column and can be dragged to the right column to create groups. The instructions of what to do in the card sorting exercise will be visible in the right column to guide the user:

After the user drag the first card on the platform, the instructions explain to the user how to create groups and labels for each group.

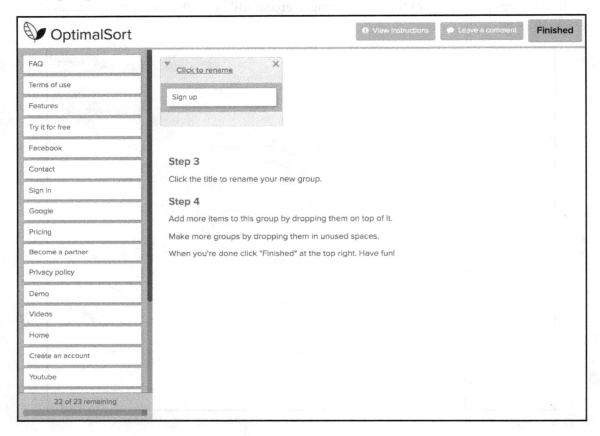

During the card sorting exercise, the cards will reduce in number on the left, and unlimited groups can be created on the right.

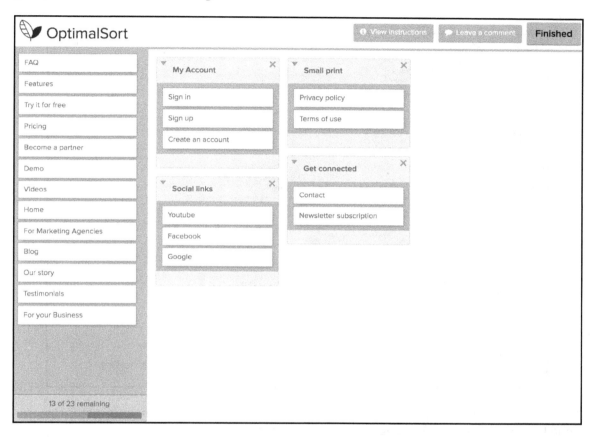

When the user is done sorting all the cards into groups and renaming the groups to what makes sense to the user, they can click on **Finished** and the results will be sent to the originator.

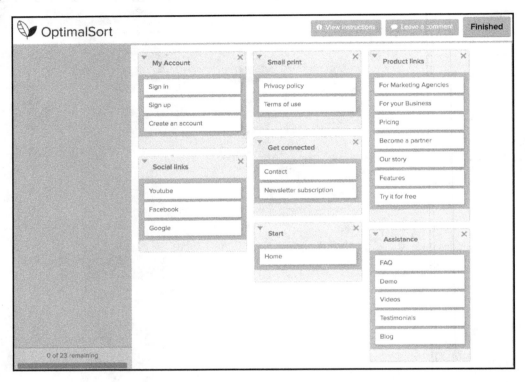

The following screenshots are only excerpts from the results of the card sorting exercise done before. The following categories table shows which cards were sorted into each category by your participants. You can standardize similar categories by highlighting multiple rows and then clicking **Standardize**. This will update the **CARDS** tab so that card placements are tallied in the context of your standardizations. Refer to the **Standardization Grid** tab for a visualization of the distribution of cards into your standardized categories.

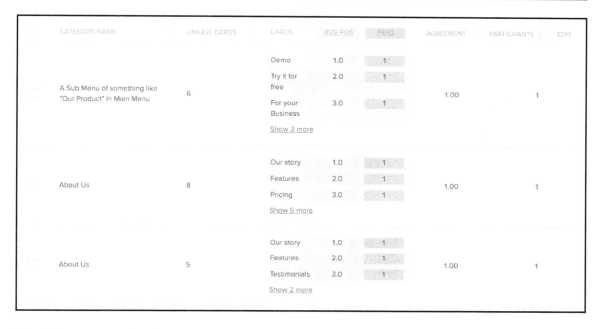

CATEGORY NAME	UNIQUE CARDS	CARDS	AVG.POS	FREQ	AGREEMENT	PARTICIPANTS	EDIT
A Sub Menu of something like "Our Product" in Main Menu	6	Demo	1.0	1	1.00	1	
		Try It for free	2.0	1			
		For your Business	3.0	1			
		Show 3 more					
About Us	8	Our story	1.0	1	1.00	1	
		Features	2.0	1			
		Pricing	3.0	1			
		Show 5 more					
About Us	5	Our story	1.0	1	1.00	1	
		Features	2.0	1			
		Testimonials	3.0	1			
		Show 2 more					

The following cards table shows which categories each card was sorted into by your participants:

CARD NAME	UNIQUE CATEGORIZATIONS	CATEGORIES	AVG.POS	FREQ
Become a partner	8	info for other businesses	1.0	1
		Join us	2.0	1
		Our Product	2.0	1
		Show 5 more		
Blog	7	Resources	1.0	1
		content to generally enrich the site and create more interest	2.0	1
		Propaganda	2.0	1
		Show 4 more		
Contact	7	Contact Us	1.0	2
		Contact	1.0	1
		need to know	1.0	1
		Show 4 more		

The following screenshot of **Participant-Centric Analysis** shows the top three most preferred groupings by your study participants, based on their similarity with other responses:

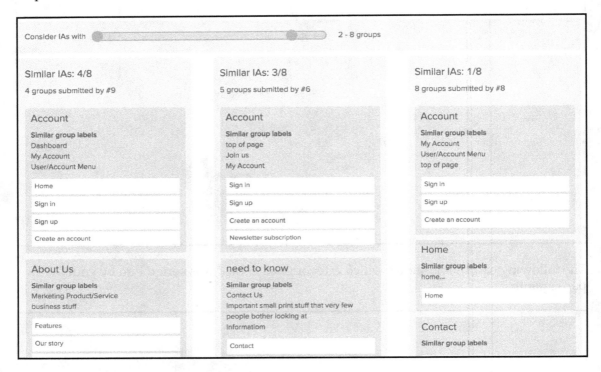

From the snippets of the preceding results it's easy to see patterns from the user's mental model, and how the content is grouped into specific patterns. Labeling and names of cards also plays a huge role in the card sorting exercise. If a user groups a specific card with a mismatch group, they might not necessary know it, and this is a clear indication that the name of the card, in this case the link in the footer, needs to be re-looked and updated to be more clear regarding the actual content that lives on that page.

Constructing a sitemap

From the early 90s when the website era started, sitemaps were used by web designers to add an online table of contents, which included a complete list of all the pages, in the footer of a website. This link will take the user to a single page that will allow users to easily find a page within a website if they fail to navigate to it through the navigation.

The sitemap has evolved from a list of content pages at the bottom of a website's footer to an essential module for the success of a website. In recent years XML sitemaps have been used for **Search Engine Optimization (SEO)**, and provide a guide for search engines to map website content and pages. This type of sitemap is not accessible to the user and can thus not be used for navigation purposes by a human, it is specifically created for the search engine.

In the UX context, sitemaps have developed into a key component in the UX process when designing a website. A **sitemap** is a basic diagram illustrating the grouping of related content as well as the hierarchical structure of a website, thus how the pages within the website relate to one another and what dependencies exist between them. Depending on who creates the sitemap and for what particular project, the UX sitemap can vary from the basic diagram version to a fusion of the basic sitemap with a focus on task flows or user journeys to indicate the user's flow through the pages. In this book, we'll look at the basic diagram sitemap.

In addition to the high level use of a sitemap as a basic diagram of all the pages within a website, this diagram can be interpreted differently by various teams with specific outcomes within a company:

- **Structure**: The overview of all sections gives the development a clear scope of the website in totality
- **Flow**: The hierarchical structure gives the UX team a high level view of all the available pages as well as hidden pages (password protected sections such as when a login is required) and their possible user journeys
- **Relationship**: The collection of content gives the content team a clear understanding of the relationship between content sections, as well as dependencies and duplicate content

Steps to creating a solid sitemap

Creating a sitemap seems like a simple task. However, there is much more to creating a solid sitemap than listing all the available pages and linking them together to make up the website's content. Firstly, a sitemap is a key deliverable of the IA and cannot be created independently from the other IA dependencies such as task flows and user journeys. The following are the steps to creating a sitemap:

1. **Objective of the website**: Determine the purpose and main goal of the website. The value proposition created in the beginning of the UX process will give clear guidance to where the main focus of the website will be.

2. **Do the necessary research**: Collect the necessary data regarding personas created from the potential target markets and what information these personas will need from the website. This should tie in closely with the objective of the website.

3. **Define the types of content**: After deciding what type of content the personas will need from the website, the next step would be to determine how to provide this content to the user. Depending on the type of content, it can be served in video format, audio podcasts, FAQs, product details, and so on.

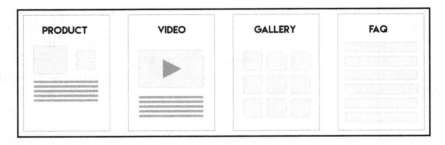

4. **Establish global navigation**: The sitemap consists of a hierarchical structure whereby global navigation will be represented in the first level of this structure. All pages within the website should logically flow from the main navigation. This first level of the structure can be tweaked throughout the creation of the sitemap to ensure all content is easily accessible to the user.

5. **Build content sections from global navigation**: From the first level of the hierarchical structure, the content will be structured in a second and third level to ensure all content fits into a logical flow and is accessible to the user. Don't make the structure too complicated by creating a fourth, fifth, or even sixth level. Going too deep in to the hierarchical structure will make the user journey unnecessarily complex and can easily lose or annoy the user if they cannot find the content they're looking for.

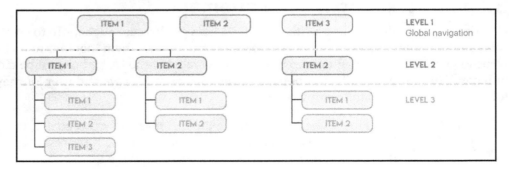

After *step 5*, the sitemap is tweaked and reiterated until it's molded into a solution that caters for all the persona's needs. These steps to create a sitemap are merely a guideline and can be adjusted based on the project's needs and stakeholders involved. Never take UX methodologies as absolute and expect the given guidelines to always give a successful outcome. The winning recipe is to act and adjust to fit your project, and repeat.

The following is an example of a sitemap done for a concept of an online financial advisory tool. As you can see, the layout of your sitemap can change to fit your website's needs:

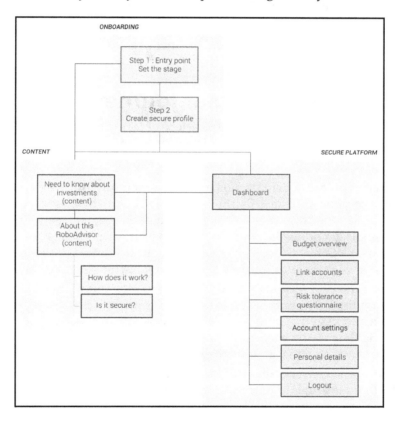

Creating user journeys

A user journey is a visual representation of the step-by-step path the user takes through a website to reach their end goal. Each of these steps consists of decisions made by the user to continue to the next step.

The UX team will dissect the user journey and revise each step to make the journey as smooth as possible. User journeys can be divided into the following types of flows:

- The current flow of how the user is interacting with the website
- The potential flow, how the user can interact with the website

Benefits of creating user journeys:

- Understand user behavior in relation to the product/website
- Pinpoint obstacles that prohibit the user from reaching their end goal
- Validate the value proposition and business vision

Key components of a user journey

While user journey maps can take on a wide variety of forms and directions, there are key elements that are always present in the foundation of a successful user journey map, which are:

- **Personas**: You cannot create a user journey map for your website if you do not know who your users are. By the time you start creating user journeys, the personas for your brand or website should already have been formed and settled into a stable set of needs, emotions and goals these personas are after. To build strong user journeys, focus on creating one user journey per persona per entry point to ensure the user journey has a strong narrative and clear end goal.
- **Context**: The user journey narrative needs to play out within a set environment. By giving the user journey context through time and phases, it's easy to pick up positive and negative points within the narrative. A user journey can play out in a specific time frame such as 30 minutes to buy a book at an online retailer or 3 months for online investments through an online financial advisory website.
- **Emotion**: Within a specific user journey there are different emotional phases the user will go through to reach the end goal, some may be positive and some negative. Ideally there should be no to minimal negative feeling within the user journey, but in the end the sum of positive feelings the user has within the user journey should outweigh the potential negative feelings the user might have.

- **Touchpoints**: Earlier in the book we discussed the customer journey and how users would interact with different aspects of Apple when buying an iPhone, for example. The user's interaction with various touch points within the user journey such as social media channels, in-store experience, or customer care plays a significant role in finding the gaps within the user journey and addressing any negative emotions that might surface during the user journey. It's fairly common for users to have unnecessary negative experiences in omnichannel journeys (channels across different mediums such as website, telephonic, or in-store) because the user journey across channels is often overlooked.

Four steps in creating an effective user journey

Creating different user journeys for your website is as simple as finding all the possible ways the user can navigate to their end goal through various steps, and the emotional connection with these touch points:

1. Do sufficient research by collecting all results from qualitative and quantitative research done on the target market.
2. Create personas and establish their needs by consolidating all research and creating a value proposition.
3. Determine what motivates the user to reach their goal by mapping out all possible options and decisions the user will have to make during their journey on the website to reach their end goal.
4. Highlight any obstacles that the user might face during their journey on the website to reach their end goal.
5. Find a solution to eliminate the obstacles within the user's journey through the website to allow the user to reach their end goal as effortlessly as possible.

If you're not keen to use the traditional pen-and-paper technique, there are several useful tools online to assist in creating your user journeys. One such tool is called UXPRESSIA, and can be found here: `https://uxpressia.com`.

Case study - Book Galaxy online book retailer

Book Galaxy is an online book retailer that offers thousands of titles that can be shipped to anywhere in the world. This case study is based on Jason, an anthropologist, who's been searching for a very rare book on a specific tribe in the Amazon. We'll look at Jason's user journey through the entry point of a Google search to purchasing the desired book.

Use the following illustration as a reference to the steps given to explain the user's decisions and emotional phases during the user journey to purchase the book:

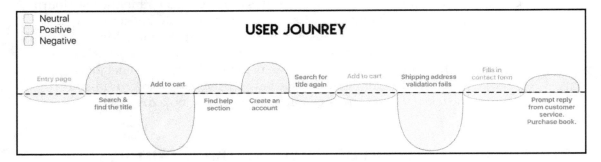

- Jason lives in Kenya in Africa and has been looking for a specific book called *The lost secrets of the Neolithic Tribe*. Once a week he searches Google for online book shops that would possibly have this title and be able to ship it to Kenya. This week Jason stumbled upon Book Galaxy through a Google search and lands on the home page--*neutral emotion*.
- With a quick glance over the website, Jason found the search bar and typed in the title of the book he's been looking for. He's overwhelmed with joy when he finds out the title he's searched for is stocked by Book Galaxy--*positive emotion*.
- Jason opens the product page to make sure this is indeed the book he's been searching for and is delighted to see that it is. He wants to add the book to his cart, but cannot continue until he has created an account. The add cart CTA does not redirect Jason to a register page, and Jason is struggling to find the register button to create an account. There is only a login button--*negative emotion*.
- He decides to go to the contact page to send a support email requesting for help and finds the help section with a link to the register page. He creates an account with Book Galaxy--*positive emotion*.
- After spending 20 minutes trying to register, Jason has to go back in to the search widget to search for his book again as the website did not bookmark the previous search and the book he wanted to add to his cart--*negative emotion*.
- Jason find the title again and successfully adds it to his cart, and continues to the checkout. He patiently goes through all the steps by filling in all his details but on the shipping address section he gets stuck again. The website states they ship worldwide but the address form forces the user to add an American state and ZIP code to be able to continue. Jason is very annoyed and goes back to the help section again to send an email through the contact form--*neutral emotion*.

- Within 10 minutes, someone from customer service replies to Jason and assists him in processing his purchase online. Jason is very happy and looking forward to receiving his book--*positive emotion*.

This a high level example of how a user journey can be mapped out. Within this case study there are several other steps that could influence the user's decision-making and emotional phases such as the search component not resulting in the correct results, currency and shipping issues, or, on a more positive note, the checkout could potentially offer Jason similar books on the Neolithic tribe that could potentially have a really positive impact on Jason's experience on Book Galaxy. As you can see from the case study, the positive experience should always outweigh the negative experience.

Creating task flows

User journeys and task flows seem very similar and a lot of people confuse the one with the other, or settle on only one of the two when doing a UX strategy. User journeys focus on the unique journey specific personas will follow to reach their end goal. This user journey is based on the different context of that specific persona, whereas task flows cover all possible routes a user can follow to reach a goal, irrespective of the person, context or entry point. If we look at the previous case study of Jason, who wants to buy a specific book, a task flow will focus on any possible way Jason could have found the book he's looking for. In the case study, Jason searched for the book, but he could've potentially browsed through a list of categories and found the book, or he could have stumbled upon the Book Galaxy Facebook page and seen that the book was advertised on Facebook. As you can see, all entry points are also covered, thus task flows cover all possible flows within a website to reach a specific end goal.

Key components of a well-constructed task flow

The five key components of a well-constructed task flow look at all the different approaches from the user:

- **The ignition point**: What is it that prompts a user to begin a task?
- **The focus point**: What is it that will tell the user that the task is finished?
- **What do they already know?** What knowledge does the average user have when they begin the task?

- **What do they need to know?** In order to reach the focus point what additional knowledge will the user require?
- **What do they use?** Which tools, processes, or information will the user utilize during the completion of the task?

Example of a task flow

The following figure is an uncomplicated example of a task flow for a login flow on a website. There are a couple of other elements such as register, reset password, and system notifications that should be included in a typical task flow. In this case they were omitted to demonstrate the basic flow and look of a task flow compared to a user journey:

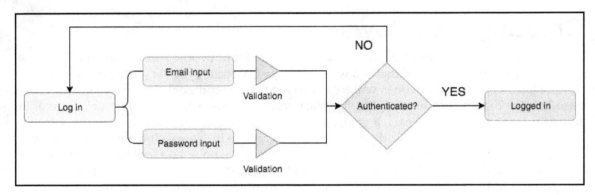

Just remember that UX methodologies implemented are unique and owned by the individual who executes them as well as the project they serves.

Summary

From the topics covered in this chapter it's clear that a comprehensive understanding of your users, their behavioral patterns, and how they will possibly interact with your product, in this case a website, is crucial. Structuring the website's content in a logical manner that will make sense to the user can be achieved by conducting card sorting exercises and creating a sitemap to support a solid and structured IA. In the next chapter, we'll look at creating effective prototypes using wireframes, and storyboards to display scenarios of interaction with the user. The importance of moodboards and style tiles for steering the look and feel of a website will also be discussed.

7
Bring Your UX Strategy to Life with Wireframes and Prototypes

A UX designer works with various stakeholders to research, create, test, refine, and implement designs. These include graphic designers, developers, business analysts, managers, and target users. UX designers use various deliverables to document and communicate their work at different stages of a project.

As well as documenting and communicating a designer's work, well-created deliverables can persuade stakeholders about the value or effectiveness of designs, educate the team about a user's needs and contexts-of-use, test ideas before too much time and effort have been spent on implementing them, and ensure quality and consistency of the current website and future redesigns.

We have already looked at some deliverables in previous chapters, for example, content audit spreadsheets, heuristic analysis reports, sitemaps, personas, and user journey maps. In this chapter, we will describe how to create effective prototypes for different audiences, focusing on those most commonly used during design and testing--wireframes and interactive prototypes. We will also cover moodboards and style tiles for the look and feel of the website; storyboards for scenarios of interaction for your personas; and pattern libraries for reuse and consistency. Finally, we will discuss how to incorporate responsive and accessible design into your prototypes. The topics covered in this chapter are:

- Setting up moodboards and storyboards
- Deciding what, when, and how to prototype
- Creating wireframes and interactive prototypes
- Setting up a pattern library
- Designing for responsiveness and accessibility

Setting up moodboards and storyboards

Moodboards and storyboards are typically used during the concept phase of a website's design. Moodboards help stakeholders understand and agree on the look and feel of the website. Storyboards present stories about people interacting with the website, which help stakeholders think about a user's concerns and needs. Both feed into prototypes.

Neither of these deliverables is critical for a good website design. However, they are useful for communicating early design ideas and creating a shared understanding among stakeholders. Both are powerful tools for persuading stakeholders about design ideas, as they concretize abstract ideas and have an emotional impact.

Defining moodboards

Moodboards visually present the style or theme of an idea. They are used in various creative industries, for example, interior design, film making, photography, and graphic design.

A **moodboard** is a collection of colors, images, words, textures, and so on, which suggest or describe a proposed style or theme. In web design, they describe the look and feel of a website.

Pinterest is a popular site for visually collecting and exploring ideas, which uses the moodboard form. Users post or pin items with a common theme, to collect and share with others.

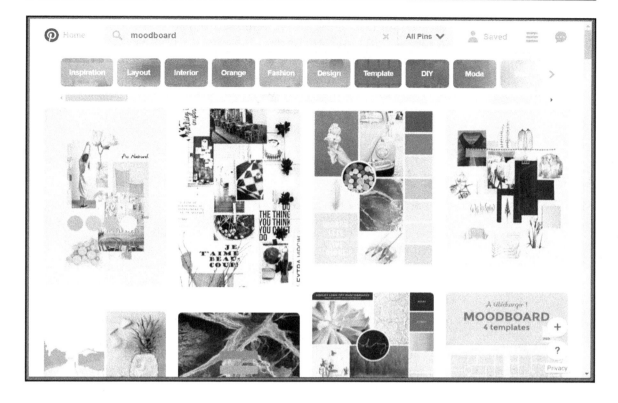

Screenshot of the Pinterest web site

Moodboards can have various purposes in a web design project. These include:

- **Inspiration**: Present visuals from the external world and other sites that have inspired the team. Another name for a moodboard is an *inspiration board*.
- **Persuasion**: To show stakeholders the design ideas in an attractive and compelling manner.
- **Clarity**: Nail down the theme of the website so that all stakeholders have a clear mental image of what it will look like in the end.
- **Comparison**: Create multiple boards to compare different ideas for the look and feel of the site, and choose the one that resonates best with the stakeholders. For example, dark and moody versus light and airy.
- **Consistency**: A moodboard can be referred to throughout the design project when new images, colors, fonts, and so on, are added to the website, to ensure that the additions are consistent with the chosen theme of the website.

A moodboard might be created for one of the aforementioned purposes, or for all of them. There is a large variety in the content and form of moodboards, depending on their purpose, the nature of the project, and the amount of time available. For example, in the early stages of a new website, moodboards might just be a collage of inspirational images, fonts, textures, and words. Later in the project, moodboards could include typography, color schemes, and screen layouts. Another name for these more formal moodboards is *style tiles*.

Creating a moodboard

Moodboards might contain any or all of the following elements:

- **Inspiration**: These can be photographs, illustrations, sketches, or screenshots of other websites that are inspiring for the theme.
- **Typography**: Fonts or font families that should be used on the website. This could include fonts and sizes for different levels of text, for example, headings and body text.
- **Design elements**: Examples of icons, logos, buttons, and other elements of the website.
- **Color schemes**: The color palette that will be used on the website, possibly divided into primary, secondary, and tertiary colors
- **Key words**: Words that describe the proposed theme, for example slick, modern, edgy or restful, elegant, soft.
- **Sample layouts**: Ideas for how the content, visual, and navigation areas of the website could be laid out in ways that support the theme and style.
- **Textures**: Drawn or collected textures that are suggested for styling the website.
- **Annotations**: Comments next to sections or elements of the moodboard describing why choices were made and how they relate to the theme, or detailing how elements could be used on the website.

Moodboards can incorporate many different elements. They can be laid out more casually, like a collage, or more formally with a template and labeled sections, depending on their audience and purpose. The following is an example template for a formal moodboard:

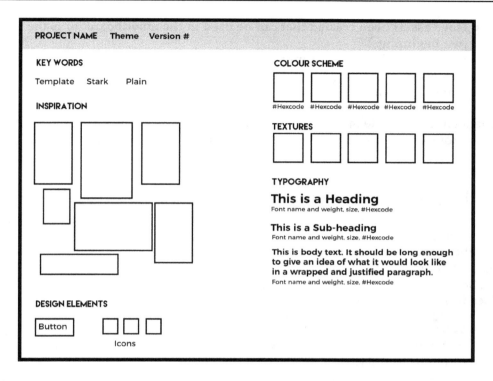

Template for a moodboard

Here are some questions to ask when creating a moodboard:

- **What is the theme of the moodboard?**
  This may already exist as part of the brand identity of the client. In this case, gather or brainstorm adjectives to describe the theme, which will inspire the team. You may want to show the client a few different ways of interpreting their brand. In this case, brainstorm around three different themes that work with the client's brand, but are distinct enough to encourage preferences.

- **Why is the team creating the moodboard?**
  This will influence its presentation and elements. For example, a collage may be best for inspiration, but a moodboard created for clarity or consistency will require more careful layout and annotation.

- **Who is your audience?**
  A large corporate client may respond better to a more formal moodboard, whereas a less formal client such as a startup might prefer a more casual, creative board.

- **Have assets been created that can be used in the moodboard, or is the project just beginning?**
  If you are still looking for inspiration, explore images and websites on the internet in a relatively unstructured way, guided by your theme(s). Save anything that grabs your attention into a shared space.

If the client has a corporate or brand document, there may be elements that you can or should use, for example, color palettes, design element styles, and language styles.

Defining storyboards

Storyboards are like comic strips: they visually present a story, scene by scene, with notes for what is happening in each scene. They were first used in the film industry to visualize and plan the scenes of a movie before filming took place. In web design, a **storyboard** is an ordered, visual representation of a user's experience while using a website, or part of a website. Storyboards are a good tool for persuading your stakeholders to focus on their user's needs, for several reasons:

- **Story**: Storyboards tell a story. When people are told things through a story, they remember them better. Stories also inspire empathy and capture attention through curiosity.
- **Visualization**: Storyboards use images to show the story. It is well understood that showing people things works much better to gain their attention and persuade them, than just telling them.
- **Disruption**: Combining the steps to use your interface with a compelling story works to disrupt thinking. When you are trying to find solutions to difficult design problems, this works very well to help stakeholders think about things differently.

If we look at the definition, it should be clear what storyboards are not. Storyboards are not ordered sketches of the pages of your website. They can include sketches of your website or application, but these must be put in context of a specific person using the site for a purpose, their story, and their feelings about it. Diagramming the pages of your website is an important part of design; we will discuss it later in the section on creating wireframes and interactive prototypes. However, at this stage you should not be thinking too much about how the system will work.

The best storyboards tell a compelling story about users and include their context and motivations during the interaction. This helps stakeholders empathize with their target audience and understand its problems, needs, and contexts. This in turn helps the designer to gain acceptance for designs based on these needs.

The story must be based on actual user behaviors and feelings, otherwise you could easily be designing for needs that are not real. The personas, user journeys, and task flows that we discussed in the previous chapter will be useful here. These are all based on user research and will inform the storyboard. In fact, a user journey or a path of the task flow can provide the backbone of the story you want to create.

Storyboards take time to create well. Most designers will not have time to create a storyboard for every scenario of interaction with a website. Therefore, carefully select which interactions, if any, should be storyboarded. If there are important, emotional, difficult, or controversial interactions in your website design, consider storyboarding those. These are the tasks where it is most necessary to empathize with users, so you and other stakeholders can create interactions that properly address the needs of the user.

Creating a storyboard

A misconception is that you must be able to draw to create a storyboard. This is not the case. The most important part of the storyboard is a well told story based on a real interaction scenario.

These are the steps to creating a storyboard:

1. Choose the set of interactions or tasks that you want to highlight. These will have emerged from user research or concept design.

 It is very important that the story is rooted in real UX research and data, otherwise it may distract the team's attention from the real problems of your users.

2. Gather the story elements. A compelling story has several elements:
   - **Character**: A character should have personality, a history, emotions, and motivations. Ideally, use one of the personas you've created from user research.
   - **Context**: A story happens in a specific situation. Interactions are triggered in context. Where and when would your persona be doing the task?
   - **Plot**: The events of the story create the narrative that make it compelling. This is the persona performing the tasks that leads them to their goal. If you have already created user journeys or task flows, these will form the building blocks of your plot.

3. Create the story. Now you have the elements, combine them into a compelling story arc. If you think about good stories, you will realize that this arc has a typical progression:

    -   **A character with goals and motivation in a context**: There may be more than one character, but the main actor should be your persona.
    -   **A trigger for the action**: What makes the character start the interaction?
    -   **Struggles and conflicts**: These may be problems in the context that your design solves, or problems in the current interaction that you want to highlight.
    -   **The climax or crisis**: This is the solution that your design provides, or the trouble that is caused by the current design.
    -   **The resolution**: This is the result of the climax or crisis. What are the consequences for the character?

4. Break the story up into scenes or steps. Each step will correspond to a panel on the storyboard:

    -   For each scene, make sure that you consider what the character's feelings and reactions would be, and include them. This creates empathy.
    -   The last panel should provide a clear outcome to confirm the impact of the story, and the benefits or fallout from the climax/crisis.

5. Create the storyboard:

    -   Create a framework for the storyboard. All you need are rectangular panels for the diagrams, possibly with space for descriptive text underneath each panel.
    -   Write the description that will appear on or below each panel. This will guide what you want to draw.
    -   Plan what you want to appear in each panel. In some cases, the panel might be an interface sketch. Make sure you include an idea of the character as well, so the panel is not impersonal.
    -   Draw the storyboard to your ability, or use existing assets. There are many sites that provide comic-style assets for storyboarding.

6. Present the storyboard. Ideally, you want to present your storyboard to stakeholders, so you can back it up immediately with nuggets from your user research. This highlights that it is not just a fun cartoon, but has real-world impact.

Case study - creating a storyboard

In this example, we will create a storyboard for the feature in mapping software, such as Google Maps, where a user can share their real-time route information with others:

- **Character**: Susan is a sales representative. She uses mapping software on her phone all the time to find her way to clients. She is a busy, single mom to Simon.
- **Context**: She is in her car, stuck in traffic. Her phone is in its holder on the dashboard. Simon, the second character, is waiting at school.
- **Plot**: Susan is rushing back from a client to fetch Simon from school (Characters). She sees that she is late. Because of the unexpected traffic, she will be very late fetching Simon. Simon is waiting at school, anxious and upset (Struggle). Susan remembers that she can send her real-time location to Simon with the click of a button on her phone. Then he will know that she is coming. She is relieved (Trigger). Simon gets the notification and is immediately relieved because he knows when Susan will be arriving and that she is thinking of him (Climax + Resolution).

The next step is to separate the story into panels. We are going to create a short panel sequence for illustration purposes:

1. Susan driving from an appointment to fetch her son, Simon, from school. She is late and the traffic is bad. She is upset and worried.
2. Closeup of Susan realizing that she can share her location with Simon, so he can see where she is and know when she's going to arrive.
3. Simon waiting at school. He is sad and anxious because he doesn't know when Susan will arrive and she is late. His phone buzzes with a message.
4. Simon sees Susan's progress and ETA on his phone. He is happy because he sees that Susan is on her way and knows when she will arrive. He feels cared for because he knows she thought of him.

The following figure shows the storyboard created, based on the sequence of panels:

Storyboard example

Deciding what, when, and how to prototype

Moodboards and storyboards are mostly used in the concept stages of design, when the team is deciding what features to include in the design and roughly what they might look like. The next stage of design is when you begin working out exactly what the web pages will look like and how they will work. This is where prototypes come into the picture.

A prototype is an early, unfinished version of a product, built to test one or more aspects of that product.

For website design, anything from a rough sketch on paper to HTML and CSS code can serve as a prototype, depending on what you want to test and with whom. Although prototypes don't have to be inherently interactive, they are usually made to test interaction with some part of the product.

Prototypes take time to create and are not the final product; they are usually thrown away. There are several benefits to prototyping that make this time and effort worthwhile:

- **Concrete**: Prototypes are concrete versions of a design idea. They help stakeholders to visualize what the final product will look and feel like.
- **Interactable**: Stakeholders can physically interact with prototypes. It is easier to judge problems with an interaction when stepping through it than when imagining it.
- **Less risk**: Prototypes take less time and energy to create than the final product. This means that it is less costly to explore design options. Design teams are less likely to roll out an inferior design.

Prototypes vary widely in form and function, and the amount of effort required to create them. Therefore, it is important to be clear about what kind of prototype you will be creating, so that the whole design team has the same expectation. You can do this by specifying the **fidelity**. This is the realism and accuracy of the prototype. It can sub-divided into interactive, graphical, and content fidelity:

- **Interactive fidelity**: It refers to the interactivity of the prototype. It can range from a static image to a *clickable prototype* to a fully interactive simulation, where all interactions and animations seem to work like they would on the real website. For example, swipes, drags, dropdowns, edit boxes, forms, and so on.
- **Graphical fidelity**: It refers to the visual quality of the prototype. It can range from a sketch to a wireframe to a pixel-perfect representation, where all images are production quality, and fonts, colors, and textures are accurate to the finished product. A pixel-perfect representation is also known as a mock-up.

- **Content fidelity**: It refers to the accuracy of the text and images on the website, and the degree to which all the content of the website can be accessed. This can range from placeholder text and images, to parts of the website being completely and accurately formed and others not at all, to complete fidelity where all content is present.

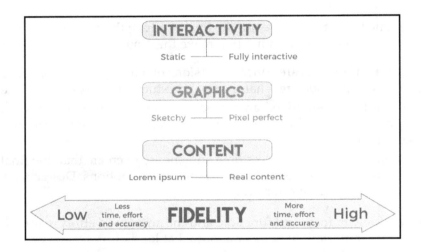

Fidelity of prototypes

Choosing what and when to prototype

During the life cycle of a website development project, the team should be prototyping and testing repeatedly. What you prototype and how, depends on where you are in the cycle. The stages of the cycle and related prototype demands are as follows:

- **Research**: For a new website, this stage does not use prototypes. If a website is being redesigned, then the existing website can be tested to discover *existing problems*. This is high fidelity because it is the product.
- **Concept**: In this phase, *interface flows, ideas, and specific interactions* are being tested. Prototypes are typically low fidelity, although small high interaction fidelity prototypes can be created to test technical constraints. At this stage, sketches, moodboards, and storyboards are more useful design aids.

- **Design**: In this phase, *detailed designs* are created and tested for *usability, discoverability, and desirability*. This is where most prototyping will happen. You can test *screen layouts, visual designs, interaction flows, specific UI features,* and so on. The fidelity that you choose depends on your team and what you are testing.
- **Build**: If you are building code, then prototypes will be high fidelity as you are more likely to have high fidelity content and graphics available. You will be creating small snippets of code to test *parts of the interface or backend for small changes*.
- **Deploy**: Here, any testing will be done with the *final product*, or with *alternative versions*. Therefore, this is high fidelity.

Choosing how to prototype

We have discussed prototype fidelity, form, and place in the product life cycle. Four other considerations in prototyping are:

- **Audience**: Who is the prototype for? Is it external users or the internal team? Is it everyday team members or the client?
- **Resources**: What are your resources in terms of time, money, and skills? Does your team have the skills and time to code HTML for a prototype? What prototyping software does your team have access to, do they have skills with this software? If not, what is the learning curve of the software?
- **Reuse**: Is the prototype being used for another purpose, such as documentation, communication, or a building block of the finished product?
- **Process**: What is the software development process that your design team follows? This varies considerably, depending on preference and project resources. You might move from sketch to wireframe to high fidelity interactive and graphical prototype to code, or you might move straight from sketch to code, or anything in between.

High fidelity prototypes take longer to create, are more unstable (you need pilot tests to make sure the prototypes do what they are supposed to do), require more skill, and the software to create them typically costs more and has a higher learning curve. However, it is easier to get accurate responses from testers, as they look and behave more like the real website. Clients also respond better to high fidelity prototypes as they can more easily visualize the finished product and they can see the work that has been done.

Another consideration is whether the prototype will be used for another purpose:

- **Internal documentation**: Wireframes and sketches work well here. They can be annotated with design details and are easy to timestamp, so you can pinpoint when the design happened. Wireframes can be a blueprint for the layout and structure of your website.
- **Presentation**: Clients tend to respond better to high fidelity graphical prototypes.
- **Specification**: High fidelity graphical prototypes can be used as specifications for developers and are easy to annotate. Wireframes are useful for specification of layout and content, and are also easy to annotate.
- **Code**: Interactive prototypes and HTML code can be reused for the final product. However, this can backfire as the code is not typically production quality. Also, prototyping in code can lead to designers becoming too fixed on ideas or elements that are easier to create with the code.

It is easy to spend too much time on a prototype. The primary decider for fidelity should be the quality you need to test with. For example, if you are testing two concepts for onboarding users onto your website, sketches on paper will work well to show the concepts to users. However, if you are testing the usability and enjoyability of your website's touch interface on mobile devices, a high fidelity HTML prototype is the best option. Even interactive prototypes created using prototyping software don't provide enough interaction fidelity to simulate the feeling of more embodied interactions, such as swipes and drags.

 A rule of thumb
Plan the prototypes you will create during the software process. At each stage, create the lowest fidelity prototype necessary to gain the primary result.

Creating wireframes and interactive prototypes

In the previous section, we discussed how to decide what, when, and how to prototype. In this section, we will focus on creating two very useful kinds of prototypes for UX design-- wireframes and interactive prototypes. Wireframes help the team to plan the layout and flow of the website precisely, without the distraction of colors, images, and fonts. Interactive prototypes help the team to understand how users will interact with the website.

Prototyping tools

There are many tools available to create wireframes and prototypes, from lightweight and easy to use but with less functionality, to fully featured but with a high learning curve. It can be difficult to know which to choose. The trick is to choose those that work for you and your team, and stick with them until they don't. Some teams seem to change tools with every project. However, even the simplest tools take time to master; and even if the underlying task and workflow are similar there is always some cost to learning a new interface.

The following diagram shows some of the more common prototyping methods or tools, along the axes of purpose and learnability. Typically, tools that are **what you see is what you get (WYSIWYG)** are easier to learn, for example, paper. However, they also tend to provide no or fewer options for adding interactivity.

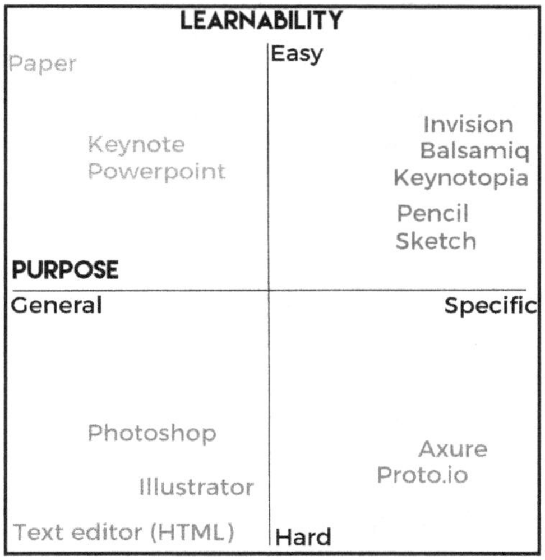

	LEARNABILITY	
Paper	Easy	
Keynote Powerpoint		Invision Balsamiq Keynotopia
		Pencil Sketch
PURPOSE		
General		Specific
Photoshop Illustrator		Axure Proto.io
Text editor (HTML)	Hard	

Prototyping software

Here is some more detail on these options:

- **Paper**: This is the most generic tool. Paper is used for sketching interfaces and can be used to prototype. It is very cheap. Because it is generic, your team will probably already have paper, pens, and rulers available. There is no learning curve, as everyone knows how to use paper. The designer does not have to draw well, but some practice to instill confidence will be useful. There is no interactivity here, except what is provided by a human talking through the sketches.

- **Text editor**: This is almost as generic as paper. Text editors are used for coding prototypes and for anything else involving text. Code can be used to wireframe and prototype. The learning curve is high here, because the designer must learn to code to use a text editor for wireframes and prototypes. Some text editors are free, but in general they are inexpensive. Some provide syntax highlighting and others support for coding. The prototype could have complete interactive fidelity, seamless with the finished product, depending on time and skill.

- **Presentation and drawing software**: Such as Keynote, PowerPoint, Illustrator, and Photoshop. These are generic, and are typically used for other purposes. They can be used to draw wireframes and create prototypes with very limited interactivity, based on the animation systems provided by the software. Depending on their primary purposes, they may be easier or more difficult to learn to use.

- **Wireframing tool**: There are several products for wireframing and creating high fidelity visual designs. These are specific; they are only used for wireframing. If they do provide options for interactivity, it is low fidelity--limited to linking between pages or components. Typically, they are quite easy to learn. Examples include Balsamiq, Sketch, OmniGraffle, and Pencil.

- **Prototyping tool**: There are a few tools that are only used for prototyping, where the screen elements must be imported. This is a small category as most prototyping tools also provide for wireframing and visual design. They are generally easy to learn, often including plug-and-play components for adding interactivity to imported visual designs. Examples include Invision and Keynotopia.

- **Wireframing and prototyping tools**: These tools provide a one-stop shop for design of wireframes, high quality visual designs, and interaction design. Many of them also automatically turn your designs into code. They usually support import of designs from a different source. However, this code will usually need to be redeveloped or refactored, as it may not be optimized and may be messy. They are typically harder to learn. Examples include Axure, Proto.io, Justinmind, and Adobe XD.

Available prototyping and wireframing tools are changing and being redesigned constantly. Some of the preceding information might change.

Other considerations when choosing a prototyping tool are:

- **Devices supported**: Some prototyping tools are better at supporting mobile design or desktop design, and some do both.
- **Collaboration**: Many prototyping tools offer ways to make collaboration easier, such as sharing and annotation on the internet so that stakeholders can comment on designs. The alternative for this is to create a PDF, Google doc, or other file type with screen designs, that allows comments, and email/share this with stakeholders.
- **Operating systems**: Some prototyping and wireframing tools are only available for specific operating systems. For example, Sketch is only available for Apple products.
- **Tools ecosystems**: Some tools work together seamlessly, so the outputs of one can easily be imported into another. This streamlines the design process. For example, using Illustrator for wireframing means you can easily create a high fidelity visual prototype directly from the wireframe, or export it to Photoshop; Sketch works with various prototyping tools, such as Invision and Proto.io; and Axure works with **Subversion (SVN)** for version control.

We cover wireframing and prototyping in a tool-agnostic way as much as possible. We use Axure for illustration as it is used for both wireframing and interactive prototyping, so we can use one tool to illustrate both processes. It is also available on all operating systems. However, this section is not meant to provide a tutorial. It is an introduction to the processes of creating wireframes and interactive prototypes. The examples we provide are simple and incomplete.

Creating a wireframe

A **wireframe** is a specification of the layout and structure of a web page design.

In this section, we will describe how to go from a rough sketch to a complete wireframe specification of your website.

Designing the interface

It is always a good idea to sketch interface ideas on paper first, for several reasons:

- **Flexibility**: Paper is the most flexible design medium. All others will guide your designs in some way, because of the frameworks or widgets they provide.
- **Low investment**: Drawing designs on paper is low investment. It is easy to throw away designs or pivot to a new design direction.
- **Lack of detail**: With prototyping tools, it is too easy to add too much detail to early designs, as the tools support this. When you are creating a rough idea or concept of what your web page could look like, it is too early for detail.

Designing an effective interface and user experience is a complex, difficult task. This can be especially daunting at the beginning when faced with a blank canvas. It helps to break it into smaller, more manageable subtasks. Here are some ways to approach the problem and guide design:

- Beginning the design work by doing rough sketches allows designers to approach the problem in a casual, unstructured way.
- The UX designer should already have information about the problem, from the business plan for the project and the user research that has been conducted. This should have informed the team about user's expectations and goals with regards to their product. For example, the information users expect to see and how this product might fit into their lives.
- Competitor research into similar kinds of websites is useful, for example, e-commerce, company websites, news and entertainment sites, or social networking sites. Researching successful similar sites, such as Amazon for e-commerce, will indicate common elements and what works for them, for example how checkout works, how they build trust, and providing comprehensive, multifaceted search and filter options.

- The design team's knowledge about usability conventions, psychology, design patterns, and so on, is a primary input to the design process. This comes from experience and following research by organizations such as the Nielsen-Norman group about how users interact with websites. For example, eye-tracking studies show that people typically read web pages on a computer in an F-pattern—two horizontal bands across the top and a vertical stripe down the left side. Therefore, the most important content and navigation should ideally fall into these areas.
- Focusing on your information hierarchy and messaging flow is a good way to begin thinking about the design--which content you want to emphasize most and how you want users to experience it. Think about the first thing you want users to see when they open your website, your main message, and your calls to action.

Components of a wireframe

Wireframes can be created at various levels of detail, from simply blocking out areas of the page to a complete specification. A complete wireframe specification should have the following elements:

- **Key pages**: There should be a wireframe for every type of page of your website. If you have multiple pages that follow the same format, it is less important to wireframe every example.
- **Screen elements**: For example, buttons, dialogs, menus.
- **Layout**: Grid size, spacing between elements, footer and header, content areas, image placeholders.
- **Annotations**: Notes about aspects not captured visually, for example usability of elements and possible interactions.
- **Site map**: A flow indicating how the wireframes connect to each other and other parts of the system that have not been wireframed. Many wireframing tools provide the ability to create flow diagrams.

The following elements are optional:

- **Interactivity**: Limited interactivity between wireframes to give some idea of flow. However, at this stage you shouldn't be focusing on interaction even if your software allows you to create more complex interactions.
- **Copy**: If you have copy already, use it instead of placeholder text to make your wireframes more accurate. However, wireframes should not be used to record copy as it is too difficult to keep different versions accurate. A **copy spreadsheet** should be used to record exact copy and its location. This is a single document that can be referenced by the whole team. It provides a single source of truth about the website copy. In addition, copy can be easily cut and pasted from a spreadsheet, as opposed to a wireframe.

We'll discuss these elements and how to create them as we step through creating a wireframe.

Components of a wireframing tool

Although you can wireframe on paper, we are going to use a wireframing tool. Wireframing tools tend to have similar interfaces, which make them easier to move between than other tools.

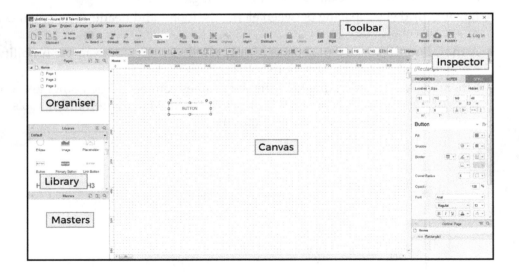

Axure interface

This is shown in the preceding and the following screenshots, which show the interfaces of Axure and Balsamiq with a simple Button element. Similar sections are annotated:

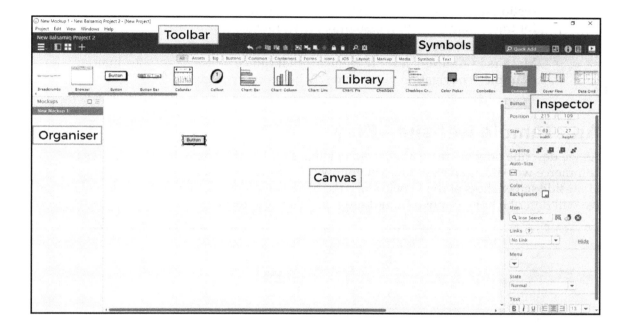

Balsamiq interface

As can be seen, they provide:

- **Canvas**: A canvas or artboard on which the designer draws, or drags-and-drops interface elements.
- **Layer or page organizer**: A list of all the pages and/or layers that have been created.
- **Inspector**: A panel to edit properties of the currently selected element, for example x and y placement, color, font, borders, alignment. For tools that provide interactions on elements, these will be available here.

- **Toolbar**: This typically handles import and export of elements, file handling, and whole-page properties.
- **Libraries**: For tools that provide custom elements or widgets, there will be a section for selecting these. External libraries or stencils can usually be imported for things like operating system widgets, for example, iOS-styled widgets.
- **Elements for reuse**: These are called Symbols in Balsamiq and Sketch and Masters in Axure. These are elements that can be reused across the interface, for example, a navigation menu that will be on every page.

An example website - Etsy

As we describe how to create a wireframe, we use part of the home page of the Etsy e-commerce website as an example. The following screenshots show rough sketches alongside screenshots of the Etsy home page on desktop and mobile. In the following steps, we will describe how to move from these sketches to the website:

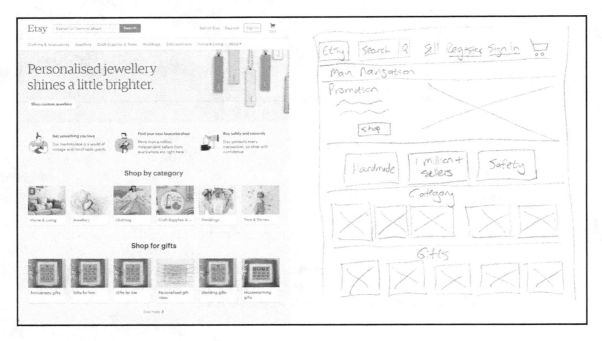

Sketch vs website-desktop

These sketches have been copied from the Home pages of the website. They are therefore more accurate to the finished product than many sketches would be; in a real-world process, the layout could change during wireframing because of design issues that emerge from the wireframing. The team would also have multiple sketches of different parts of the site. We will focus on the landing page in this exercise, but the steps should be performed for all key pages and complex components.

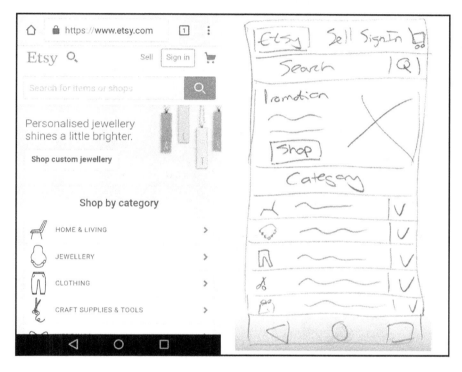

Sketch versus website--mobile

In the Etsy example, if we only consider the part of the site aimed at buyers, the key pages and components are--the landing page; mega-menu on the landing page; a category page; the filters on category pages; a product page; registration and login pages; checkout pages and flow; search results page.

A note about responsiveness

Every website will be viewed on various devices; the interface and interaction consequences must be considered. We will discuss responsive design in the next chapter. Here, we note that the team should design with multiple devices in mind, to consider how the design works on different devices and rules for moving between devices. A rule of thumb is to design mobile-first, as this is the more difficult design because of the smaller screen size. Designers are also forced to think about the priority and hierarchy of information with mobile designs, as the smaller screens require a more linear vertical arrangement of the content. This insight can then be translated to bigger screen designs. In the example, we will focus on desktop design to explain the basics, as we discuss mobile design issues in the next chapter.

A typical wireframing process

There are many ways to design a wireframe; each designer will have their own process. The process shown here is a basic one to use as a guide if you don't know where to begin. Although we use Axure to create the wireframe, you can wireframe on paper to complete the following steps:

1. **Create and name the pages**: Create and name those pages that you will be using for wireframing. Create two groups of pages--one for mobile and one for desktop. This helps you to keep the different screen sizes in mind while positioning elements:
   - Some tools will help you with responsive design. For example, Axure provides Adaptive Views, which allows you to create a base view and then specify linked versions for different screen sizes.
2. **Create grids and guides** to give structure to the design area. These will ensure your design is consistent, accurate, and neat. Grids are intersecting vertical and horizontal lines or dots. Guides are lines that you can add to the page to specify where elements should be placed:
   - Most desktop web designs work on a 960 or 1200 px grid size, with guides that create 12 or 16 columns. These are standard and allow easy translation to CSS. For mobile portraits, 360 px grid size is often used.
   - Canvases tend to have rulers around the edges, defaulting to pixels as the units, so you can compare positioning. For example, when designing on the desktop pages, you can see where the edges of your mobile interface would be.
   - The grids and guides will not appear when the wireframe is printed or previewed.

3. Once you have set up the design area of your page, block out the main areas to break up the space. You will continue to define these areas in increasing detail while designing your wireframes:

   - Initially, the division will be simple, for example, header, footer, main content area, and secondary content areas. You will probably already have sketched this. The difference is that these blocks are pixel-accurate in size because of your grids and guides.

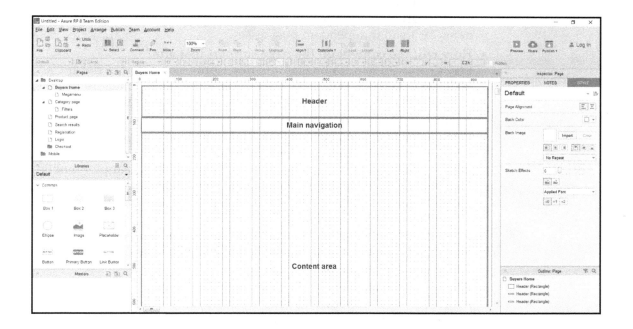

Axure screenshot, showing grid, guides, page structure, and main website blocks

4. Think about the page content and where it might be placed in your broad areas. Then subdivide and add to your original block layout to add more descriptive blocks indicating content areas. We will consider these questions using the Etsy Home page as a reference:

- **What is the aim of this page?**
  The aim of most landing pages is to introduce users to the site, attract them into exploring, and show them what is possible. Consider what users expect to see here, for example, secure payment process, prices. Etsy want to showcase themselves as a secure and comprehensive online marketplace with a difference: a focus on handmade and custom items by small independent businesses.

- **How will the content on the page support that aim?**
  Etsy's content includes images and descriptions of different products, featured collections with editorials, other promotions, category listings, customer reviews, and so on. They provide users with multiple entry points into their catalogue.

- **What information do you want to highlight on the page?**
  This information should be near the top of the content area, which is the first thing users will see on entering the page on desktop or mobile. Etsy has chosen to highlight their current promotion: custom jewelry with a hero image and call to action. On desktop, Etsy use the space just below the hero image to deliver important messages about craft, range of products, and security. These highlight important Etsy values, but provide no immediate calls to action, therefore they are a luxury that is not present on the mobile site.

- **How do you want users to interact with the page?**
  In other words, what calls to action should you provide? It should be obvious where and when users can interact. Etsy provides a call to action to "Shop custom jewelry" in the prime viewing area. The search bar and primary menu (or category listing for mobile) are also immediately obvious. Every product or category image is clickable/tappable. The links to sign in, register, sell, and subscribe to newsletter are all noticeable.

- **What other content or information do you need to provide?**
  Most of the content we've been describing would fit in the main content area of the Home page. Less important information is often displayed in headers and footers. For example, contact links, social media share options, sign in and register, the company name and logo, related blogs and forums, a shopping cart, company details, privacy statement, and FAQ. Keep a list of these elements.

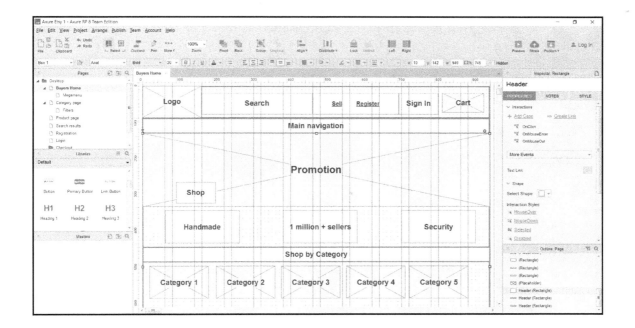

Axure screenshot, showing refinement

5. Now that you have blocked out the rough location of all the elements on the page, begin adding detail using elements from the wireframing tool instead of placeholders and draft content. Be precise about the visual hierarchy, layout, and spacing with this step:
   - Use usability conventions to help place items effectively. For example, search boxes are usually placed on the header.
   - Fill in the navigation with menu items. If your navigation is complex, for example, a mega menu that slides down over content, then you may want to create a separate page to show an open menu.

- Add buttons, links, images, edit boxes, and so on, from the Widget Library of your tool. Use the Inspector to refine them and add detail.
- Create image or video frames that are the correct size, possibly containing proposed images.
- Replace placeholder or simulated text with real copy. This doesn't have to be polished, but you want an idea of the message of each piece of text and roughly how long it will be. Copy includes all the text on the page, such as paragraphs, menu items, headings, microcopy such as labels and help text, copyright, and privacy links.
- Add typography so headings are differentiated from body text.

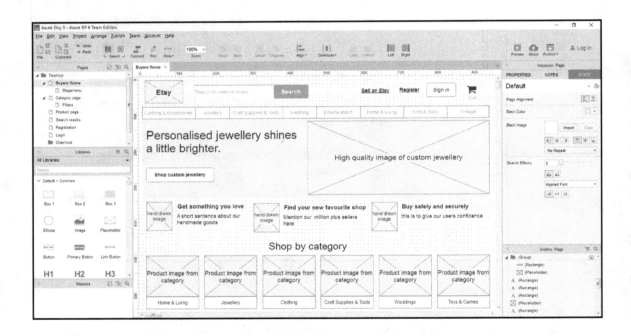

Axure screenshot, showing wireframe detail

6. At this point, you have created an accurate wireframe of the elements and layout of a page. This is a complete wireframe of one page. If you are planning to reuse any of these elements, for example the navigation menu, then set this up now:
    - In Axure, you will select the widget, for example, a navigation bar, and turn it into a *master*. It will appear in the Masters panel, where it can be selected and added to any page.

7. If the wireframe is being used for design and documentation, annotation is crucial for accurately communicating the design. As a rule of thumb, consider whether there is anything that you would need to explain about the design if you were not there to present it. Typical areas for annotation are *content* that is missing or hidden, *behavior* of the interface, and any *constraints* on the design. For example, the content of hidden menus or dropdowns; notes about missing content; error messaging guidelines; proposed interactivity or animations and their effects; visual design, CSS, or HTML suggestions; responsiveness and accessibility guidelines:
    - In the Etsy example, the page changes when a visitor returns to the website. A new section for recently viewed items is added. You can indicate this addition with an annotation pointing at the position where it would be inserted.

8. There are three optional steps relating to increasing fidelity:
    - You can finetune the appearance of the wireframe. You may choose to just add greyscale, borders, and shadows to show visual strength and highlights, or you may choose to add color, fonts, and so on for increased graphical fidelity.
    - You could add improved content, so that the real text and images are in place. This would increase the content fidelity of the wireframe.
    - You can choose to add interactions to the wireframe. These can be simple links that show the flow of the wireframes or you could increase the interaction fidelity of the wireframe and simulate the real actions users would take, for instance, swipes, drags, working dropdowns, and so on. This will be discussed further below.

9. This is an optional step too. If you want to show flow of interaction through your wireframes, consider creating wireflows. These are a cross between wireframes and flowcharts, which are especially useful in mobile UX design because of the small screen size. Each node or box on a flowchart is replaced with a wireframe, which provides context for interactions.

Best practices for wireframing

Before we move on to discussing how to create an interactive prototype, here are a few best practices for creating wireframes:

- **Use color sparingly, if at all**: Wireframes are simple line drawings at their most basic. This is one of the reasons they are useful for layout and interaction design. Color can be distracting, both to the designer and to the client, who may feel the need to comment on the look and feel of the design prematurely.

- **Name widgets descriptively**: If you are creating wireframes for more than a couple of web pages, you will end up with a lot of widgets or elements in your design. These can become confusing and difficult to find and specify unless you name them descriptively. For example, Sign in button and Hero image button instead of Button 1 and Button 2.

- **Reuse elements early**: In website design, there are typically a lot of elements that appear on multiple pages. To save yourself time and keep your design consistent, reuse these. For example, convert widgets to masters in Axure as soon as you create them to save time. It will be more time consuming to do this later.

- **Be flexible**: Wireframing should be fast and agile. If you discover problems as you add elements, content, or interactivity, be prepared to change your design. This is the time to do it, when changes are relatively easy to make.

- **Collaborate**: Design is difficult. It is also always improved when more people are involved in thinking about it. This is one of the reasons user testing is so important. Make time to check your designs with colleagues informally and formally. Be open to feedback and prepared to change.

- **Interact**: Step through your wireframes as you imagine a user would. Think of your scenarios and storyboards for user experiences. Then try to put yourself in this position and see the design with fresh eyes. Step through each proposed interaction to test if it makes sense and is complete.

- **Step off the default path**: People do not interact with websites in the same way. One of the values of testing with users is that they will interact with your website in ways that you did not intend. An important part of interaction design is trying to foresee all the ways users can interact with your interface. Then you can make sure that your interface always provides a pleasant, recoverable, and clear response, rather than providing a confusing, unpleasant experience for the user. Critically examining your wireframes for edge interactions is a good way to approach this.

We have described how to create a wireframe in this section. In the next section, we will explain how to turn your wireframe or visual design into an interactive prototype.

Creating an interactive prototype

We have defined a prototype as an early, unfinished version of a product, built to test one or more aspects of that product.

An **interactive prototype** is one where the interactions have been built into the prototype so they can be tested, either internally by the team or externally with users.

You can test interactions without building them into the prototype. For example, you can create a sequence of sketches, wireframes, or high graphical fidelity mockups, and simulate the interactions and screen responses by stepping through manually. However, in this case the prototypes themselves are not interactive.

There are three ways to understand the meaning of an interactive prototype, shown here in order of increasing interaction fidelity:

- **Clickable**: This is a series of wireframes or mockups that are linked, so clicking on part of one opens another, possibly with animated transitions. A clickable prototype shows the flow of screens and consequences of interaction, but the interaction itself is very limited. Invision, Balsamiq, and Keynotopia are examples of tools that provide this kind of interaction.
- **Complex interactions**: These are wireframes where widgets have associated interactions that simulate those in the real product more closely. The interaction fidelity will be much closer to the real thing, but the transitions, feeling, and exact form of the interactions will not be the same, especially with more embodied interactions. They may vary in the kind of interactions they support. Examples here are Axure and Proto.io. Proto.io has more support for mobile interactions than Axure does.
- **CSS + HTML**: This is where the designer codes directly in HTML and CSS to create an interactive prototype. This is the closest fidelity to the real thing, but it may be a stripped down or simpler version.

We will broadly describe how to create interactions for the first two cases. Interactions usually follow an event-action form:

- **Trigger:** This is a discrete event on the interface. For example, click or tap, a swipe, double-tap, key up or down, showing or hiding an element, and so on.
- **Conditions**: These are optional. They specify the circumstances under which the triggering event will cause actions to happen. They are if...then statements. If the condition is active when the trigger occurs, then the action will happen, otherwise not. For example, if a key is pressed (trigger) while an image is visible (condition), then the image will hide (action).
- **Actions**: These are the outcomes that occur when the triggering event happens. For example, setting text, moving or rotating an element, opening a page, or hiding or showing an element.

The form is much simpler for clickable prototypes than more complex interactions: clicking on the chosen widget is the trigger; there are no conditions possible; and the only action is opening another page. You would specify this by linking the second page to the widget, using the Inspector. In tools that act on images, such as InVision, you would create a **hotspot** on the image, and link to the hotspot.

Creating complex interactions is more complicated, but based on similar principles. More complex interactions allow you to simulate a website much more closely. Clicking on a widget to open a page is possible, but there are typically many other types of triggers and actions.

Examples from Axure include:

- **Triggers by page-level events**: Interactions triggered by page-level events, not triggers on widgets. These events include: when the page loads, if the window resizes or scrolls, and if a context menu opens on the page. The following Axure screenshot shows page-level options for triggering interactions (Cases is the Axure term for actions and their conditions):

Partial Axure screenshot, showing page-level interactions

- **Triggers on widgets**: They depend on the type of widget, or the part that is selected, and include a wide variety. For example, for a *menu* widget, you can trigger actions with an event on the whole menu, such as moving the menu, hiding or showing it, or when it loads. When you select the individual menu items, different triggers are offered. These include when the item is clicked, selected, unselected, or when it gains or loses focus.
- **Actions that are triggered**: They depend on the type of widget, and include a wide variety. You can also specify multiple actions connected to one trigger. Action examples include opening a page in the current window or a new tab, changing the text or image on a widget, moving or rotating a widget, and setting the focus of a widget.

- Because there are so many options for interaction, a new page may open where the actions and conditions will be specified. In Axure, this is the Case Editor. The following is a screenshot of the Axure editor, showing two actions that have been set up when a menu item is clicked (in the central column): opening a link, and hiding a widget. The Case Editor looks complicated when you first see it, as it provides a lot of functionality. The left-hand column shows you all the actions that are possible; the center column shows the actions that have been added (and possible conditions); the right-hand column shows ways to fine-tune the actions.

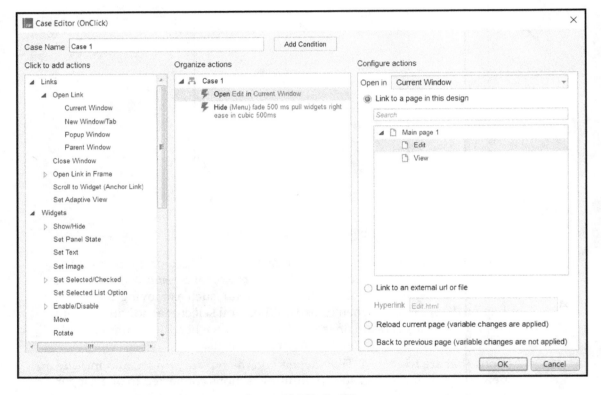

Axure screenshot of the Case Editor

- **Fine tuning actions** are part of what makes an interaction simulation compelling. These allow you to specify how, where, and when transitions happen. For example, in Axure you can specify the speed of a transition, and whether a page link should be opened in the current tab or a new one. A specific example from the preceding screenshot is--hide the Menu widget with a fade transition that will last 500 ms, and the action will pull widgets to the right into the space with a cubic ease in transition that will last 500 ms. In this example, we specified the speed of the fade transition, what would happen to the empty space when this widget disappeared, and the transition effect.
- **Conditions** also add to the realism and power of an interaction simulation. In Axure you can add zero to many conditions on every triggering event, and specify whether all or just one of them needs to be present for the action to happen. Examples include visibility of a widget, text on a widget, a key press, and the cursor position. In our menu example, you might specify the following trigger-condition-action triad: when the menu item is clicked (trigger), if a specific image is not visible (condition), then the image becomes visible (action).

You can usually preview interactions created in prototyping tools on the web, from within the tool. This is very important for testing your interactions, to make sure they work the way you intended. In Axure, you do this with the **Preview** button. You can also create a shareable URL for the preview, so you can share it with stakeholders.

Best practices for creating interactive prototypes

Here are some best practices for prototyping interactions:

- **Transitions**: If a tool allows you to design transitions, such as fading or easing in and out, these can make your interactions look much more professional and real, which increase your interaction fidelity.
- **Reduce complexity**: Interactions can rapidly become very complex when using a prototyping tool like Axure. Therefore, carefully consider the interactions that you are adding to your prototype and whether you really need them. Ideally, create simple connections linking your wireframes and increase the fidelity for a few important interactions. Attempting to create high interaction fidelity for an entire website could become unmanageable.

- **Pilot test**: Pilot test your prototype thoroughly before testing with it, or sharing it with stakeholders. This is like debugging code when the interactions become complicated--you must make sure it all works.
- **Single path**: Be careful not to only create interactions for the perfect user path. This will interfere with proper testing of findability on your website, as it will quickly become obvious to users where they can interact. We will discuss this further in `Chapter 9`, *Optimize your UX Strategy with Iterative User Testing*.

When creating wireframes and prototypes, it is easy to lose track of changes over a project. Version control is important to prevent this, but often overlooked until it is too late.

Version control

This is a familiar concept among developers. If you have been part of a team in a software project, you have probably been exposed to it. Version control (also known as source control) means managing your files and other documents so that changes over time are recorded. This means that you can return to specific versions of each file at a later stage. Version control is crucial when a team is working on a software project, as it prevents work from being duplicated and helps to ensure that team members are communicating accurately and referencing the correct documents in their work.

Version control is less well-performed with visual documents than with code files. It is more difficult to note the changes in each new diagram. But it is especially important if both developers and designers are working on the designs, as is usually the case in an agile project: developers are using the designs as specifications and designers are creating new designs or changing designs based on feedback.

There are various ways of keeping version control of visual designs:

- At a basic level, the team should decide on a version control numbering scheme and the designers should use these in their file naming schemes.
- Designs should be in a repository shared with the team. There should be a method of describing the contents of the repository, which any team member can easily view to understand which document they should be working with.
- There are more formal version control systems, such as GIT and Subversion (SVN), which are used by most larger teams.

Setting up a pattern library

We've discussed reuse of elements in your prototyping or wireframing software, with Masters in Axure and Symbols in Balsamiq. The next step is creating a pattern library. Creating and maintaining a pattern library is important, if not crucial, for any long-running website or business. Pattern libraries make reuse of elements easier and quicker, they ensure that your interfaces are consistent, and they make maintenance of your site easier by different stakeholders.

A **pattern library** is a collection of website design elements with details about their appearance, behavior, and implementation.

Examples of such elements are buttons, menus, forms, and so on. They can also include visual design elements, such as icon sets and stylings, color, and typography.

Pattern libraries are easy to set up:

- **Document and template**: All you need is a document that contains the patterns and a template for how each pattern will be recorded.
- **Online**: Because your whole team will be using the pattern library as a reference, whether they are current or future members, co-located or distributed, it is best to host the library online where everyone can access it.
- **Hyperlinked**: Your pattern library can easily become large and unwieldy. Create an index that can easily be referenced, with hyperlinks to the items.

The template for patterns should ideally contain the following sections:

- **Title**: Name of the pattern.
- **Description**: A brief description of the pattern, and when and where you would use it. This can include images for clarity.
- **Image**: An image of the pattern. If possible, this should be a live instance rather than a static image, so that it can show behavior and responsiveness.
- **Visual details**: Details about the colors, typography, and other stylings for the pattern, including how it looks in different states if necessary. For example, selected, unselected, and inactive for a button.
- **Behavior**: A description of interactions possible with the element and the effects of the interaction, including animations.

- **Code**: How the pattern will be implemented. Consider creating a link to a common code repository, so that the code does not have to be updated in multiple places when it is changed.
- **Author and version**: Some historical data about who created the pattern and when it was updated can be useful.

Here are some tips for setting up an effective pattern library:

- **Start early**: Think about setting up a pattern library as soon as you begin reusing elements in your design. You can add details as they become available.
- **Be selective**: For ease of maintenance, be selective about the elements that you include. Everything in a pattern library will have to be maintained and updated for the library to be current and effective.
- **Responsive guidelines**: Add in guidelines for how the pattern responds to different devices and screen sizes.
- **Accessibility guidelines**: Include pointers for how the pattern should be made accessible.

Designing for responsiveness and accessibility

Design takes place in the real world, which is messy. In creating a website, the ideal is to create an experience that all potential users will find enjoyable and usable.

We've indicated how you should consider the fact that people will interact with your designs in unexpected ways. Taking this further, we need to consider responsiveness and accessibility.

We've already discussed responsiveness briefly. This refers to people accessing your website using different devices, browsers, and operating systems. Your website will potentially look and behave differently in each of these contexts. If you control the experience by designing for these different contexts, then you can deliver a good experience no matter the context. We will discuss this in detail in Chapter 8, *Build your Product*.

Designing for accessibility means making sure that anyone who wants to access your website can do so. This includes people with disabilities or injuries that make our default interactions and designs difficult for them to access. Some examples are older people with poor vision, blind people, people with muscular disabilities, people who are deaf or hard of hearing, people with dyslexia, and people with low literacy or second language speakers.

By carefully following usability guidelines, such as color contrasts, hit target size, clean layout, and text size constraints, and designing responsively, we cater for a lot of these issues. A few additional design choices can make our websites accessible for all our users. For example:

- Including keyboard input as an alternative to mouse, which is difficult for people with certain physical disabilities
- Describing visual elements carefully in text and HTML codes, so that screen readers can interpret them
- Ensuring a logical tab order

We discuss accessibility and how to design for it in detail in Chapter 10, *The basics and benefits of Web Accessibility* and Chapter 11, *A Designer's Guide.*

Summary

In this chapter, we have looked at how to create design deliverables that communicate your designs effectively to different stakeholders in different contexts, and at different times in the design process.

We began by looking at two deliverables that communicate aspects of design persuasively and effectively during conceptual design--moodboards for the look and feel; and storyboards for interactions. We described how to create these deliverables, with examples, and provided tips for getting the most out of them.

We then defined and categorized prototypes, which are core to a UX designer's process, as they facilitate testing with users. We described the various tools that designers use to create these prototypes, and how and when different tools are most effective. The most important design artifacts for laying out your design are wireframes, so we looked at how to create a great wireframe in detail.

Interaction design is one of the most important parts of UX design. We discussed how to create effective interactions in interactive prototypes, both for low- and high-fidelity interactions, and where you might want to do each.

We described the usefulness of pattern libraries for ensuring that long-term, consistent designs are maintained. Finally, we briefly described the importance of responsive and accessible design, and highlighted how we will focus on these in later chapters.

In the next chapter, we will delve into responsive design, looking at technologies, devices, browsers and operating systems, including assistive technologies, and how we can design for these effectively.

8
Building Your Product - Devices, Browsers, and Assistive Technologies

Designing a website that will potentially be accessed by anyone with an internet connection is a complex task, especially if you want to provide every user with an enjoyable and user-friendly experience. Like any complex task, it is made achievable by breaking it down into sub-tasks: In previous chapters, we have discussed some of these sub-tasks, the elements of UI design, branding awareness, researching and analyzing the results, and creating a content strategy and an information architecture. In the previous chapter, we explored how to design and define the structure and detail of each page in a website.

In this chapter, we consider the technologies that people use to experience our websites-- devices, browsers, operating systems, and assistive technologies, and how to design responsively for them. This is a crucial step in website design, as the web can only be experienced through technology. This means that the way each person views the website and interacts with it is filtered through the technology that they use. If we have not considered that technology in our designs, then we might be delivering a deficient experience.

Awareness of the varied technologies people use can be considered under the umbrella of responsive, accessible, and universal design. Therefore, we begin by discussing the importance of these design guidelines. Then, we describe how to design for varied technologies. Finally, we discuss how to test your design's effectiveness on different technologies.

The topics covered are as follows:

- Understanding the importance of responsive, accessible, and universal design
- Designing for varied technologies
- Testing your designs on multiple technologies

Understanding the importance of responsive, accessible, and universal design

The responsive, accessible, and universal design guidelines are similar in that they promote creating designs that are usable and enjoyable by a variety of end users, especially those who are not like you.

They are different in that they focus on different end user characteristics, although there are some overlaps. Let's take look at the following definitions:

- **Responsive design** is about creating fluid designs through HTML and CSS that adapt seamlessly to screen size, resolution, and aspect ratio, so that the layout remains optimally usable and attractive
- **Accessible design** is about creating designs that are usable and enjoyable by people with disabilities, including physical, sensory, cognitive, and neurological problems
- **Universal design** is about creating designs that are usable and enjoyable by everyone, regardless of age, status, culture, ethnicity, or ability

Interestingly, none of these ideas originated in the web or even technology design fields. They originated in architectural and product design:

- Accessibility could be considered to have originated with the ANSI Barrier Free Standard (ANSI A117.1, *Making Buildings Accessible to and Usable by the Physically Handicapped*) in 1948, which specified minimum requirements for barrier-free access to facilities for the physically disabled.
- Responsive web design was coined in 2010 by Ethan Marcotte, a web designer. He was inspired by responsive architecture, which explored how physical spaces and people could interact with each other and how spaces could respond to this.
- Universal design was defined by a group of architects and product designers in 1997, led by Ronald Mace. It referred to the design of any environment to be accessible, understandable, and usable to the greatest possible extent by everyone.

Ethan Marcotte's description of responsive web design can be used for all three, if we focus on technology needs, rather than the qualities of people.

 Rather than tailoring disconnected designs to each of an ever-increasing number of web devices, we can treat them as facets of the same experience. We can design for an optimal viewing experience, but embed standards-based technologies into our designs to make them not only more flexible, but more adaptive to the media that renders them.

Responsive design focuses on technology, accessible design on disability. Universal design creates a space to think about designing for marginalized people who are not considered disabled. Their problems with finding websites usable and enjoyable stem from factors such as culture, ethnicity, language, and poverty.

Increasingly, disability is defined to include universal design issues; it is a mismatch between a person and the situation, rather than something inherent to the person. This encompasses the fact that anyone can and probably will be disabled at some point or in certain situations, for example, older people experiencing loss of vision, hearing, and mobility; breaking an arm and being unable to use a keyboard or mouse; lack of sleep causing loss of concentration, such as in insomniacs or new parents; being ill with the flu causing physical weakness and mental disorientation; or being in a noisy environment that affects hearing. In addition, people using mobile phones often use them in difficult contexts, which affects their ability to engage with the content on the phones, for example in queues, while performing other tasks such as shopping or watching TV, or while commuting.

While responsive, accessible, and universal design are obviously morally and socially important paradigms, maximizing the accessibility of your website also has business and legal benefits:

- **Bigger market**: A quick look at various statistics shows how much you can increase your potential market by designing for a variety of end-users:
  - According to the WHO, 15% of the world is disabled. This is rising because of aging populations and the rapid spread of chronic diseases.

- The UN Broadband Commission's report in 2015 indicated that for every broadband user in the developed world, there are two users in the developing world, and this difference is growing; there are big differences in the affordability of broadband and, in some countries, it remains prohibitively expensive for most of the population; 31% of people live outside 3G coverage; and future internet users are likely to come from less educated and more rural backgrounds, and speak languages that are not currently supported.
  - In 2016, Google reported that over 50% of internet searches come from mobile devices.
- **Visitor retention**: If people have a bad experience on your website, they are less likely to use it again and they are more likely to develop a negative perception of your brand. The Nielsen Norman group reports that websites have about 10 seconds to show clear value to users, otherwise they will leave. Since universal accessibility focuses on usability and enjoyability, designing for marginalized users will improve your website for all users.
- **Positive image**: By supporting accessibility for marginalized groups or on a large variety of devices, you generate positive feelings towards your brand.
- **Crossover benefits**: By making your website usable and enjoyable for a greater variety of people and devices, you will create features and experiences that are appreciated by groups you had not considered.
- **Legality**: Increasingly, rights to accessibility are being legislated.

The problem with designing for people who are not you is that they will experience your website using a seemingly endless range of devices, operating systems, browsers, and assistive technologies:

- **Operating systems**: The main options are Apple (macOS and iOS), Windows, Android, and Linux. These may display websites differently, for example, how fonts and UI components are displayed. They also have different interface guidelines, which govern how interfaces should look and work.
- **Browsers**: Some common browsers are Chrome, Firefox, Internet Explorer, Safari, Edge, Opera, and Opera Mini. Websites display differently on browsers based on the APIs browsers support, and other features. For example, Opera Mini uses compression technology to save data costs and speed up transfer on slow networks; however, this means that sites relying on JavaScript do not work properly.

- **Devices**: People may access your website using a range of devices, including mobile phones, tablets, laptop and desktop computers, game controllers, and TVs. These have a wide variety of screen sizes and dimensions. OpenSignal reported in 2015 that there were over 24,000 mobile device types. Android devices had widely diverging screen sizes, from 2 inches by 2 inches to 6.5 inches by 12 inches.
- **Assistive technology**: People may interact with your website using various assistive technologies, which have different consequences for input and output. For example, screen readers, magnifiers, Braille embossers, and eye trackers.

For each of these categories, we must consider the capabilities of both the newest versions and much older versions. For example, many businesses still run Microsoft XP, which was released in 2002 and has not been supported for years. This complexity is shown in the following figure:

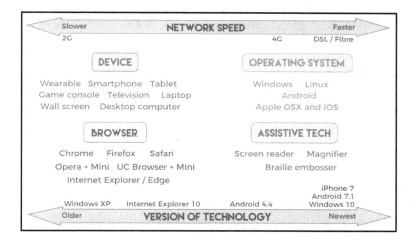

Technology ecosystem

How do you begin to consider all of these technologies? Luckily, there are many guidelines, APIs, and frameworks that will help your design and development team.

Designing for varied technologies

In the previous chapter, we discussed how to create and document a website design effectively. However, apart from a brief discussion of responsiveness and mobile design, we did not consider the technologies through which people would be viewing and interacting with your website.

Here are some examples of people who may be visiting a typical e-commerce website, using very different technologies:

- A teenager using a game console and a 5-year-old TV
- A blind accountant using a keyboard and screen reader on a laptop
- A color-blind developer with a desktop computer and two large external monitors
- A 70-year-old retiree using a tablet
- An Arabic speaker who understands basic English, on a smartphone with the language set to Arabic (right to left reading order)

There are various dimensions with which we can consider technologies. In this section, we will discuss designing for input and output; responsive design; designing for different browsers, operating systems, and assistive technologies; and following universal design principles. We discuss accessibility and assistive technologies in detail in Chapter 10, *The Basics and Benefits of Web Accessibility*, and Chapter 11, *A Practical Guide to Web Accessibility*.

Designing for input and output

Luke Wroblewski, a well-known proponent of mobile-first design, suggested categorizing technology according to device experience. This comprises three elements:

- **Usage/posture**: How a device is used in terms of frequency and duration, and body position and the context of the person using it
- **Input method**: Keyboard/mouse, touch/sensors, gesture/remote, keypad/trackpad
- **Output/screen**: Wall-sized, desk-sized, lap-sized, palm-sized, or wrist-sized

This division is valuable for considering the different experiences that users may have accessing the same website. However, the input method and output/screen sub-categories must be broadened to consider assistive technologies--voice is now a recognized input method; and alternatives to screen-based output, such as sound and haptics, are not considered.

Anne Gibson, a proponent of designing for accessibility, suggests that we categorize technological requirements according to input and output devices, rather than the disabilities that require them. This approach is similar to device experience, but Gibson also provides us with a method for ensuring that we design for different experiences--the accessibility test matrix for input and output devices. This idea makes it easier to design optimal interfaces for a variety of devices.

It is a useful exercise to explore the technologies that will be used to access your website. The following is a diagram of an accessibility matrix of input and output devices:

INPUT	OUTPUT										
	Computer monitor	10-inch Tablet	7-inch Tablet	Smartphone	Speakers	Screen reader	Braille embosser	Printer	Smartwatch	Television	Wall screen
Keyboard + Mouse											
Keyboard											
Mouse											
Touch screen											
Game controller											
Joystick											
Microphone											
Touch pad											
Remote											
Camera (gestures)											
Stylus											

Accessibility matrix

To create it, perform the following steps:

1. Create a matrix of input and output devices that might be used to access your website. Make sure you add common assistive technologies. Start broader, then become more specific. For example, start with a computer monitor, and then break that into the various dimensions of laptop and desktop computer monitors:
   - This matrix should be made into a large-scale poster and placed where the whole team can see it. This will help the team to think more broadly about how people might interact with the website.

2. You can annotate the intersecting cells in various ways:
   - For each intersection, consider whether the combination makes sense for your website. If it doesn't, cross it out.
   - If your base designs work for certain combinations, check the intersecting cells.
   - Each time you change or add to your designs to cater for a new technology, check the intersecting cells.

- Indicate which combinations intend catering for, so you can see the gaps.
- As designs are reviewed, refined, or developed, they can be checked against the matrix to make sure that different options are covered. Where there are problems with the design or development for a combination, this can be indicated.

3. The accessibility matrix becomes part of the documentation for your website, and will assist in future maintenance. It can easily be updated as new input or output technologies are included.

An example of a common input difference to be aware of is mobile touchscreens versus desktop keyboard and mouse input. Most website designs should include at least mobile and desktop designs; therefore, your team must be aware of the differences these two inputs make to design.

- Touchscreens do not have a hover state, so tooltips shown on a desktop in this way will not be seen on a mobile
- Touchscreens can pinch to zoom, swipe, and so on, which do not directly translate to keyboard and mouse interaction

You can use this spreadsheet to help set up your test suite when designs are being tested. We'll discuss this further when we consider testing on multiple technologies.

Designing responsively

Recall that responsive web design means that the same HTML is served to every device, and displayed optimally on that device using CSS with fluid grids, flexible images, and media queries:

- **Fluid grids**: They reshape depending on the shape of the viewport, so your layout changes as the screen dimensions change. They are based on relative screen proportions such as percentages, not absolute units such as pixels.
- **Flexible images**: They display at a size that is appropriate for the device resolution and screen size. Their sizes in the HTML are relative, not absolute. Typography is defined relatively as well.
- **Media queries**: They check the type of device and send different CSS styling depending on its dimensions and resolution. The viewport meta tag and breakpoints are used to know when to change.

The CSS can change the layout of web pages in this way, such as adding rows, removing columns, changing image size, and so on. Interactions can also be changed with JavaScript.

It is important to consider how your content will be displayed and accessed because of different device experiences. People will view content differently depending on the context. For example, you may read an entire article while at a desktop computer, but only skim its main points while standing in a queue with your smartphone. Different inputs, such as gestures on a Wi-Fi remote as opposed to keyboard and mouse, change how you interact.

Luke Wroblewski identifies some of the simpler responsive layouts that are used when moving from desktop to tablet to smartphone:

- **Mostly fluid**: This layout remains the same, with smaller size, until the smallest screen when it becomes more linear.
- **Column drop**: Columns are dropped from the desktop design until a single column is presented on the smartphone.
- **Off canvas**: The layout remains mostly the same, but the screen acts as a window onto it. On a desktop, you see the whole screen, but on a smartphone, you must swipe left or right to see more.
- **Layout shifter**: Parts of the design, such as the menus, shift around to better suit the dimensions and size of the new screen.

The following figure shows a responsive layout changing from laptop to tablet and smartphone, with a flexible image. This is a combination of column drop and off canvas:

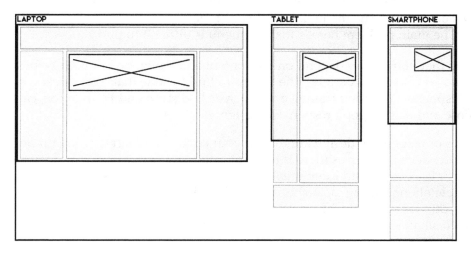

Responsive screen layout on laptop, tablet, and smartphone

One of the most important aspects of layout when designing responsively is *navigation*. This is how people find their way. It should be obvious, but not get in the way of the content. You always want to expose content, to show value immediately to a website visitor. This becomes more of a problem on a smaller screen. On a desktop, the main navigation is usually at the top or down the left-hand side. This is so that it can be seen immediately to help users find their way. On smaller screens, putting the menu at the top or left pushes the content off screen.

Look at your information architecture carefully and work out the most important areas to expose. If you have analytics of where people spend time on your website, this will help you prioritize content sections. Brad Frost, a well-known web designer, has detailed some typical simple navigation layout patterns for mobiles:

- **Top nav**: Nothing changes from desktops. This works for simple menus but longer menus will take up too much screen space and may wrap badly.
- **Footer anchor**: The menu is anchored at the top with a widget, so users can find it, but it appears at the footer of the page. This can create an unpleasant jump from the top to the bottom of the page.
- **Select menu**: This is a drop-down menu at the top of the page. It takes up very little space, but users must recognize it as a menu. The menu items are also hidden, which is not ideal.
- **Toggle**: This has a menu anchor at the top, like the footer anchor, but the menu slides out from the top.
- **Left nav flyout**: This has a menu anchor. The menu slides out from the left.
- **Footer only**: The menu only appears at the bottom of the page, with no anchors. The main problem here is that the menu is difficult to find.

The layouts that you choose depend on the content and navigation of your website. There are pros and cons to every pattern. The trick is to find the one that works best with your content. Responsive frontend frameworks, such as Bootstrap and Foundation, can help your team choose and deliver good responsive design.

The benefits of responsive design are that all your content and strategy are unified in one place. Maintenance is easier as there is no duplication. Designs are also more future-friendly, as it is easier to add more breakpoints as new device types emerge, than it is to create completely new designs. Responsive design highlights the importance of designing to display your content in the best way possible. It has given us some great techniques for dealing with small screens, for example, sticky navigation and back-to-top buttons.

Responsive design has also led to some design difficulties. Simple layout changes may create very long pages, especially on a mobile, that users must endlessly swipe. This is not a good user experience, because of the fatigue of repeated swiping and the lack of feedback. For larger screens, responsive design has led to too much white space. Designs are simply upsized from mobiles, rather than being optimized for the extra width and height.

There are three deeper problems with responsive design:

- **Limited optimization of layout and content**: If you deliver the same HTML to multiple devices, there is a limit to how much you can customize and optimize the design for a specific device. For example, smartphones typically have built-in sensors and features that laptops and desktop computers do not have: GPS, accelerometers, pointable camera, and so on.
- **Poor performance and large file sizes**: Responsive design can lead to poorer performance and heavy downloads. By designing specifically for mobiles, you can choose not to send larger images or content that is not currently necessary. If you serve the same HTML, this is more difficult. For example, images typically have very large file sizes, so that they look good on high-resolution screens. There are solutions to change this, but they require server-side code and/or JavaScript.
- **Poor user experience on low-end devices or browsers**: Low-end devices and browsers may not support JavaScript or media queries. They do not understand them and so are unable to gracefully degrade the experience. Therefore, the richly designed experiences fail to load and there is nothing to replace them.

Adaptive design and **progressive enhancement** are alternatives to responsive design. Adaptive design chooses breakpoints and creates different designs for those breakpoints, to leverage differences in technologies. Progressive enhancement (as opposed to graceful degradation) works very well for low-cost delivery--design the minimum interface that delivers core content and functionality successfully, then add richer experiences for devices that can support them.

The problem with these techniques is that they lead to multiple repositories of code and potentially diverging designs across different media. To have a good and consistent brand experience, users must feel that the content, voice, and features of each device experience are similar.

Going back to Luke Wroblewski's device experience concept, devices that give you a dramatically different experience based on usage/posture, input, or output probably need specifically adapted designs. Vastly different screen sizes, such as wall screens or wearables, cannot show the same information in the same way. You may need a different information architecture for these. A compromise is to be adaptive for big breakpoints and responsive for everything in between. There is a lot of variation in resolution, aspect ratio, and capabilities within each larger breakpoint. The simpler and more standard your website, the more you can use responsive design across devices without adaptation.

Designing for different browsers and operating systems

Browsers and OSes may show content differently, although the differences here are not as large as for different devices.

In terms of operating systems, Apple, Windows, and Android have different UI guidelines and styles that they support.

For browsers, such as Chrome, Safari, Firefox, UC Browser (very popular in India and the Philippines), and Edge, the differences are about particular code APIs that are supported or not. These are not typically very big differences. However, there are other browsers, such as Opera Mini and UC Browser Mini, which operate very differently and are used by millions of people. For example, Opera Mini is used by people who have basic phones and want to control data usage. It proxies all websites to make transfers quickly and cheaply. It doesn't support a lot of JavaScript and so will probably break it on a web page.

As with responsive design, frontend frameworks such as Bootstrap and Foundation help you deal with different browsers. The code that they produce is also OS independent, so it will work the same on different operating system.

However, there are problems that frameworks are less able to help you with, such as blocking of sites and features. This can happen on a country basis. For example, China blocks much of JavaScript and many of Google's services, such as Maps, Gmail, and Docs. If your site depends on any of these services, it will not work well in China.

Blocking can also happen on an individual basis. More people are using apps that block certain features and deliveries to speed up their browsing or make it cheaper. For example, ad blockers often block content delivery services that deliver CSS and JavaScript, so people using these will not receive your rich experiences. Content blockers are becoming more common; these block but do not disable JavaScript so it is harder to automatically detect what content to deliver to them.

They can also block web fonts and custom fonts used on websites.

There is no single method of handling these differences and blockers. Designers must be aware of the apps that are popular on various stores and design with these restrictions in mind. Progressive enhancement can solve a lot of these problems--by making sure that the experience that you deliver is good on the most basic device, you can make sure that you never deliver an unpleasant experience, no matter what has been stripped from your design.

Designing for accessibility and assistive technologies

Assistive technologies, such as screen readers and magnifiers, are technologies that *read* websites and translate them, usually for people who are blind, partially sighted, dyslexic or illiterate; for example, screen readers provide output via text to speech synthesizers or Braille displays. There are many good screen readers, such as **NonVisual Desktop Access (NVDA)**, which is an excellent open source option. Most operating systems have built-in screen readers, for example, Microsoft Narrator, VoiceOver for Apple, and TalkBack for Android.

We discuss designing for accessibility in detail in Chapter 10, *The Basics and Benefits of Web Accessibility*, and Chapter 11, *A Practical Guide to Web Accessibility*. Therefore, we will not spend very much time on it here. The most important way to design for assistive technologies is to design with users in mind, following usability guidelines. Here are some examples:

- Careful color and color contrast choices make our websites viewable by people with various forms of color-blindness.
- Designing for keyboard input, with clear focus states and a logical tab order, supports screen readers and keyboard-only input.
- Using semantic HTML, alternative text for images, transcriptions for video, and creating a logical document structure with headings makes it easier for everyone to access and understand your content.
- Make sure that the readability of your site is not too high for most people to understand. There are various reading-level formulas that you can use to analyze the copy on your website and check the level of reading ability required to understand it.

Using universal design principles to guide design

The seven principles of universal design created by Ronald Mace and his collaborators can also help designers to evaluate their designs from an accessibility point of view:

- **Equitable use**: The design is useful and attractive to people with different abilities and situations. Examples are using alt text to help screen readers and users on slow or unstable connections (where images may not download); using high contrast, which helps people with weak vision and people using technology in sunlight; and not providing mouse-only interactions such as hover.
- **Flexibility in use**: The design allows interaction with a range of abilities and preferences. Examples are making sure that magnifying text does not ruin the layout of your website; providing novice and expert interaction options; and customization so users can choose how they want to experience your website.
- **Simple and intuitive use**: It is easy to understand the design, regardless of experience, knowledge, language skills, or concentration level. Examples of how to accomplish this include providing useful prompting and feedback on actions, consistent interfaces, and strong information hierarchy. Testing with users will help you refine your designs in this way.
- **Perceptible information**: The design communicates necessary information, regardless of the context and the user's abilities. You can accomplish this by providing redundant information in different modalities, enough contrast, legible text, and a good information architecture.
- **Tolerance for error**: Minimize the negative effects of incorrect actions. Provide warnings and easy recovery. Allow the user to undo actions.
- **Low physical effort**: Users should be able to use your design comfortably, with minimum effort mentally and physically. Minimize repetitive actions by placing hit targets carefully and creating links to navigate long pages. Group items that refer to the same content together.
- **Size and space for approach and use**: There should be enough space for effective and error-free action, regardless of size or mobility. For example, hit targets should be big enough for easy selection.

The preceding list is very similar to Nielsen's 10 heuristics for good interface design, which we discussed in `Chapter 5`, *Set a Solid Foundation - Research and Analyze*: visibility of system status; match between system and user's world; user control and freedom; consistency and standards; error prevention; recognition rather than recall; flexibility and efficiency of use; aesthetic and minimalist design; helping users recognize, diagnose, and recover from errors; and providing help and documentation. This makes it obvious that designing for universal accessibility is, for the most part, designing by following usability guidelines.

Testing your designs on multiple technologies

We have described how to consider the external world when designing a website, both technologically and from a user perspective. It is also important to test your designs against the external world. In the next chapter, we discuss how to test with users. Here, we will briefly look at testing internally on different technologies. Simulating the real world, where your website will be experienced, is crucial when testing your designs.

Gibson's **accessibility matrix** is useful to guide the testing. Wherever you have different input/output combinations, you should test them. You can add devices, operating systems, and browsers to this matrix to complete the test suite. For example, you may begin with screen reader as an option, then note exactly which screen reader(s) you tested against. If differences emerge with other readers, you can add them as separate items for your next design/test cycle.

There are many tools that help performance, accessibility, and network testing, and emulate different experiences. However, the best way to test (such as testing with real users) is to test on actual devices, operating systems, and browsers. Do this as much as possible, and as completely as possible:

- **Browsers**: Cross-browser testing is the easiest to accomplish. Simply download the main browsers, such as Chrome, Firefox, Safari, UC Browser, and Edge, and test your website on them. Test your website on basic browsers, such as Opera Mini, to see what breaks. Turn off JavaScript on your browser and see what your website looks like and how it performs. Turn off fonts and see what happens.
- **OS**: Find people within your team with Windows, iOS, macOS, Android, and Linux operating systems and test on their devices.
- **Assistive technology**: Download a screen reader or use the built-in one for your OS and view your website through it; calculate your readability score; navigate your website using only a keyboard and make sure that you can see the focus and access everything; simulate color-blindness on your website with an app; enlarge your fonts to 200% and see what it does to your website.
- **Devices**: Use emulators on websites or within your own browser. Test on as many differently sized devices as possible. It is worth checking Amazon and other technology e-commerce sites to find out what the popular mobile devices are. Then you can test on those, or at least check their specifications.

Your browser can help you. Chrome, Safari, and Firefox offer responsive and accessible design tools. The following is a screenshot of Chrome's inbuilt Developer Tools window, showing emulated devices and network throttling options:

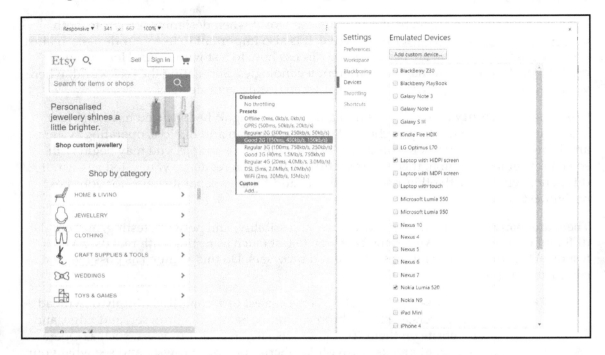

Screenshot of Chrome Developer Tools, showing responsive emulation and network throttling

- Change the viewport to **Responsive**, then adjust it to any size and see what happens to your website. You can also select from a list of predefined devices, or add a custom device, so you can see how that device would render your website. Within each device option, you can choose to view the device in portrait or landscape and with or without a keyboard, if applicable. For touch devices, Chrome shows the hit target size as well.
- Set the network speed through the network throttling tool, so you can test how your website will work on a 2G or 3G connections.

Summary

In this chapter, we discussed how to make sure your website design works in the real world, for anyone who wants to access it.

As part of this, we described the importance of and differences between responsive, accessible, and universal design. We then looked at how to use these paradigms and their related tools to design effectively for different technologies and people. We specifically looked at how to design for different inputs and outputs, responsively, for different operating systems and browsers, for assistive technologies, and with universal design in mind.

Finally, we briefly looked at how to test your designs using technology. In the next chapter, we describe how to test your designs with users.

9

Optimize your UX Strategy with Iterative User Testing

A UX practitioner's primary goal is to provide every user with the best possible experience of a product. The only way to do this is to connect repeatedly with users and make sure that the product is being designed according to their needs. At the beginning of a project, this research tends to be more exploratory. Towards the end of the project, it tends to be more about testing the product.

We have previously discussed various ways of connecting with users in Chapter 5, *Set a Solid Foundation,* when we described UX research. In this chapter, we explore in detail one of the most common methods of testing a product with users--the usability test. As we describe the steps to plan, conduct, and analyze usability tests, this will provide insights into how to practically plan, conduct, and analyze any user research.

We begin by describing how to make sure that you get the most value out of user testing. Then we delve into usability testing in detail, including how to identify and find representative users, design a test with useful tasks and interview questions, make sure you manage all the administration that needs to happen around the test, conduct a test effectively, and successfully analyze the results. Finally, we will briefly explore a more quantitative approach to testing--applying analytics effectively to test website usage. We will look at A/B testing as an example of analytics being used.

The topics covered in the chapter are:

- Maximizing the value of user testing
- Planning, conducting, and analyzing usability tests
- Applying analytics effectively--constructing a useful A/B test

Maximizing the value of user testing

Testing with users is not only about making their experience better; it is also about getting more people to use your product. People will not use a product that they do not find useful; and they will choose the product that is most enjoyable and usable if they have options. This is especially the case with the web. People leave websites if they can't find or do the things they want. Unlike with other products, they will not take time to work it out. Research by organizations such as the Nielsen Norman group generally shows that a website has between 5 and 10 seconds to show value to a visitor.

User testing is one of the main methods available to us to ensure that we make websites that are useful, enjoyable, and usable. However, to be effective it must be done properly. Jared Spool, a usability expert, identified seven typical mistakes that people make while testing with users, which lessen its value. The following list addresses how not to make those mistakes:

- **Know why you're testing**: What are the goals of your test? Make sure that you specify the test goals clearly and concretely so that you choose the right method. Are you observing people's behavior (usability test), finding out whether they like your design (focus group or sentiment analysis), or finding out how many do something on your website (web analytics)? Posing specific questions will help to formulate the goals clearly. For example, will the new content reduce calls to the service center? Or what percentage of users return to the website within a week?
- **Design the right tasks**: If your testing involves tasks, design scenarios that correspond to tasks users would actually perform. Consider what would motivate someone to spend time on your website, and use this to create tasks. Provide participants with the information they would have to complete the tasks in a real-life situation; no more and no less. For example, do not specify tasks using terms from your website interface; then participants will simply be following instructions when they complete the tasks, rather than using their own mental models to work out what to do.

- **Recruit the right users**: If you design and conduct a test perfectly, but test on people who are not like your users, then the results will not be valid. If they know too much or too little about the product, subject area, or technology, then they will not behave like your users would and will not experience the same problems. When recruiting participants, ask what qualities define your users, and what qualities make one person experience the website differently to another. Then recruit on these qualities. In addition, recruit the right number of users for your method. Ongoing research by the Nielsen Norman group and others indicate that usability tests typically require about five people per test, while A/B tests require about 40 people, and card sorting requires about 15 people. These numbers have been calculated to maximize the return on investment of testing. For example, five users in a usability test have been shown by the Nielsen Norman group (and confirmed repeatedly by other researchers) to find about 85% of the serious problems in an interface. Adding more users improves the percentage marginally, but increases the costs significantly. If you use the wrong numbers then your results will not be valid or the amount of data that you need to analyze will be unmanageable for the time and resources you have available.

- **Get the team and stakeholders involved**: If user testing is seen as an outside activity, most of the team will not pay attention as it is not part of their job and easy to ignore. When team members are involved, they gain insights about their own work and its effectiveness. Try to get team members to attend some of the testing if possible. Otherwise make sure everyone is involved in preparing the goals and tasks (if appropriate) for the test. Share the results in a workshop afterwards, so everyone can be involved in reflecting on the results and their implications.

- **Facilitate the test well**: Facilitating a test well is a difficult task. A good facilitator makes users feel comfortable so they act more naturally. At the same time, the facilitator must control the flow of the test so that everything is accomplished in the available time, and not give participants hints about what to do or say. Make sure that facilitators have a lot of practice and constructive feedback from the team to improve their skills.

- **Plan how to share the results**: It takes time and skill to create an effective user testing report that communicates the test and results well. Even if you have the time and skill, most team members will probably not read the report. Find other ways to share results to those who need them. For example, create a bug list for developers using project management software or a shared online document; have a workshop with the team and stakeholders and present the test and results to them. Have review sessions immediately after test days.

- **Iterate**: Most user testing is most effective if performed regularly and iteratively; for testing different aspects or parts of the design; for testing solutions based on previous tests; for finding new problems or ideas introduced by the new solutions; for tracking changes to results based on time, seasonality, maturity of product or user base; or for uncovering problems that were previously hidden by larger problems. Many organizations only make provision to test with users once at the end of design, if at all. It is better to split your budget into multiple tests if possible.

As we explore usability testing, each of these guidelines will be addressed more concretely.

Planning, conducting, and analyzing usability tests

In this section, we will describe in detail how to practically plan, conduct, and analyze a typical formal usability test. Before starting, we will define what we mean by a usability test, and describe the different types. At the end of this section, we will briefly discuss variations on the formal usability test, such as guerrilla testing and unmoderated remote testing.

 Usability testing involves watching a representative set of users attempt realistic tasks, and collecting data about what they do and say. Essentially, a usability test is about watching a user interact with a product. This is what makes it a core UX method: it persuades stakeholders about the importance of designing for and testing with their users.

Team members who watch participants struggle to use their product are often shocked that they had not noticed the glaringly obvious design problems that are revealed. In later iterations, usability tests should reveal fewer or more minor problems, which provides proof of the success of a design before launch. Apart from glaring problems, how do we know what makes a design successful? The definition of usability by the **International Organization for Standardization (ISO)** is: *Extent to which a product can be used by specified users to achieve specified goals with effectiveness, efficiency and satisfaction in a specified context of use*. This definition shows us the kind of things that make a successful design.

From this definition, usability comprises:

- **Effectiveness**: How completely and accurately the required tasks can be accomplished.
- **Efficiency**: How quickly tasks can be performed.
- **Satisfaction**: How pleasant and enjoyable the task is. This can become a delight if a design pleases us in unexpected ways.

There are three additional points that arise from the preceding points:

- **Discoverability**: How easy it is to find out how to use the product the first time.
- **Learnability**: How easy it is to continue to improve using the product, and remember how to use it.
- **Error proneness**: How well the product prevents errors and helps users recover. This equates to the number and severity of errors that users experience while doing tasks.

These six points provide us with guidance on the kinds of tasks we should be designing and the kind of observations we should be making, when planning a usability test.

There are three ways of gathering data in a usability test--using metrics to guide quantitative measurement, observing, and asking questions. The most important is observation. Metrics allow comparison, guide observation, and help us design tasks, but they are not as important as why things happen. We discover why by observing interactions and emotional responses during task performance. In addition, we must be very careful when assigning meaning to quantitative metrics because of the small numbers of users involved in usability tests. Typically, usability tests are conducted with about five participants. This number has been repeatedly shown to be most effective when considering testing costs against the number of problems uncovered. However, it is too small for statistical significance testing, so any numbers must be reported carefully.

If we consider observation against asking questions, usability tests are about doing things, not discussing them. We may ask users to talk aloud while doing tasks to help us understand what they are thinking, but we need the context of what they are doing.

> *"To design an easy-to-use interface, pay attention to what users do, not what they say. Self-reported claims are unreliable, as are user speculations about future behavior."*
>
> *- Jakob Nielsen*

This means that usability tests trump questionnaires and surveys. It also means that people are notoriously bad at remembering what they did or imagining what they will do. It does not mean that we never listen to what users say, as there is a lot of value to be gained from a well-formed question asked at the right time. We must just be careful about how we understand it. We need to interpret what people say within the context of how they say it, what they are doing when they say it, and what their biases might be. For example, users tend to tell researchers what they think we want to hear, so any value judgement will likely be more positive than it should. This is called experimenter bias.

Despite the preceding cautions, all three methods are useful and increase the value of a test. While observation is core, the most effective usability tests include tasks carefully designed around metrics, and begin and end with a contextual interview of the user. The interviews help us to understand the user's previous and current experiences, and the context in which they might use the website in their own lives.

Planning a usability test can seem like a daunting task. There are so many details to work out and organize, and they all need to come together on the day(s) of the test. The following diagram is a flowchart of the usability test process. Each of the boxes represents a different area that must be considered or organized:

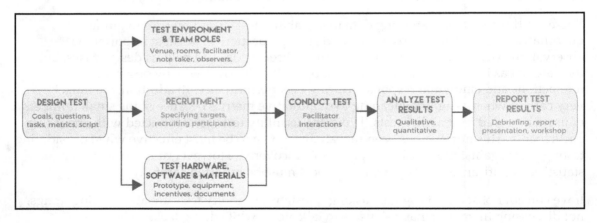

Usability test process

However, by using these areas to break the task down into logical steps and keeping a checklist, the task becomes manageable.

Planning usability tests

In designing and planning a usability test, you need to consider five broad questions:

- **What**: What are the objectives, scope, and focus of the test? What fidelity are you testing?
- **How**: How will you realize the objectives? Do you need permissions and sign off? What metrics, tasks, and questions are needed? What are the hardware and software requirements? Do you need a prototype? What other materials will you need? How will you conduct the test?
- **Who**: How many participants and who will they be? How will you recruit them? What are the roles needed? Will team members, clients, and stakeholders attend? Will there be a facilitator and/or a notetaker?
- **Where**: What venue will you use? Is the test conducted in an internal or external lab, on the streets/in coffee shops, or in users' homes/work?
- **When**: What is the date of the test? What will the schedule be? What is the timing of each part?

Documenting these questions and their answers forms your test plan. The following figure illustrates the thinking around each of these broad questions:

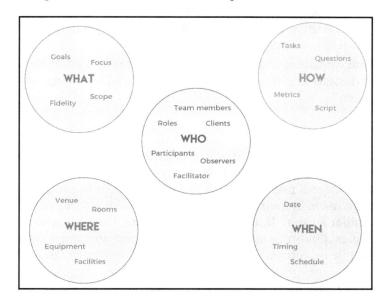

Test plan questions

It is important to remember that no matter how carefully you plan usability testing, it can all go horribly wrong. Therefore, have backup plans wherever you can. For example, for participants who cancel late or do not arrive, have a couple of spares ready; for power cuts, be prepared with screenshots so you can at least simulate some tasks on paper; for testing live sites when the internet connection fails, have a portable wireless router or cache pages beforehand.

Designing the test - formulating goals and structure

The first thing to consider when planning a usability test is its goal. This will dictate the test scope, focus, and tasks and questions. For example, if your goal is a general usability test of the whole website, the tasks will be based on the business reasons for the site. These are the most important user interactions. You will ask questions about general impressions of the site. However, if your goal is to test the search and filtering options, your tasks will involve finding things on the website. You will ask questions about the difficulty of finding things. If you are not sure what the specific goal of the usability test might be, think about the following three points:

- **Scope**: Do you want to test part of the design, or the whole website?
- **Focus**: Which area of the website will you focus on? Even if you want to test the whole website, there will be areas that are more important. For example, checkout versus contact page.
- **Behavioral questions**: Are there questions about how users behave, or how different designs might impact user behavior, that are being asked within the organization?

Thinking about these questions will help you refine your test goals.

Once you have the goals, you can design the structure of the test and create a high-level test plan. When deciding on how many tests to conduct in a day and how long each test should be, remember moderator and user fatigue. A test environment is a stressful situation. Even if you are testing with users in their own home, you are asking them to perform unfamiliar tasks with an unfamiliar system. If users become too tired, this will affect test results negatively. Likewise, facilitating a test is tiring as the moderator must observe and question the user carefully, while monitoring things like the time, their own language, and the script.

Here are details to consider when creating a schedule for test sessions:

- **Test length**: Typically, each test should be between 60 and 90 minutes long.
- **Number of tests**: You should not be facilitating more than 5-6 tests in one day. When counting the hours, leave at least half an hour cushioning space between each test. This gives you time to save the recording, make extra notes if necessary, communicate with any observers, and it provides flexibility if participants arrive later or tests run longer than they should.
- **Number of tasks**: This is roughly the number of tasks you hope to include in the test. In a 60-minute test, you will probably have about 40-45 minutes for tasks. The rest of the time will be taken with welcoming the participant, the initial interview, and closing questions at the end. In 45 minutes, you can fit about 5-8 tasks, depending on the nature of the tasks. It is important to remember that less is more in a test. You want to give participants time to explore the website and think about their options. You do not want to be rushing them on to the next task.

The last thing to consider is moderating technique. This is how you interact with the participant and ask for their input. There are two aspects: *thinking aloud* and *probing*. Thinking aloud is asking participants to talk about what they are thinking and doing so you can understand what is in their heads. Probing is asking participants ad-hoc questions about interesting things that they do. You can do both concurrently or retrospectively:

- **Concurrent thinking aloud and probing**: Here, the participant talks while they do tasks and look at the interface. The facilitator asks questions as they come up, while the participant is doing tasks. Concurrent probing interferes with metrics such as time on task and accuracy, as you might distract users. However, it also takes less test time and can deliver more accurate insights, as participants do not have to remember their thoughts and feelings; these are shared as they happen.
- **Retrospective thinking aloud and probing**: This involves retracing the test or task after it is finished and asking participants to describe what they were thinking in retrospect. The facilitator may note down questions during tasks, and ask these later. While retrospective techniques simulate natural interaction more closely, they take longer because tasks are retraced. This means that the test must be longer or there will be fewer tasks and interview questions. Retrospective techniques also require participants to remember what they were thinking previously, which can be faulty.

Concurrent moderating techniques are preferable because of the close alignment between users acting and talking about those actions. Retrospective techniques should only be used if timing metrics are very important. Even in these cases, concurrent thinking aloud can be used with retrospective probing. Thinking aloud concurrently generally interferes very little with task times and accuracy, as users are ideally just verbalizing ideas already in their heads.

At each stage of test planning, share the ideas with the team and stakeholders and ask for feedback. You may need permission to go forward with test objectives and tasks. However, even if you do not need sign off, sharing details with the team gets everyone involved in the testing. This is a good way to share and promote design values. It also benefits the test, as team members will probably have good ideas about tasks to include or elements of the website to test that you have not considered.

Designing tasks and metrics

As we have stated previously, usability testing is about watching users interacting with a product. Tasks direct the interactions that you want to see. Therefore, they should cover the focus area of the test, or all important interactions if the whole website is tested.

To make the test more natural, if possible create scenarios or user stories that link the tasks together so participants are performing a logical sequence of activities. If you have scenarios or task analyses from previous research, choose those that relate to your test goals and focus, and use them to guide your task design. If not, create brief scenarios that cover your goals. You can do this from a top-down or bottom-up perspective:

- **Top down**: What events or conditions in their world would motivate people to use this design? For example, if the website is a used goods marketplace, a potential user might have an item they want to get rid of easily, while making some money; or they might need an item and try to get it cheaply secondhand. Then, what tasks accomplish these goals?
- **Bottom up**: What are the common tasks that people do on the website? For example, in the marketplace example, common tasks are searching for specific items; browsing through categories of items; adding an item to the site to sell, which might include uploading photographs or videos, adding contact details and item descriptions. Then, create scenarios around these tasks to tie them together.

Tasks can be exploratory and open-ended, or specific and directed. A test should have both. For example, you can begin with an open-ended task, such as examining the home page and exploring the links that are interesting. Then you can move onto more directed tasks, such as finding a particular color, size, and brand of shoe and adding it to the checkout cart. It is always good to begin with exploratory tasks, but these can be open-ended or directed. For example, to gather first impressions of a website, you could ask users to explore as they prefer from the home page and give their impressions as they work; or you could ask users to look at each page for five seconds, and then write down everything they remember seeing. The second option is much more controlled, which may be necessary if you want more direct comparison between participants, or are testing with a prototype where only parts of the website are available.

Metrics are needed for task, observation, and interview analysis, so that we can evaluate the success of the design we are testing. They guide how we examine the results of a usability test. They are based on the definition of usability, and so relate to effectiveness, efficiency, satisfaction, discoverability, learnability, and error proneness. Metrics can be qualitative or quantitative. Qualitative metrics aim to encode the data so that we can detect patterns and trends in it, and compare the success of participants, tasks, or tests. For example, noting expressions of delight or frustration during a task. Quantitative metrics collect numbers that we can manipulate and compare against each other or benchmarks. For example, the number of errors each participant makes in a task. We must be careful how we use and assign meaning to quantitative metrics because of the small sample sizes.

USABILITY COMPONENT	METRICS
EFFECTIVENESS	Task success Task completion
EFFICIENCY	Time on task Steps to complete task
SATISFACTION	Rating scale for enjoyment, ease of use, usefulness Expressions of satisfaction / frustration
DISCOVERABILITY	First clicks First impressions Expressions of satisfaction / confusion
LEARNABILITY	Time on task for repeat tasks Task success for repeat tasks Number of errors for repeat tasks Expressions of mastery / confusion
ERROR PRONENESS	Number of errors Severity of errors

Tasks and metrics to test usability

Here are some typical metrics:

- **Task success or completion rates**: This measures effectiveness and should always be captured as a base. It relates most closely to *conversion*, which is the primary business goal for a website, whether it is converting browsers to buyers, or visitors to registered users. You may just note success or failure, but it is more revealing to capture the degree of task success. For example, you can specify whether the task is completed easily, with some struggle, with help, or is not completed successfully.
- **Time on task**: A measure of efficiency. How long it takes to complete tasks.
- **Errors per task**: A measure of error-proneness. The number and severity of errors per task, especially noting critical errors where participants may not even realize they have made a mistake.
- **Steps per task**: A measure of efficiency. A number of steps or pages needed to complete each task, often against a known minimum.
- **First click**: A measure of discoverability. Noting the first click to accomplish each task, to report on findability of items on the web page. This can also be used in more exploratory tasks to judge what attracts the user's attention first.

When you have designed tasks, consider them against the definition of usability to make sure that you have covered everything that you need or want to cover. The preceding diagram shows the metrics typically associated with each component of the usability definition.

A valid criticism of usability testing is that it only tests first-time use of a product, as participants do not have time to become familiar with the system. There are ways around this problem. For example, certain types of task, such as search and browsing, can be repeated with different items. In later tasks, participants will be more familiar with the controls. The facilitator can use observation or metrics such as task time and accuracy to judge the effect of familiarity. A more complicated method is to conduct longitudinal tests, where participants are asked to return a few days or a week later and perform similar tasks. This is only reasonable to spend time and money on if learnability is an important metric.

Planning questions and observation

The interview questions that are asked at the beginning and end of a test provide valuable context for user actions and reactions, such as the user's background, their experiences with similar websites or the subject-area, and their relationship to technology. They also help the facilitator to establish rapport with the user.

Other questions provide valuable qualitative information about the user's emotional reaction to the website and the tasks they are doing. A combination of observation and questions provides data on aspects such as ease of use, usefulness, satisfaction, delight, and frustration.

For the initial interview, questions should be about:

- **Welcome**: These set the participant at ease, and can include questions about the participant's lifestyle, job, and family. These details help UX practitioners to present test participants as real people with normal lives when reporting on the test.
- **Domain**: These ask about the participant's experience with the domain of the website. For example, if the website is in the domain of financial services, questions might be around the participant's banking, investments, loans, and their experiences with other financial websites. As part of this, you might investigate their feelings about security and privacy.
- **Tech**: These questions ask about the participant's usage and experience with technology. For example, for testing a website on a computer, you might want to know how often the participant uses the internet or social media each day, what kinds of things they do on the internet, and whether they buy things online. If you are testing mobile usage, you might want to inquire about how often the participant uses the internet on their phone each day, and what kind of sites they visit on mobile versus desktop.

Like tasks, questions can be open-ended or closed. An example of an open-ended question is: *Tell me about how you use your phone throughout a normal workday, beginning with waking up in the morning and ending with going to sleep at night.* The facilitator would then prompt the participant for further details suggested during the reply. A closed question might be: *What is your job?* These generate simple responses, but can be used as springboards into deeper answers. For example, if the answer is *fireman*, the facilitator might say, *That's interesting. Tell me more about that. What do you do as a fireman?*

Questions asked at the end of the test or during the test are more about the specific experience of the website and the tasks. These are often made more quantifiable by using a rating scale to structure the answer. A typical example is a Likert scale, where participants specify their agreement or disagreement with a statement on a 5- to 7-point scale. For example, a statement might be: I can find what I want easily using this website. #1 is labeled *Strongly Agree* and #7 is labelled *Strongly Disagree*. Participants choose the number that corresponds to the strength of their agreement or disagreement. You can then compare responses between participants or across different tests.

Examples of typical questions include:

- **Ease of use** (**after every task**): *On a scale of 1-7, where 1 is really hard and 7 is really easy, how difficult or easy did you find this task?*
- **Ease of use** (**at the end**): *On a scale of 1-7, how easy or difficult did you find working on this website?*
- **Usefulness**: *On a scale of 1-7, how useful do you think this website would be for doing your job?*
- **Recommendation**: *On a scale of 1-7, how likely are you to recommend this website to a friend?*

It is important to always combine these kinds of questions with observation and task performance, and to ask *why* afterwards. People tend to self-report very positively, so often you will pay less attention to the number they give and more to how they talk about their answer afterwards.

The final questions you ask provide closure for the test and end it gracefully. These can be more general and conversational. They might deliver useful data, but that is not the priority. For example, *What did you think of the website?* or *Is there anything else you'd like to say about the website?*

Questions during the test often arise ad hoc because you do not understand why the participant does an action, or what they are thinking about if they stare at a page of the website for a while. You might also want to ask participants what they expect to find before they select a menu item or look at a page.

In preparing for observation, it is helpful to make a list of the kinds of things you especially want to observe during the test. Typical options are:

- Reactions to each new page of the website
- First reactions when they open the Home page
- The variety of steps used to complete each task
- Expressions of delight or frustration
- Reactions to specific elements of the website
- First clicks for each task
- First click off the Home page

Much of what you want to observe will be guided by the usability test objectives and the nature of the website.

Preparing the script

Once you have designed all the elements of the usability test, you can put them together in a script. This is a core document in usability testing, as it acts as the facilitator's guide during each test. There are different ideas about what to include in a script. Here, we describe a comprehensive script that describes the whole test procedure. This includes, in rough order:

1. The information that must be told to the participant in the welcome speech. The welcome speech is very important, as it is the participant's first experience of the facilitator. It is where the rapport will first be established. The following information may need to be included:
    - Introduction to the facilitator, client, and product.
    - What will happen during the test, including the length.
    - The idea that the website is being tested, not the participant, and that any problems are the fault of the product. This means the participant is valuable and helpful to the team developing a great website.
    - Asking the participant to think aloud as much as possible, and to be honest and blunt about what they think. Asking them to imagine that they are at home in a natural situation, exploring the website.
    - If there are observers, indication that people may be watching and that they should be ignored.
    - Asking permission to record the session, and telling the participant why. Assuring them of their privacy and the limited usage of the recordings to analysis and internal reporting.
2. A list of any documents that the participant must look at or sign first, for example, an NDA.
3. Instructions on when to switch on and off any recording devices.
4. The questions to ask in thematic sections, for example, welcome, domain, and technology. These can include potential follow - on questions, to delve for more information if necessary.
5. A task section, that has several parts:
    - An introduction to the prototype if necessary. If you are testing with a prototype, there will probably be unfinished areas that are not clickable. It is worth alerting participants so they know what to expect while doing tasks and talking aloud.

- Instructions on how to use the technology if necessary. Ideally your participants should be familiar with the technology, but if this is not the case, you want to be testing the website, not the technology. For example, if you are testing with a particular screen reader and the participant has not used it before, or if you are using eye tracking technology.
- An introduction to the tasks, including any scenarios provided to the participant.
- The description of each task. Be careful not to use words from the website interface when describing tasks, so you do not guide the participant too much. For example, instead of: *How would you add this item to your cart?*, say *How would you buy this item?*
- Questions to include after each task. For example, the ease of use question.
- Questions to prompt the participant if they are not thinking aloud when they should, especially for each new page of the website or prototype. For example: *What do you see here? What can you do here? What do you think these options mean?*

2. Final questions to finish off the test, and give the participant a chance to emphasize any of their experiences.
3. A list of any documents the participant must sign at the end, and instructions to give the incentive if appropriate.

Once the script is created, timing is added to each task and section, to help the facilitator make sure that the tests do not run over time. This will be refined as the usability test is practiced.

The script provides a structure to take notes in during the test, either on paper or digitally:

- Create a spreadsheet with rows for each question and task
- Use the first column for the script, from the welcome questions onwards
- Capture notes in subsequent columns for the user
- Use a separate spreadsheet for each participant during the test
- After all the tests, combine the results into one spreadsheet so you can easily analyze and compare

The following is a diagram showing sections of the script for notetaking, with sample questions and tasks, for a radio station website:

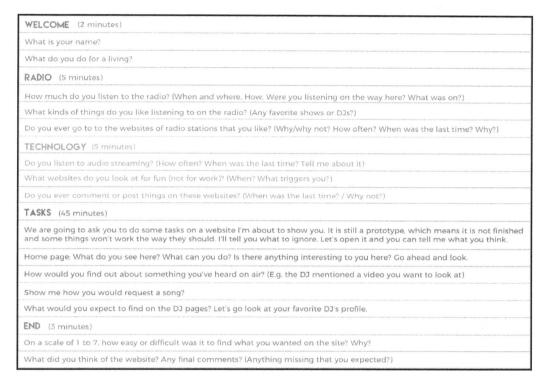

WELCOME (2 minutes)
What is your name?
What do you do for a living?
RADIO (5 minutes)
How much do you listen to the radio? (When and where. How. Were you listening on the way here? What was on?)
What kinds of things do you like listening to on the radio? (Any favorite shows or DJs?)
Do you ever go to to the websites of radio stations that you like? (Why/why not? How often? When was the last time? Why?)
TECHNOLOGY (5 minutes)
Do you listen to audio streaming? (How often? When was the last time? Tell me about it)
What websites do you look at for fun (not for work)? (When? What triggers you?)
Do you ever comment or post things on these websites? (When was the last time? / Why not?)
TASKS (45 minutes)
We are going to ask you to do some tasks on a website I'm about to show you. It is still a prototype, which means it is not finished and some things won't work the way they should. I'll tell you what to ignore. Let's open it and you can tell me what you think.
Home page: What do you see here? What can you do? Is there anything interesting to you here? Go ahead and look.
How would you find out about something you've heard on air? (E.g. the DJ mentioned a video you want to look at)
Show me how you would request a song?
What would you expect to find on the DJ pages? Let's go look at your favorite DJ's profile.
END (3 minutes)
On a scale of 1 to 7, how easy or difficult was it to find what you wanted on the site? Why?
What did you think of the website? Any final comments? (Anything missing that you expected?)

Sample of usability test script

Securing a venue and inviting clients and team members

If you are testing at an external venue, this is one of the first things you will need to organize for a usability test, as these venues typically need to be booked about one-two months in advance. Even if you are testing in your own offices, you will still need to book space for the testing.

When considering a test venue, you should be looking for the following:

- A quiet, dedicated space where the facilitator, participant, and potentially a notetaker, can sit. This needs surfaces for all the equipment that will be used during the test, and comfortable space for the participant. Consider the lighting in the test room. This might cause glare if you are testing on mobile phones, so think about how best to handle the glare. For example, where the best place is for the participant to sit, and whether you can use indirect lighting of some kind.
- A reception room where participants can wait for their testing session. This should be comfortable. You may want to provide refreshments for participants here.
- Ideally, an observation room for people to watch the usability tests. Observers should never be in the same space as the testing, as this will distract participants, and probably make them uncomfortable. The observation room should be linked to the test room, either with cables or wirelessly, so observers can see what is happening on the participant's screen, and hear (and ideally see) the participant during the test. Some observation rooms have two-way mirrors into the test room, so observers can watch the facilitator and participant directly. Refreshments should be available for the observers.

We have discussed various testing roles previously. Here, we describe them formally:

- **Facilitator**: This is the person who conducts the test with the participant. They sit with the participant, instruct them in the tasks and ask questions, and take notes. This is the most important role during the test. We will discuss it further in the *Conducting usability tests* section.
- **Participant**: This is the person who is doing the test. We will discuss recruiting test participants in the next section.
- **Notetaker**: This is an optional role. It can be worth having a separate notetaker, so the facilitator does not have to take notes during the test. This is especially the case if the facilitator is inexperienced. If there is a notetaker, they sit quietly in the test room and do not engage with the participant, except when introduced by the facilitator.
- **Receptionist**: Someone must act as receptionist for the participants who arrive. This cannot be the facilitator, as they will be in the sessions. Ask a team member or the office receptionist to take this role.

- **Observers**: Everyone else is an observer. These can be other team members and/or clients. Observers should be given guidelines for their behavior. For example, they should not interact with test participants or interrupt the test. They watch from a separate room, and should not be too noisy so that they can be heard in the test room (often these rooms are close to each other). The facilitator should discuss the tests with observers between sessions, to check if they have any questions they would like added to the test, and to discuss observations. It is worth organizing a debriefing for immediately after the tests, or the next day if possible, for the observers and facilitator to discuss the tests and observations.

It is important that as many stakeholders as possible are persuaded to watch at least some of the usability testing. Watching people using your designs is always enlightening, and really helps to bring a team together. Remember to invite clients and team members early, and send reminders closer to the day.

Recruiting participants

When recruiting participants for usability tests, make sure that they are as close as possible to your target audience. If your website is live and you have a pool of existing users, then your job is much easier. However, if you do not have a user pool, or you want to test with people who have not used your site, then you need to create a specification for appropriate users that you can give to a recruiter or use yourself.

To specify your target audience, consider what kinds of people use your website, and what attributes will cause them to behave differently to other users. If you have created personas during previous research, use these to help identify target user characteristics. If you are designing a website for a client, work with them to identify their target users. It is important to be specific, as it is difficult to look for people who fulfill abstract qualities. For example, instead of asking for *tech savvy* people, consider what kinds of technology such people are more likely to use, and what their activities are likely to be. Then ask for people who use the technology in the ways you have identified. Consider the behaviors that result from certain types of beliefs, attitudes, and lifestyle choices. The following are examples of general areas you should consider:

- **Experience with technology**: You may want users who are comfortable with technology or who have used specific technology, for example, the latest smartphones, or screen readers. Consider the properties that will identify these people. For example, you can specify that all participants must own a specific type or generation of mobile device, and must have owned it for at least two months.

- **Online experience**: You may want users with a certain level and frequency of internet usage. To elicit this, you can specify that you want people who have bought items online within the last few months, or who do online banking, or have never done these things.
- **Social media presence**: Often, you want people who have a certain amount of social media interaction, potentially on specific platforms. In this case you would specify that they must regularly post to or read social media such as Facebook, Twitter, Instagram, Snapchat, or more hobbyist versions such as Pinterest and/or Flickr.
- **Experience with the domain**: Participants should not know too much or too little about the domain. For example, if you are testing banking software, you may want to exclude bank employees, as they are familiar with how things work internally.
- **Demographics**: Unless your target audience is very skewed, you probably want to recruit a variety of people demographically. For example, a range of ages, gender ethnicity, economic, and education levels.

There may be other characteristics you need in your usability test participants. The previous characteristics should give you an idea of how to specify such people. For example, you may want hobbyist photographers. In this case, you would recruit people who regularly take photographs and share them with friends in some way. Do not use people who you have previously used in testing, unless you specifically need people like this, as they will be familiar with your tests and procedures, which will interfere with results.

Recruiting takes time and is difficult to do well. There are various ways of recruiting people for user testing, depending on your business. You may be able to use people or organizations associated with your business or target audience members to recruit people using the screening questions and incentives that you give them. You can set up social media lists of people who follow your business and are willing to participate. You can also use professional recruiters, who will get you exactly the kinds of people you need, but will charge you for it.

For most tests, an incentive is usually given to thank participants for their time. This is often money, but it can also be a gift, such as stationery or gift certificates.

A **recruitment brief** is the document that you give to recruiters. The following are the details you need to include:

- Day of the test, the test length, and the ideal schedule. This should state the times at which the first and last participants may be scheduled, how long each test will take, and the buffer period that should be between each session.
- The venue. This should include an address, maps, parking, and travel information.
- Contact details for the team members who will oversee the testing and recruitment.
- A description of the test that can be given to participants.
- The incentives that will be provided.
- The list of qualities you need in participants, or screening questions to check for these.

This document can be modified to share with less formal recruitment associates. The benefit of recruiters is that they handle the whole recruitment process. If you and your team recruit participants yourselves, you will need to remind them a week before the test, and the day before the test, usually by messaging or emailing them. On the day of the test, phone participants to confirm that they will be arriving, and that they know how to get to the venue. Participants still often do not attend tests, even with all the reminders. This is the nature of testing with real people. Ideally you will be given some notice, so try to recruit an extra couple of possible participants who you can call in a pinch on the day.

Setting up the hardware, software, and test materials

Depending on the usability test, you will have to prepare different hardware, software, and test materials. These include screen recording software and hardware, notetaking hardware, the prototype to test, screen sharing options, and so on.

The first thing to consider is the prototype, as this will have implications for hardware and software. Are you testing a live website, an electronic prototype, or a paper prototype?

- **Live website**: Set up any accounts or passwords that may be necessary. Make sure you have reliable access to the internet, or a way to cache the website on your machine if necessary.

- **Electronic prototype**: Make sure the prototype works the way it is supposed to, and that all the parts that are accessed during the tasks can be interacted with, if required. Try not to make it too obvious which parts work and which parts do not work, as this may guide participants to the correct actions during the test. Be prepared to talk participants through parts of the prototype that do not work, so they have context for the tasks. Have a safe copy of the prototype in case this copy becomes corrupted in some way.

- **Paper prototype**: Make sure that you have sketches or printouts of all the screens that you need to complete the tasks. With paper prototype testing, the facilitator takes the role of the computer, shows the results of the actions that the participant proposes, and talks participants through the screens. Make sure that you are prepared for this and know the order of the screens. Have multiple copies of the paper prototype in case parts get lost or destroyed.

For any of the three, make sure the team goes through the test tasks to make sure that everything is working the way it should be.

For hardware and other software, keep an equipment list, so you can check it to make sure you have all the necessary hardware with you. You may need to include:

- **Hardware for participant to interact with the prototype or live site**: This may be a desktop, laptop, or mobile device. If testing on a mobile device, you can ask participants to use their own familiar phones instead of an unfamiliar test mobile device. However, participants may have privacy issues with using their own phones, and you will not be able to test the prototype or live site on the phone beforehand. If you provide a laptop, include a separate mouse as people often have difficulty with unfamiliar mouse pads.

- **Recording the screen and audio**: This is usually screen capture software. There are many options for screen capturing software, such as *Lookback*, an inexpensive option for iOS and Android, and *CamStudio*, a free option for the PC. Specialist software that handles multiple camera inputs allows you to record face and screen at the same time. Examples are *iSpy*, free CCTV software, *Silverback*, an inexpensive option for the Mac, and *Morae*, an expensive but impressive option for the PC.

- **Mobile recording alternative**: You can also record mobile video with an external camera that captures the participant's fingers on screen. This means you do not have to install additional software on the phone, which might cause performance problems. In this case, you would use a document camera attached to the table, or a portable rig with a camera containing the phone and attached to a nearby PC. The video will include hesitations and hovering gestures, which are useful for understanding user behavior, but fingers might occlude the screen. In addition, rigs may interfere with natural usage of the mobile phone, as participants must hold the rig as well as the phone.
- **Observer viewing screen**: This is needed if there are observers. The venue might have screen sharing set up; if not, you will have to bring your own hardware and software. This could be an external monitor and extension cables to connect to a laptop in the interview room. It could also be screen sharing software, for example, *join.me*.
- **Capturing notes**: You will need a method to capture notes. Even if you are screen recording, notes will help you to review the recordings more efficiently, and remind you about parts of the recording you wanted to pay special attention to. One method is using a tablet or laptop and spreadsheet. Typing is fast and the electronic notes are easy to put together after the tests. An alternative is paper and pencil. The benefit of this is that it is least disruptive to the participant. However, these notes must be captured electronically.
- **Camera for participant face**: Capturing the participant's face is not crucial. However, it provides good insight into their feelings about tasks and questions. If you don't record face, you will only have tone of voice and the notes that were taken to remind you. Possible methods are using a webcam attached to the computer doing screen recording, or using inbuilt software such as Hangouts, Skype, or FaceTime for Apple devices.
- **Microphone**: Often sound quality is not great on screen capturing software, because of feedback from computer equipment. Using an external microphone improves the quality of sound.
- **Wireless router:** A portable wireless router in case of internet problems (if you are using the internet).
- Extra extension cables and chargers for all devices.

You will also need to make sure that you have multiple copies of all documents needed for the testing. These might include:

- **Consent form**: When you are testing people, they typically need to give their permission to be tested. You also typically need proof that the incentive has been received by the participant. These are usually combined into a form that the participant signs to give their permission and acknowledge receipt of the incentive.
- **Non-disclosure agreement (NDA)**: Many businesses require test participants to sign NDAs before viewing the prototype. This must be signed before the test begins.
- **Test materials**: Any documents that provide details to the participants for the test.
- **Checklists**: It is worth printing out your checklists for things to do and equipment, so that you can check them off as you complete actions, and be sure that you have done everything by the time it needs to be done.

The following figure shows a basic sample checklist for planning a usability test. For a more detailed checklist, add in timing and break the tasks down further. These refinements will depend on the specific usability test. Where you are uncertain about how long something will take, overestimate. Remember that once you have fixed the day, everything must be ready by then.

USABILITY TEST CHECKLIST	
☐ What to test (scope, fidelity)	☐ Participants recruited
☐ Date confirmed	☐ Script
☐ Venue booked	☐ Prototype ready (including dummy data if necessary)
☐ Facilitator and other key roles filled	☐ Equipment ready (ref Equipment checklist)
☐ Stakeholders and team members invited	☐ Incentives ready
☐ Task and scenario list	☐ Documents ready (NDA, consent form)
☐ Recruitment brief	☐ Pilot test

Checklist for usability test preparation

Conducting usability tests

On the day(s) of the usability test, if you have planned properly, all you should have to worry about are the tests themselves, and interacting with the participants. Here is a list of things to double-check on the day of each test:

1. Before the first test:
    1. Set up and check equipment and rooms.
    2. Have a list of participants and their order.
    3. Make sure there are refreshments for participants and observers.
    4. Make sure you have a receptionist to welcome participants.
    5. Make sure that the prototype is installed or the website is accessible via the internet and working.
    6. Test all equipment, for example, recording software, screen sharing, and audio in observations room.
    7. Turn off anything on the test computer or device that might interfere with the test, for example, email, instant messaging, virus scans, and so on. Create bookmarks for any web pages you need to open.
2. Before each test:
    1. Have the script ready to capture notes from a new participant.
    2. Have the screen recorder ready.
    3. Have the browser open in a neutral position, for example, Google search.
    4. Have sign sheets and incentive ready.
    5. Start screen sharing.
    6. Reload sample data if necessary, and clear the browser history from the last test.
3. During each test:
    1. Follow the script, including when the participant must sign forms and receive the incentive.
    2. Press record on the screen recorder.
    3. Give the microphone to the participant if appropriate.
4. After each test:
    1. Stop recording and save the video.
    2. Save the script.
    3. End screen sharing.
    4. Note extra details that you did not have time for during the session.

Once you have all the details organized, the test session is in the hands of the facilitator.

Best practices for facilitating usability sessions

The facilitator should be welcoming and friendly, but relatively ordinary and not overly talkative. The participant and website should be the focus of the interview and test, not the facilitator. To create rapport with the participant, the facilitator should be an ally. A good way to do this is to make fun of the situation and reassure participants that their experiences in the test will be helpful. Another good technique is to ask more like an apprentice than an expert, so that the participant answers your questions, for example: *Can you tell me more about how this works?* and *What happens next?*.

Since you want participants to feel as natural and comfortable as possible in their interactions, the facilitator should foster natural exploration and help satisfy participant curiosity as much as possible. However, they need to remain aware of the script and goals of the test, so that the participant covers what is needed.

Participants often struggle to talk aloud. They forget to do so while doing tasks. Therefore, the facilitator often needs to nudge participants to talk aloud or for information. Here are some useful questions or comments:

- *What are you thinking? What do you think about that?*
- *Describe the steps you're doing here.*
- *What's going on here?*
- *What do you think will happen next?*
- *Is that what you expected to happen?*
- *Can you show me how you would do that?*

When you are asking questions, you want to be sure that you help participants to be as honest and accurate as possible. We've previously stated that people are notoriously bad at projecting what they will do or remembering what they did. This does not mean that you cannot ask about what people do. You must just be careful about how you ask, and always try to keep it concrete. The priorities in asking questions are:

- **Now**: Participants talking aloud about what they are doing and thinking now.
- **Retrospective**: Participants talking about what they have done or thought in the past.
- **Never prospective**: Never ask participants about what they would do in the future. Rather ask about what they have done in similar situations in the past.

Here are some other techniques for ensuring you get the best out of the participants, and do not lead them too much yourself:

- Ask probing questions such as why and how to get to the real reasons for actions. Do not assume you know what participants are going to say. Check or paraphrase if you are not sure what they said or why they said it. For example, *So are you saying the text on the left is hard to read?* or *You're not sure about what?* or *That picture is weird? How?*

- Do not ask leading questions, as people will give positive answers to please you. For example, do not say *Does that make sense?*, *Do you like that?* or *Was that easy?* Rather say *Can you explain how this works? What do you think of that?* and *How did you find doing that task?*

- Do not tell participants what they are looking at. You are trying to find out what they think. For example, instead of *Here is the product page*, say *Tell me what you see here*, or *Tell me what this page is about.*

- Return the question to the participant if they ask what to do or what will happen: *I can't tell you because we need to find out what you would do if you were alone at home. What would you normally do?* or *What do you think will happen?*

- Ask one question at a time, and make time for silence. Don't overload the participants. Give them a chance to reply. People will often try to fill silence, so you may get more responses if you don't rush to fill it yourself.

- Encourage action, but do not tell them what to do. For example, *Give it a try.*

- Use acknowledgement tokens to encourage action and talking aloud. For example, *OK, uh huh, mm hmm.*

A good facilitator makes participants feel comfortable and guides them through the tasks without leading, while observing carefully and asking questions where necessary. It takes practice to accomplish this well.

The facilitator (and the notetaker if there is one) must also think about the analysis that will be done. Analysis is time consuming; think about what can be done beforehand to make it easier. Here are some pointers:

- Taking notes on a common spreadsheet with a script is helpful, because the results are ready to be combined easily.

- If you are gathering quantitative results, such as timing tasks or counting steps to accomplish activities, prepare spaces to note these on the spreadsheet before the test, so all the numbers are easily accessible afterwards.

- If you are rating task completion, then note a preliminary rating as the task is completed. This can be as simple as selecting appropriate cell colors beforehand and coloring each cell as the task is completed. This may change during analysis, but you will have initial guidance.
- Listen for useful and illustrative quotes or video segment opportunities. Note down the quote or roughly note the timestamp, so you know where to look in the recording.
- In general, have a timer at hand, and note the timestamp of any important moments in each test. This will make reviewing the recordings easier and less time consuming.

Analyzing and reporting on usability tests

Once you have conducted usability tests, you have a lot of raw data to analyze for useful results. You should begin the analysis as soon as possible after the testing is complete, so that the tests are fresh in your mind. How do you begin? Quantitative data is easier to work with, as the numbers can easily be compared with each other or a benchmark. With qualitative data, you must extract the information that you want and use it to build up evidence. Qualitative data is therefore more difficult to work with. However, it is also more important. The quantitative data is useful, but these numbers could be gained with cheaper remote testing and analytics.

The main value of a usability test comes from the insights that we gain from observing people using a product, seeing where they have problems, and understanding why. We understand why because we have talked to the people beforehand and so understand their personal context, and we have watched the actions that lead up to the problems and so understand the interaction context. We also understand how critical the problem is because we have watched people's body language and emotional response when the problem occurs. It is important to include evidence of these emotional reactions and their consequences when analyzing a usability test.

To ensure that you remain focused on the reasons for conducting the test, frame and structure your analysis using the following guidelines:

- **Test goals**: Refer to your original goals for conducting the test, and the behavioral questions that came out of those goals. These are the questions that your findings must address.
- **Usability metrics**: Think about effectiveness, efficiency, satisfaction, discoverability, learnability, and error proneness. What metrics did you define to address these issues when you were planning the test?
- **Website pages**: Consider the usability of each separate page or important component of the website that was included in the test, for example, the search function or checkout process.

Put the preceding details somewhere visible while you do the analysis, so you can refer to them at any time. This will help to ensure that you remain focused. For each of the preceding points, you can also begin to collect evidence from the testing. If you are unsure about how to begin analyzing, here are some steps to get you started:

1. Gather all filled in scripts on the same sheet in your spreadsheet, with the first column set aside for the script.
2. On separate sheets, set up the structure for your analysis:
   1. Create headings for your goals, metrics, and the usability criteria.
   2. You may also want to create a sheet with sections for every page or component of the website.
   3. Many of these sections and sheets may overlap. You will also find that many of the tasks or questions that comprised the test relate directly or indirectly to one or more of the goals, metrics, or criteria.
   4. Look through the script to check if there are any holes in your structure. If there are tasks or questions in the script that are not covered by the headings you've created, then add further headings for these items.
3. For each heading that you've created, review all the test notes for evidence. Add evidence that you find under the appropriate heading:
   1. Gather evidence of good experiences as well as bad ones. It is important to report on what works well in a usability test, as well as what does not work.
   2. Copy across quotes that highlight emotional responses or problematic interactions.

2. Quantitative results are added to the other evidence at this point. For example, if you asked a question using a rating scale, you would gather the values that each participant chose for comparison. You would also gather the observations and discussions that happened around the participant choosing that number.

2. Review the videos, using the timestamps that are included with the notes, for more detail:
   - Take note of timestamps where good video clips can be found.

3. Identify the biggest problems, and highlight these.

4. Review the notes and videos repeatedly, from different standpoints, to discover trends and investigate problem areas, adding to your sheets as you work.

Once you have structured the results as shown previously, you have all the findings from the tests organized and at your fingertips. Now you can work with some of the results to describe and visualize them.

The most important and interesting results are the frequency and severity of usability issues during the test. These come from the task success metric. Here is a powerful technique for measuring and visualizing these:

- Copy the combined spreadsheet onto a new sheet.
- Remove all rows that do not relate to task performance. Make sure you have one row for each task, or part of a task for which you are rating success.
- Add rows for broader usability criteria for which you want to rate, that do not relate directly to a task. For example, discoverability can be rated through observation of initial interactions with the website, rather than any specific task.
- Color the spreadsheet according to task success. This may already have been done to some extent during the tests. If not, choose the metric that you will use to evaluate the severity of usability problems. A good default is four levels of success coded like a traffic light: green for success; yellow for a minor problem that causes some confusion or frustration (relatively insignificant, but you do not want too many of them); orange for a problem that takes some effort to solve and will reduce trust and credibility; and red for a major problem that is likely to significantly reduce confusion across many users. Remember to choose hues that color blind viewers can distinguish.

- When you have color coded all cells, remove the text in every cell except the first column. Then shrink all cells until you can view the whole sheet. This creates an impressive visualization of overall usability. It is easy to see many things at a glance: whether the tests went well or badly overall; how many problems there were; how severe the problems were; how many problems each participant had relative to others; which tasks were especially problematic, and which went well; and whether there were some tasks that caused problems for all participants. The result of such an analysis is shown in the following diagram:

	Participant 1	Participant 2	Participant 3	Participant 4	Participant 5
Discoverability					
Task 1					
Task 2					
Task 3					
Task 4					
Task 5					
Task 6					
Task 7					
Task 8					

Visualization of task success, showing frequency and severity of usability problems

We can also use numbers such as *time on task* and *number of steps or errors per task* to describe how participants interacted with the website. They do not tell us much by themselves; we need to compare them with benchmarks to assign value to the numbers. For example, we do not know how long a task should take, so *time on task* results only tell us how participants faired against each other, and in relation to the rest of their experience. We can make inferences from this about things such as why some participants were faster than others, and what we can do to speed up slower interactions (presuming faster task performance is a good thing). However, unless we know a benchmark number for how long this task should take or has taken in the past, we do not know whether the range of scores is fast or slow in general.

These numbers are typically manipulated to make them more meaningful: taking the average across all tests to compare this group of participants against another group; and reporting the minimum, maximum and range to show how spread the numbers were among participants. This will show if the average is influenced by extreme scores and therefore skewed in one direction.

Reporting the results of a usability test

The traditional method of reporting usability test results is the usability test report. This should have the following content:

- **A description of the test and participants**: This includes the test objectives, what was tested, details of participants, and recruitment criteria.
- **Key findings of the test**: This is an executive summary for those who do not want to read the rest of the document, stating what the key findings were.
- **Detailed findings**: This is the bulk of the document. It is generally organized by task or web pages and components. For each part, evidence from the usability test is presented. The findings are presented with quotes, links to video segments, annotated screenshots and other images, and visualizations. Suggested solutions can be included, where these are obvious from usability guidelines or design discussions.
- **Recommendations**: The report should end with recommendations. These may include solutions, or be suggestions for redesign.
- **Content listing and/or index**: Some method for readers to gain an overview of the content of the report, so they can jump to areas that interest them.

Writing a report is a time consuming, expert task. It requires skills in composition, visual organization, and writing. The writer must make the information stand out, and keep readers interested in all the content. There are other ways of reporting the results of the usability test. These relate to different reasons for reporting the test results:

- **Showing value and documenting**: In this case, a report is a good method. A report is the most detailed and complete method of reporting on usability tests. It can act as a base for all other reporting methods, as details can be extracted and used in different contexts. However, creating a great report that communicates all the test details effectively takes time. It is not an agile deliverable. Comprehensive reports are long and detailed documents, so people often do not read them properly.

- **Persuading and educating clients**: A presentation or workshop based on the usability test is a great way to persuade and educate clients of the test results. Even if you create a report, consider presenting it in some way. Then you can be sure that stakeholders have seen the information. Focus on the main findings and possible solutions, together with evidence from the tests, such as quotes, video segments and, observation details.
- **Communicating to the design and development teams**: Ideally, most of the team has observed at least some of the usability tests. Having a design review immediately after the usability tests, where various team members discuss their observations and top findings, is a great way to communicate the test results. You will not have time to analyze results before this, so follow up meetings or online discussion groups around further results may be necessary. Keeping a central *bug* or problem list derived from the test is also a good idea.

Variations on usability testing

In the previous sections, we have described a traditional, moderated usability test that happens in a lab. There are variations on this, that make usability testing more flexible as a research method:

- **Moderated remote usability tests**: Usability tests can be conducted remotely, where participants are at their own computers. The facilitator cannot observe or ask questions as effectively, but if you do not have time or a budget to set up a formal test, or participants are geographically dispersed, this is an option. A combination of video conferencing software (such as Skype, Hangouts, or FaceTime), email, and chats are used to view the screen and communicate with the participant.
- **Unmoderated usability testing**: Unmoderated usability testing is remote, and has the same advantages and disadvantages as moderated remote usability tests. Because there is no facilitator, there is less control and oversight, but you can test with a lot more people. Recruiting is much easier, as you can use *panels* of internet users that are provided by various companies. These businesses often organize, run, and potentially analyze the tests for you. You specify the tasks, the screens, and the survey questions, and they deliver the results. Some current examples are Lookback, Loop11, and UserTesting.

- **RITE**: This stands for Rapid Iterative Testing and Evaluation. These are usability tests conducted towards the end of a design project, to iron out final problems before development or deployment. Typically, about three-four testing days are organized with about three participants, one or two days apart from each other. The design team makes changes to the prototype in between the tests. Theoretically, very few to no problems should be found on the final testing day.
- **Benchmarking**: This is typically done later in a project and is a form of summative testing. It aims to create benchmarks for your usability metrics, such as time on task and task satisfaction or ease of use. It is a quantitative test, as the idea is to compare your website's progress over time against specific user performance standards. In order to compare results of two tasks, they must be the same. Therefore, tasks tend to be very specific to allow for comparison later, but they must also be generic enough that they can remain the same in future tests, when the interface has changed. You cannot refer to elements that are likely to change. Benchmarking tests need more users than usual. To create benchmarks, you ideally should be testing with at least 20 people. They also need to be more formal, as you need to repeat the process.
- **Comparative**: Comparative tests are similar to benchmark tests. These are usability tests that are conducted on competitor websites, to assess how they compare against your website, or to develop ideas about what works and does not work in the market. Because they are comparative, they also require more participants to yield effective results. All the websites must be tested with the same tasks to enable comparison.
- **Eye tracking and heat maps**: There are various ways of tracking how people browse websites while doing usability tests. You can track mouse clicks and hovers on a desktop site--these create heat maps that show where users spend time and attention on a page. They can be done remotely with automated tools. Eye tracking tracks how users' eyes move over web pages. Currently it requires specialist technology and so is only lab-based. These techniques require users to interact as naturally as possible, so facilitation must be as minimal as possible, and any questions should be asked retrospectively.

- **Corridor/ guerrilla:** This means any informal usability tests that are conducted with people in your organization who work down the corridor from you, or with random people in public spaces such as coffee shops and malls. These tests will not be as structured as formal tests, participants are not screened, they probably will not be recorded, they will be much shorter and often more specific, and the results are likely to be less accurate and generalizable. However, they are easy to conduct, as they require very little infrastructure. They also get the team into the habit and practice of testing their designs with users. Even though the results are generally less accurate, seeing how other people respond to your designs is always useful for a UX practitioner. While you should definitely conduct more formal testing, guerrilla testing at least once or twice every week is a great way to keep users in mind and practice. If you are unable to do formal usability tests because of money, time, or stakeholder resistance, then guerrilla testing is the least you can do as a UX practitioner.

The guidelines that we have shared for formal moderated usability testing can be used, with small modifications, with all of the variations discussed here.

Applying analytics effectively-constructing a useful A/B test

Analytics show us how people behave when they are on their own and not being observed or directed. However, analytics are ambiguous because we cannot identify user intentions, expectations, or satisfaction with analytics. They just show behavior and not why it is happening. For example, if the conversion rate from visitor to buyer on an e-commerce site is below expected, visitors not converting because of your terrible checkout process or the high prices of your products? If we consider page views, another popular metric; are users visiting a lot of pages because they are exploring your site, or because they cannot find what they want?

It is very easy to gather analytics with sites such as Google Analytics. There are a lot of different metrics that can be tracked. However, we should not just track metrics because we can, as this will end up being a waste of time.

We must be careful to choose meaningful metrics so they generate actionable findings:

- Consider analytics in the context of your website or webpage goals. This is what gives them meaning. Otherwise they are just numbers. For example, identify desirable actions on your site and track the percentage of visitors doing these.
- Use multiple metrics from analytics, and other research methods such as usability tests and A/B tests to triangulate with analytics for best effect.
- Use HEART and the Goals-Signals-Metrics formalism described in `Chapter 5`, *Set a Solid Foundation* to decide what metrics to capture and how to do so.

Here is a list of typical metrics used in analytics, and what they can tell you:

- **Conversion rate**: This can refer to anything you want users of your website to do, for example sign ups, using new features, or checkouts. An improved rate compared to a previous time period could mean increased engagement, or it could mean the success of a sales campaign, or seasonal differences.
- **Bounce rate**: This is where users visit only one page and then leave the site. This could indicate that the page does not interest users and invite them further into the site, or that they get everything they need from the page.
- **Visit length**: How long visitors spend on your site and on various parts of the site. These may indicate popular pages and sections, but may also just indicate pages with a lot of content. It may also indicate visitor confusion, as people may not know where to go and so do not leave a page.
- **Revisit frequency**: This shows how often visitors return, and can be a measure of user engagement and stickiness. Adding recenct data to show how quickly visitors return adds information. Compare these numbers with other information such as the timing of content updates and promotions to understand more.
- **% visitors interacting with key components or pages**: This will show you how much people use different parts of your website compared to all traffic.
- **Average time to first interaction with key components**: A high value here might indicate discoverability issues or information overload, or that you have a lot of content to read.
- **Navigational flows**: Heat maps and click streams provide behavioral navigational patterns of how visitors tend to move through the website, what they click on first, and where they drop off.

- **Top search terms used within the site**: This might indicate that visitors cannot find these items through normal navigation, or just indicate the items that people want to see most. You could also use this metric to do failure analysis by looking for top searches with zero results or searches with bounces immediately afterwards, to indicate where you are failing to provide users with information they need.

- **Filtering and sorting behavior**: Much like with tree testing or card sorting, this gives us ideas about how users typically prefer to view data on our website, and what data they are viewing most.

- **Abandonment or fallout by page or step**: This shows where people are dropping off, but does not indicate why. It may indicate problematic features on those pages.

- **Back and Undo button usage**: These metrics may indicate where users tend to make errors.

- **Task completion rates**: What is the rate of completion for different tasks? This may highlight problematic task flows, which users do not tend to complete, or tend to complete very slowly.

- **Time on task**: As previously mentioned, this may indicate problematic tasks if users take a long time to complete them. However, it may also indicate complicated tasks. Compare against benchmarks.

- **Customer support visits**: These are links to things such as contact pages, call center numbers, or online help. They show which pages or components drive customers to support. This may indicate confusing features.

- **Traffic sources, channels, referrals, and trackbacks**: How are people getting to your site? This may indicate what expectations they arrive with. It can also show which sources are generating visits and which are not.

- **Device and browser differences**: This provides useful demographic information on the browsers and devices that people use to access your site. It may also indicate which devices and browsers the website does not support well.

Since web usage analytics are in fact metrics at their core, we can use them as part of other research methods, to evaluate the effects of interventions and design choices. For example, the A/B test.

Using analytics with A/B testing

A/B testing is split testing between two versions of something--A and B. Half the people in your test use A and half use B. You measure the effect of the usage in each group and decide which version is better according to a metric. A/B testing is very popular as it is simple and fast to do, provided you have enough people. It is also great for showing which of two design decisions will have the most impact. However, it is also quite weak because you must only vary one thing at a time to be sure that it is the thing that is causing the difference between the groups.

In this way, A/B testing is an example of a controlled experiment. Everything except the test condition must remain as similar as possible in each group. For example: the two groups must be close to equal in size; they must be similar to each other; they must experience the test condition during the same time period so there are no time of day, day of the week, or seasonal differences; and everything else in the website design must remain the same.

Examples of A/B tests are: whether a promotional banner on your website increases visitor retention; whether asking users to register after checkout instead of before increases conversions; or whether changing the text of your Call To Action makes users more likely to click it. It should be clear that web usage analytics provide the evidence for these tests. In the preceding examples, you would use revisit frequency, conversion rate at checkout, and the page event of selecting the Call To Action button, respectively.

You cannot test two changes at the same time, for example, different colored buttons and different heading styles, as you will not know how much each change influenced the end result, if at all. If you want to test for differences caused by more than one condition, you need to do a *multivariate test*. However, this kind of test is more complicated to conduct and analyze.

To test for statistical significance, you should do calculations to work out exactly how many people you need to test with to be sure a change is not due to chance. However, a general rule of thumb is that you need a minimum of 20 people per group to find reasonable sized effects in an experiment, which means 40 people for an A/B test. These numbers will only find larger effects. The more people you test with, the more sensitive the test will be. If you have reasonable traffic on your website, then large group sizes should be easy to achieve. Popular websites often test with thousands in each group.

Create a test as described in this chapter, with goals, expectations, and metrics. Create the alternative design that you want to test, and then provide half your traffic with each design. Make sure that you conduct the experiment for long enough to cater for variance caused by time of day, days of the week or holidays, and for enough people to experience the two designs.

Various statistical tests are used to work out the results of the test, depending on the metrics used. For example, use *Student's t-test* when comparing two averages, such as the average % conversions for each group; use *Fisher's exact test* or the *chi squared test* when the test is binomial, which is where there are two options such as success or failure, such as whether visitors click through to a page or not. Various companies set up and analyze A/B testing for you. For example, Google Analytics Content Experiments will organize, run, and analyze A/B or multivariate tests.

A/B tests are an example of using design thinking with analytics, but they are still behavioral. They do not tell you why users preferred one version over another. To gain a clearer picture of how and why users interact with your website, combine with other methods such as usability tests.

Summary

In this chapter, we have described usability testing in detail, as an example of how to execute a user testing plan. Before this, we discussed how to maximize the value of testing with users and the definition of usability.

Then, we examined how to plan, organize, conduct, analyze, and report on a traditional, moderated usability test. As part of this, we have discussed how to design a test with goals, tasks, metrics, and questions using the definition of usability, and how to plan the practical details such as recruitment, venue, and inviting observers.

In describing how to conduct a usability test, we discussed how to facilitate effectively. Then we examined how to analyze the results qualitatively and quantitatively, and how to report on the results effectively.

Finally, we described how to employ web usage analytics effectively in user testing, and gave some examples of typical analytics. We used A/B testing as an example of how to combine web usage analytics with research methodology.

In the next two chapters, we will examine web accessibility, and how to implement it effectively.

10
The Basics and Benefits of Web Accessibility

In this chapter, we introduce the basics and benefits of web accessibility. We have already mentioned accessibility while considering other topics in previous chapters. For example, in `Chapter 7`, *Bring Your UX Strategy to Life with Wireframes and Prototypes*, we touched on keeping accessibility in mind while designing wireframes and prototypes; and in `Chapter 8`, *Build Your Product - Devices, Browsers, and Assistive Technologies*, we briefly discussed designing for assistive technologies.

Here, we focus on accessibility in more detail. After describing web accessibility, the different types of special needs to cater for, and the benefits of making sure your product is accessible, we will discuss the legal implications for non-accessible websites around the world. Thereafter, we will revisit assistive technology and explore how assistive technologies support people with disabilities. The topics covered are:

- Defining web accessibility
- Catering for different types of temporary and permanent special needs
- Benefits of ensuring your product is accessible
- Legal implications for non-accessible products
- Assistive technology and the role it plays in developing for accessibility
- Testing for accessibility

Defining web accessibility

As we described in `Chapter 8`, *Build Your Product - Devices, Browsers, and Assistive Technologies*, accessible UX design is about creating designs that are usable and enjoyable by people with disabilities. These disabilities include physical, sensory, cognitive, and neurological problems, and can be temporary or permanent.

Web accessibility is about removing barriers that prevent people with disabilities from accessing websites. Everyone should have equal access to information on any website. This means providing multiple, redundant ways of perceiving and interacting with websites. This in turn means being able to translate between different modes of perception and interaction; for example, auditory and visual modalities, or touch, pointer, and keyboard-based interfaces. **Multimodal interaction** styles, where users are provided with multiple methods for input and output in a system, are increasingly popular, as they promote more natural and rich interaction with an interface. While they are not typically designed with accessibility in mind, they benefit people with special needs, who are more likely to find an interaction mechanism that works for them in a multimodal system, than in a system that only provides one mode of interaction.

Guidelines and standards for web accessibility and how to achieve it are increasingly available, so that designers and developers can easily find out how to make their products accessible. Two of the most universally accepted guides are **WCAG** and **WAI-ARIA**, produced by the **World Wide Web Consortium** (**W3C**), which is the main international standards organization for the web. The **Web Content Accessibility Guidelines** (**WCAG 2.0**) are an extensive set of guidelines for improving web accessibility; the **Web Accessibility Initiative – Accessible Rich Internet Applications** (**WAI-ARIA**) is a technical specification for improving accessibility of web page code, especially dynamic elements.

The WCAG 2.0 defines four principles of accessibility, which help define it further. Websites should be:

- **Perceivable**: Information and other elements of the interface must be visible to everyone. An example guideline is providing text alternatives for non-text content.
- **Operable**: Everyone must be able to navigate around any website. An example guideline is providing keyboard access as an alternative to any other means of navigation.

- **Understandable**: The information on websites must be easily understandable. An example guideline is to use language that is as simple and clear as possible.
- **Robust**: The content and its interpretation must be reliable, and compatible with different devices, browsers, and assistive technologies.

It is interesting to compare these principles with those of *Universal Design* for physical systems that we described in `Chapter 8`, *Build Your Product - Devices, Browsers, and Assistive Technologies*. These are: equitable use, flexibility in use, simple and intuitive use, perceptible information, tolerance for error, low physical effort, size and space for approach and use. The overlaps are obvious. In that chapter, we related the Universal Design principles to Nielsen and Molich's usability heuristics. Again, it becomes obvious that designing for accessibility or universal access is, for the most part, designing by following usability guidelines about how to properly support any user in a system.

We will describe WCAG 2.0 and WAI-ARIA guidelines and how to use them in detail in `Chapter 11`, *A Practical Guide to Web Accessibility*.

Catering for different types of temporary and permanent special needs

We all experience disabilities or special needs at some points in our lives. As we get older, we might experience losses in all areas; everyone experiences decreased vision, hearing, and mobility as they age. Many illnesses or diseases, such as influenza and cancer, or their treatments, leave people temporarily or chronically disabled. Having young children, insomnia, or being overworked, often leads to loss of concentration and focus. In addition, we often access websites in situations which are difficult for concentration, hearing, vision, or physical accuracy, which means that we are disabled in those situations. For example, being in a noisy environment, using a mobile device while moving on the street or in a shop, or viewing a screen in the sunlight.

In this section, we categorize different types of temporary and permanent special needs, and how to cater for them. As previously mentioned, there will be times when we all rely on websites catering for the special needs we may have.

Typically, special needs can be divided into the following categories:

- **Visual**: These are sensing disabilities. Examples include color blindness, low vision, blindness, and astigmatism. Low vision can result from ailments such as macular degeneration and glaucoma.
- **Auditory**: These are sensing disabilities. Examples include deafness and hearing impairment.
- **Motor/mobility**: These are physical disabilities. Examples are low fine motor control, tremors, slowness, and/or fatigue. These can occur for many different reasons, for example Parkinson's disease, muscular dystrophy, cerebral palsy, stroke, cystic fibrosis, arthritis, and being quadriplegic.
- **Cognitive/intellectual**: These disabilities cause people to have more difficulty with mental tasks. This can manifest in various ways; for example, lack of attention, lack of memory, poor reading skills, or poor comprehension. These can be because of developmental or learning disabilities; for example dyslexia and autism. It can also be because of illness or disease; for example, cancer or dementia.
- **Neurological**: These disorders can lead to a range of symptoms, which overlap with other categories. Examples include fatigue, muscle weakness, loss of sensation, poor coordination, confusion, and seizures.

In general terms, to cater broadly for accessibility, some basic rules of thumb are:

- Never provide mouse-only interactions. Mouse interaction is inaccessible to a broad range of disabilities.
- Always provide for keyboard-only interaction. Keyboards are usable by people who are blind and people with motor difficulties. Many assistive technologies map easily to keyboards.
- Provide a clear site structure that can be navigated directly; for example, in a site map. This helps people with a broad range of special needs to understand and navigate a website.
- Make aspects such as text size, color scheme, and timing customizable if possible, so that people can adjust to what suits them.
- Error tolerance and recovery is very important. People with various disabilities may make more mistakes and find it more difficult to recover from them, because of the difficulties of basic interaction.

We will provide more specific support guidelines for each disability category in the following sections.

Catering for visual disabilities

Support for visual impairment means a few different things, depending on the impairment. It may mean enhanced visuals; for example, partially sighted people can use *magnifiers* to view websites. Make sure the text of the website can be magnified without losing its structure.

It may mean translating the screen into audio or braille format. Blind and partially sighted people use **screen readers**, which *read* a screen, and **braille embossers** for printing. There are various guidelines for ensuring a website can be *read* by a screen reader, including labeling the page structure meaningfully as lists, menus, headings, and so on, and making sure all images have associated text (since screen readers cannot *read* images). People who are deaf and blind use screen readers that output to braille devices.

People with any visual impairment may prefer to use a *keyboard* or *speech recognition software* for input, as they cannot see the mouse pointer. Therefore, make sure the website can be navigated using the keyboard alone.

The colors and contrast on the website must be designed so that both colorblind people and those with low vision can distinguish text and objects. This means carefully choosing and testing color combinations, using high contrast, and making sure that color alone is not used to convey information.

Catering for auditory disabilities

Support for auditory impairment means making sure that any videos are captioned, sound files are described, and that sound alone is not used to convey information. Providing sign language versions of audio content is problematic, because not all deaf people understand sign language, and there are many different sign languages in the world.

Catering for motor/mobility disabilities

People with mobility disabilities are unable, to some extent, to perform fine motor actions with a mouse. They may have problems selecting small links and other targets or interacting with moving elements. They may tire easily.

Depending on the severity of the disability, people may interact with a keyboard, pointing devices such as head wands or mouth sticks, foot pedals, or they may use voice recognition software. These options should be supported.

For fatigue, provide ways of avoiding lengthy content, or skipping through content quickly.

Catering for cognitive/intellectual disabilities

Support for cognitive disabilities means supporting mental tasks by making them as clear and structured as possible. This includes the following:

- Making sure that the reading level of your website is as simple and clear as possible for the intended audience
- Defining difficult terms
- Supporting recognition rather than recall so users need to remember as little as possible
- Limiting attention-grabbing, unimportant elements, such as scrolling text and popups
- Providing multiple forms of media to explain and illustrate concepts; for example, providing pictures or videos to support text

Catering for neurological disabilities

Support for these has been covered previously, since they overlap.

Seizures, dizziness, and nausea are the only examples that are specific to this category. The WCAG provides guidelines for size, frequency, intensity and contrast of flashing light and color, so that your dynamic elements do not cause seizures in those who are susceptible.

Websites that use parallax (background and foreground elements moving at different speeds or different directions) should test carefully to avoid making users nauseous.

Benefits of ensuring your product is accessible

There is often resistance to creating fully accessible websites, as it is seen as expensive and unrewarding because most target audiences include only a small percentage of disabled people. This in itself is a misconception, as the percentage is not as small as stakeholders think. According to the World Health Organization (WHO), 15% of the world is disabled. This is rising because of aging populations and rapid spread of chronic diseases. In addition, at any point, part of any audience will be temporarily disabled and have special needs when accessing websites.

Besides ensuring equal access for disabled people, there are additional benefits to making sure that your website is completely accessible. We describe some of them here:

- **Improved usability**: As we have shown previously, designing and developing for accessibility and universal access is designing for usability. If your website works beautifully for people with special needs, it will work well for all users. Improvements in usability increase the number of returning users, the number of conversions, and revenue.

- **Improved SEO**: Many of the accessibility guidelines are the same as techniques for improving your **SEO (Search Engine Optimization)** listing. For example, structured HTML, clear and descriptive link names and tags, alternative text on images, and creating a site map. Search engine bots can only consume text content, so they "see" web pages the same way a blind user would. Therefore, improving your accessibility means improving your search ranking.

- **Richer experiences**: Accessibility guidelines advocate using multiple representations to make content more understandable, and more usable by people who have problems with any single representation. This makes website experiences richer for other users, as there is a variety of content types. In addition, providing multiple modes of input and output means that anyone can choose how they want to interact. The ability to customize websites also creates a more personal, engaging experience for all users.

- **Easier maintenance**: Designing and developing for accessibility usually means following standards. It is much easier to support and maintain designs and code that have been created according to known standards.

- **Positive brand values**: By supporting accessibility for marginalized groups, you generate positive feelings toward your brand. This establishes credibility and strengthens loyalty.

Increasingly, there are also likely to be legal consequences for non-accessible websites. We discuss this trend in the next section.

Legal implications for non-accessible products

As we stated in `Chapter 8`, *Build your Product*, the 1948 ANSI Barrier Free Standard (ANSI A117.1, *Making Buildings Accessible to and Usable by the Physically Handicapped*), which specified minimum requirements for barrier-free access to facilities for the physically disabled, could be called the beginning of accessibility guidelines.

However, current standards, including WCAG and WAI-ARIA, are just guidelines. They are not laws, so there are no legal consequences to not following them. This is beginning to change in many countries. Increasingly, countries are implementing legislation about accessibility of digital products. This is often based on applying existing human rights laws to the digital space, and often refers explicitly to the WCAG guidelines. Here are some of the legal changes happening in countries and global organizations around the world, as examples of the trend:

- **Australia**: This country provides the most famous case of a successful accessibility lawsuit. A blind man sued the Sydney Olympic Committee in 2000 under their 1992 Disability Discrimination Act, because the official website was not fully accessible to the blind.
- **Brazil**: In 2007, accessibility guidelines based on the WCAG became compulsory for all government websites.
- **European Union**: In 2016, a directive (a legal act instructing member countries to achieve an outcome, but not instructing how) required that all government websites and mobile apps be accessible by 2018.
- **United Kingdom**: The Equality Act of 2010 makes it illegal to discriminate against people with disabilities. Accompanying documents refer specifically to websites.
- **United Nations**: The Convention on the Rights of Persons with Disabilities is a treaty adopted in 2006 and ratified by most member countries. Article 9, titled Accessibility, recognizes the right of people with disabilities to full access of information and communication technologies and systems. This provides a framework and pressure for all member countries to implement accessibility legislation.

- **United States**: The Section 508 Amendment to the Rehabilitation Act of 1973 made it compulsory for all government websites to be fully accessible. Section 504 of the act enhanced this by including all organizations that receive government funds. Several public companies have been successfully sued for inaccessible websites, under the 1990 Americans with Disabilities Act, which requires consumer-facing businesses to be accessible to disabled people, for example, Netflix, Target, and Disney. These were generally settled out of court.

Assistive technology and the role it plays in developing for accessibility

As we have seen, not all people with disabilities require assistive technology to access websites. In many cases, people use standard technology, such as keyboard and trackballs, and rely on websites being designed well. Some people with disabilities require assistive technology to access the web; this is especially the case with visual and mobility disabilities. We will discuss these next.

People with *mobility disabilities* use a range of assistive technologies, depending on the severity of the disability. Most of these work through the keyboard, so providing full keyboard access to a website is an important first step in accessibility. Technologies used by people with mobility problems include:

- **Trackball**: This is not an assistive technology, but trackballs are easier to use than mice. They can be manipulated with pointing devices, such as mouth sticks, or with feet.
- **Mouth stick or head wand**: These are simple sticks that are placed in the mouth or strapped to the head, and used by quadriplegics to manipulate keyboards or trackballs. Fatigue is an issue with these technologies, so design websites where content can easily be skipped, and follow usability guidelines such as making forms as short as possible.
- **Sip-and-puff switch or single-switch access**: These are technologies for people with very limited mobility. They operate by interpreting the user's breath or head-press as on/off signals, which are used to navigate physically and digitally.
- **Eye tracking**: This is very expensive technology which tracks the user's eye movements to navigate.
- **Voice recognition software**: Website access is controlled through speaking to the computer. However, this requires that the user can speak in a clear and understandable manner.

People with *visual disabilities* use magnifiers and screen readers. **Magnifiers** magnify text on websites so it can be read. Designing and developing for these means making sure that the text on websites can be increased without losing its structure.

Screen readers require the biggest changes to website development of accessible technologies. However, as we have shown above, there are general benefits, such as improved usability and SEO rankings. Screen readers "read" websites and translate them to output via text-to-speech synthesizers or Braille displays. For screen readers to be effective, websites must be designed and developed in a structured way. Here are some guidelines for designing or developing for screen reader access:

- **Linear viewing**: Screen readers present content linearly to users. Therefore, users cannot scan a page to gain an overview; they must step through it one item at a time, and remember what has already been covered. The website should be designed and HTML-written with this in mind. For example, do not create long menu listings, as users with screen readers will have to remember the whole list before selecting an option.
- **Specify language**: If a foreign language is used in the text, screen readers will not know this unless it is specified with an HTML tag.
- **Navigation**: There are various ways that navigation elements speed up website interactions for sighted users. They can do the same for those who use screen readers. For example, screen readers provide the *Tab* key for jumping between links. Since these are read out of context, link labels should make sense out of context. The tab order of web pages should also be logical. Screen readers jump between headings, so structuring the web content logically with headings is helpful. Screen readers can also jump between other page elements, such as paragraphs, tables, lists, forms, images, and buttons, so use semantic HTML to define these elements properly.
- **Images**: Screen readers can "read" images or video content. Therefore, make sure that all visual content has alt-text that describes it usefully.

The most important way to design for assistive technologies is to design well and follow usability and accessibility guidelines. We will discuss this further in `Chapter 11`, *A Practical Guide to Web Accessibility*.

Testing for accessibility

In order to know that you have catered for accessibility and assistive technologies in your website, you need to test. This will be time consuming. It often takes longer to view and interact with websites if you have disabilities, so if you are simulating disabilities, you will experience the same delays. This is useful, as it is valuable to be aware of the difficulties experienced by users. However, you will also not be familiar with the techniques and tools, so they will take you longer to use than they would a disabled person who is more familiar with them. So, set aside a good amount of time to do this testing, and share it out among the team so that everyone involved in building the website is aware of the issues.

Here are some of the ways of testing the accessibility of your website:

- **Keyboard only**: Check if you can access all parts of your website while only using the keyboard. Especially, check the tab order while doing this, to make sure it is logical. Can you open and close all dialogs? Can you see where the focus is?

- **Screen reader**: Download a screen reader or use the built in one for your OS and view your website through it. Screen readers take time to learn and are confusing and disorienting initially, so it is worth spending time using a screen reader before testing, so you are comfortable with the process. Otherwise, your content may seem inaccessible because you do not know how to use the screen reader.

- **Magnification**: Enlarge your font to 200%. Can you still read and use all the page content?

- **Color blindness**: Check for different types of color blindness and low vision accessibility by checking your colors and contrasts against standards.

- **Checklists**: There are many accessibility checklists available to check your designs and HTML against, based on the WCAG guidelines. Two examples are those provided by WebAIM (http://webaim.org/standards/wcag/checklist/) and the A11Y Project (http://a11yproject.com/checklist.html).

- **WAVE**: WebAIM also provides the WAVE extension for Chrome and Firefox, which checks accessibility automatically. It evaluates the accessibility of any web page by embedding feedback into the content. It checks images, headings, contrast, HTML5 regions and ARIA landmarks, form controls, and tables.

Summary

In this chapter, we have introduced web accessibility. We began by defining it and describing the different types of special needs that users of a website might have. We discussed in general terms how to cater for these different special needs.

Thereafter, we looked at the benefits of providing an accessible website, including the moral value of making your information and services available to everyone. Legal implications for non-accessible websites are increasing across the world; we briefly examined trends in this area.

We examined assistive technologies, and how to design and develop for them. Finally, we provided some guidelines about testing for accessibility.

In the next chapter, we look at how to measure accessibility with the Web Content Accessibility Guidelines (WCAG 2.0) and how to implement WAI-ARIA roles effectively. We also examined designing for accessibility and using tools to implement accessible websites in more detail.

11
A Practical Guide to Web Accessibility

Web accessibility is usually seen as something you only prioritize if your product is focusing on people with special needs, but this is a distorted point of view of what web accessibility truly means for your product and the users who will interact with it. Someone once gave the example of a wheelchair ramp: the wheelchair ramp was originally built for the person with a wheelchair, but that does not stop the everyday person from using the ramp instead of the stairs. In fact, it's easier to walk up the ramp than the stairs as it's the path of least resistance. Web accessibility is based on the same principle.

Even though the majority of the WCAG and WAI-ARIA guidelines are to accommodate compatibility with assistive technology, these same rules will make the overall experience of the product even more enjoyable to every user interacting with the product. This chapter will focus on the following topics to effortlessly analyze and implement web accessibility on a website:

- Implementing the WCAG 2.0
- Understanding the WAI-ARIA guidelines
- The web accessibility approach to design as a visual aid
- Conducting a web accessibility analysis on a digital product

Where to start with web accessibility?

Web accessibility can seem quite complex and overwhelming, and can be mistaken for something only expert designers and developers should tackle, but this perception of accessibility is not true. In any area of expertise, something can be intimidating if it's unknown, but as soon as you start looking into it, it becomes attainable. The first step to getting started in an area of expertise you're not familiar with is to find reliable resources. In this chapter, we'll provide you with some great resources and guidelines to get started in creating a usable and accessible website for all users, despite limitations. The following three resources form the foundation to web accessibility:

1. The **Web Content Accessibility Guidelines (WCAG) 2.0**are the ultimateWeb Accessibility guidelines when designing or developing an accessible website. We'll discuss these guidelines in detail in this chapter. You can view the full WCAG 2.0 at `https://www.w3.org/TR/WCAG20/`.

2. The **Accessible Rich Internet Applications (WAI-ARIA)** is an addition to the WCAG 2.0 guidelines and focuses on accessibility of web content that requires semantic information about widgets, structures, and behaviors in order to allow assistive technologies to read and interpret the correct information to the user. You can view the full WAI-ARIA at `https://www.w3.org/TR/wai-aria/`.

3. **WebAIM (Web Accessibility In Mind)** is a non-profit organization founded in 1999 and offers web accessibility services to companies as well as a solid library of web accessibility resources on tools, laws, and guidelines for web accessibility. You can find WebAIM's website at `http://webaim.org/`.

Practical guidelines for analyzing a website's web accessibility status

The extensive list of web accessibility guidelines can be quite overwhelming as some of the criteria is quite complex, and you'll need an advanced understanding of development to implement these correctly. In most cases, it will not be necessary to implement all the criteria as the type of website may not include all the elements that need catering for. A good start is to establish what limitations the website has. This will give guidance as to which part of the WCAG 2.0 guidelines need to be implemented. There are several tools available to run web accessibility analysis on a website, although we'll look at the **WebAIM browser extension** in this book. You can find the resources for Chrome and Firefox at `http://wave.webaim.org/extension/`.

Using the WebAIM browser extension is as simple as opening the website in the browser and activating the extension by clicking on the WebAIM icon in the top-right of the browser. A pane will open on the left-hand side with a list of **Errors**, **Alerts**, **Features**, **Structural Elements**, **HTML 5 and ARIA**, and **Contrast Errors**:

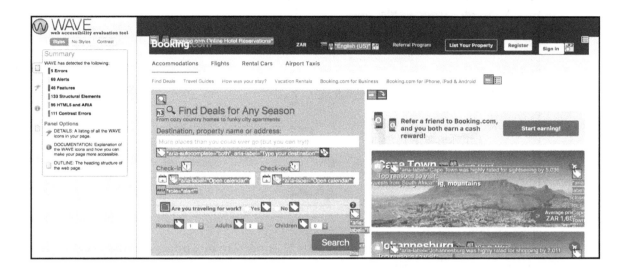

By tapping on the tab icons to the left of the container, the information pertaining to that specific area will be available:

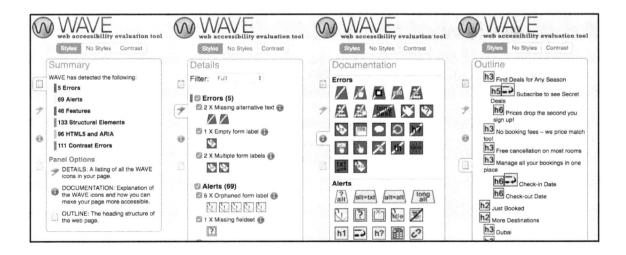

When clicking on either the icons in the WebAIM extension panel on the left or on the icons within the web page, a popup will appear, explaining the status of the element and providing more information on how to improve the element for web accessibility:

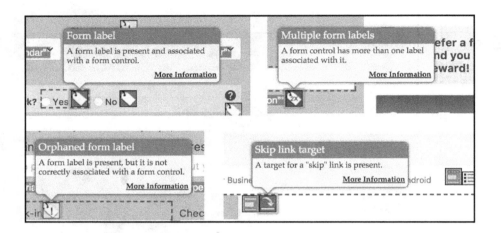

After identifying the elements within the website that need to be addressed, the WCAG 2.0 guidelines will give detailed instructions on how to proceed. As mentioned, the WCAG 2.0 is an in-depth collection of technical standards, and it won't be possible to address everything in this book. In the next section, a high-level overview will be discussed and some practical examples will be covered to give context.

An overview of the WCAG 2.0

Keep in mind that WCAG 2.0 is not an introduction to accessibility, but a reputable technical standard guideline created by the W3C to make web content more accessible to all people, especially to people who have to use assistive technology to access websites. The WCAG consists of twelve guidelines that are divided into four principles, namely **Perceivable**, **Operable**, **Understandable**, and **Robust**. Each of the four principles are measured against three levels--**A**, **AA** and **AAA**--of which **A** represents the lowest compliance to the web accessibility standard and **AAA** the highest.

Perceivable

The first principle from the Web Content Accessibility Guidelines, **Perceivable**, focuses on making content available and recognizable for all users, despite the user's way of perceiving information or the tools they use to access this information; for example, screen readers. In short, content can't be invisible to all of the user's senses. Here's an excerpt from WCAG 2.0:

"All web content and UI elements must be presentable in a way that the users can perceive, and cannot be hidden from all of the user's senses."

- **Provide text alternatives for non-text content**:
  If visual elements are key for the user to interact with the web page, it should be accompanied by alternative text (sometimes called **ALT TEXT**) for the screen reader to understand the visual elements. In the HTML code, just add the alt text attribute with a description of what the main purpose of the image is. The opposite is true if visual elements are present, and are purely used for decorative purposes. These decorative images need to be hidden from assistive technology. To hide visual content from a screen reader, leave the **ALT TEXT** attribute empty.

Image formats, such as SVG, do not have an **ALT TEXT** attribute; instead, a title and description is added in the XML structure of the SVG:

```
<?xml version="1.0"?>
<svg width="300" height="300" viewBox="0 0 300 300"
xmlns="http://www.w3.org/2000/svg">
 <title>Adidas</title>
 <desc>An infographic illustrating the history of Adidas shoe
styles</desc>
 </svg>
```

- **Provide captions and other alternatives for multimedia**:
  For videos, add transcript files for the audio and ensure that it's in sync with the visual. The transcript file should always be in the language of the video. If non-English languages are being included in a transcript file, follow the respective platform's guideline of how to save and upload the transcript files. Here are the basic guidelines from one of the world's largest video platforms--YouTube:
  - A blank line indicates the start of a new caption
  - Square brackets indicate that background sounds are present
  - Double chevrons to the right (>>) indicate a change of speaker
  - Non-English languages should be saved with UTF-8 encoding

    - ```
      >> MARLI: Web Accessibility is really not as
      complicated as it seems.
      >> CARA: It's not! The WCAG 2.0 guidelines are very
      straightforward and really logical if you think about
      it.
      >> MARLI: I hope this chapter will equip our readers
      to always design and develop accessible websites.
      [intro music]
      Maybe we should ask them to send links to their
      websites they designed based on this book?
      ```
      ```

- **Create content that can be presented in different ways, including by assistive technologies, without losing meaning**:
  The way sighted users perceive content in a logical manner is through visual cues such as headings styled as bold or in caps. In the same way, web content must be structured in a logical way for assistive technology to process and translate it to the user. Originally, HTML was developed to create clean separation of content for easy readability. It was never intended to be displayed in a visual manner, but as the internet evolved, the relationship between the HTML structure and the visual elements became more critical. The WAI-ARIA gives guidelines on how to keep complex functional elements as a single unit, in the UI as well as in the code, for assistive technologies to make sense of the purpose and required interaction for the user with these elements.

- **Make it easier for users to see and hear content**:
  Never use color only to convey important information such as error messages, especially for validation of forms. If the only indication of an error message within a form is a red border for the input field, it may not be noticed by someone with partial sightedness, such as Protanopia (red-green color confusion). The border of the input field will look just like all the other input fields, and it will be impossible for them to continue. Instead, ensure that there is clear text to accompany the visual indicator, explaining that there is a validation error that needs to be addressed. In some cases, adding a descriptive visual element such as an icon can improve usability. In the following example, the original design on the left is using red as a visual indicator for the validation of the input field. On the right is what the user (with Protanopia) will see. It's clear that a red border alone is not sufficient to convey important information. The validation message is sufficient, but the validation message with a visual indicator is even more clear. Later in this chapter, we'll discuss the available tools to measure your designs against.

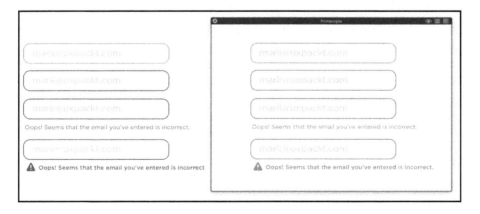

Operable

The second principle, **Operable**, focuses on the way the user navigates through the user interface to perceive the content. All the content should be easily navigable in a logical and structured manner through a keyboard. In short, give users different options to navigate and interact with the website. Let's look at an excerpt from WCAG 2.0:

"All web content, UI elements, and navigation must be operable within the UI by the user."

- **Make all functionality available from a keyboard**:
  By default, the standard HTML structure caters for all assistive technology. When referring to the standard HTML structure, this is the basic HTML 5 structure:

  -
    ```
    <!DOCTYPE HTML>
    <html>
    <head>
    Content
    </head>
    <body>
    Content
    </body>
    </html>
    ```

  A user can navigate through a web page with just the *Tab* key on the keyboard. By tapping the *Tab* key, the focus of the cursor will jump from one tag to the next within the HTML structure (this is also called the tab flow). By implementing custom scripts, such as JavaScript, to change the position of an element or hiding an element within the HTML structure, the hierarchical structure of the page is obstructed, and it has a direct impact on how the user navigates on the page through the tab flow.

  The document flow and the tab flow should always be in line; however, there are some exceptions. In the case of these exceptions, the tab flow can be manipulated by adding a `tabindex` value to an element to give it priority. By default, all elements have a `tabindex` value of 0; any `tabindex` value higher than 0 will be prioritized. If elements have been allocated a `tabindex` value of 1, these elements will be prioritized and when the user has navigated through all the elements with the `tabindex` of 1, the remaining elements with the `tabindex` value of 0 will receive focus.

- Making changes to the `tabindex` is a critical change to how the web page will be perceived by assistive technology and should only be attempted by individuals who have an advanced understanding of web accessibility and the impact that making these changes will have.

- **Give users enough time to read and use content**:
If it's not absolutely necessary to have time limits on actions online, this should not be used at all. If an action requires a time limit, give the user an option to pause, resume, or control the time of the component manually. The most well-known example is when the user's session is about to expire while interacting with a banking website. The user should always be given the option to continue the session and not just be logged out without warning.

- **Do not use content that causes seizures**:
We tend to forget that while browsing websites online, we are looking into a light and sometimes for long periods of time. There are millions of people who are sensitive to light, such as people with Epilepsy, Autism, **Attention-deficit/hyperactivity disorder** (**ADHD**), and **Sensory Processing Disorder** (**SPD**), to only name a few. Flashing lights on a computer screen can have a serious negative impact on their health and cause seizures. There should be no elements on a web page that flash for more than 3 times in a 1-second period, and ideally there should be no flashing lights at all.

- **Help users navigate and find content**:
By ensuring that all web pages have explanatory titles and the purpose of links is described in the text of the link, the user will have clear context of their journey through the website. Another excellent way to help the users navigate a website is to give them information about where they are on the website. Breadcrumbs are a secondary navigation that give the user a visual representation of their exact location on the site. It's a good practice to make these steps clickable to allow the user to move forward or backward in their journey:

Understandable

The third principle from the Web Content Accessibility Guidelines, **Understandable**, focuses on simplifying content by keeping the writing style on a level that the user will understand by not using words and phrases that will be misunderstood. In short, the content and user interface cannot be beyond their understanding. Here's an excerpt from WCAG 2.0:

> *"All web content and UI elements must be understandable to the user; thus, the user should fully know how to operate the UI and access information."*

- **Make text readable and understandable**:
  Due to the fact that screen readers read content differently than a normal person would, it is important to guide the screen reader to read the content correctly by adding the `lang` attribute to the appropriate HTML page or tag. Every language has its unique set of semantic and pronunciation rules, and the screen reader needs to be aware of this to be able to translate the content correctly for the user. The `lang` attribute for an HTML page looks like this:`<html lang="en">`. The `en` is the language code for English and can be replaced by the appropriate language code. The full list of language codes can be found at `https://www.w3schools.com/tags/ref_language_codes.asp`.
  It's a good practice to set the language of an HTML page at all times. Do not assume that English is default and that it will automatically be translated correctly. In the case of an HTML page with more than one language present, the language should be set in the `<html>` tag and the specific `lang` attributes to the tags that contain a different language. The following examples are from the WebAIM website:
    - In Matanzas, we tried a dish called ropa vieja, which literally translates to "old clothes":

        ```
        In Matanzas, we tried a dish called <span
        lang="es">ropa vieja</span>—which literally translates
        as "old clothes."
        ```

    - "C'est la vie," Harold sighed, as he watched his Volvo tumble off the cliff:

        ```
        <span lang="fr">"C'est la vie,"</span> Harold sighed, as
        he watched his Volvo tumble off the cliff.
        ```

- In Rome, Ellen was shocked by a film called La Donna Nella Doccia:

  ```
  • In Rome, Ellen was shocked by a film called <span
    lang="it">La Donna Nella Doccia</span>.
  ```

- **Make content appear and operate in predictable ways**:
  Opening a new window while browsing a website can become disorientating for the user if they don't have any visual context as to what is happening. Thus, opening new windows or tabs should be avoided as far as possible, except in the situation of the user being logged into a secure area of a site, and the action will redirect the user away from the secure logged-in area. Then, a new window or tab is acceptable with a clear message that a new window or tab will be opened. The user should always be notified if a particular action will change the context of the user's browsing experience on the website; for example, if there is a form control at the top of a web page to change the language or country of the site.

- **Help users avoid and correct mistakes**:
  The saying *"Prevention is better than cure"* also rings true when it comes to usability. It is better to put all potential checks in place to prevent opportunities for making errors than to let the user make a mistake and offer assistance to recover from the error state afterward, which can potentially just annoy the user. The submission of online forms is one of the areas with the biggest room for errors:

  - Prevent the user from filling in incorrect details by clearly labeling the input fields with visible (for assistive technology) and descriptive labels. Placeholder text in input fields should not be used as an alternative for labels. Set the input type of the input fields according to the information needed; for example, if the user is expected to fill in a contact number, do not allow alphabetical characters to be typed in, allow only numerical values. Structure the online form in a logical manner and ensure that the labels are correctly linked to the input field.

- Its not possible to prevent all mistakes made by the user, but helping the user recover as effortlessly as possible is key to ensure that the user still has a good user experience. All error messages must accompany the input field in question. Do not display an error message for a specific field in a location that doesn't make sense or is not visible to the user. Ensure that all error messages are clear; explain to the user exactly what went wrong as well as how to rectify the error to continue.

COMPULSARY FIELDS

* Full name

⚠ You have not provided a full name. We need your full name to continue with the registration process.

* Mobile number
+27 66 567 0990

* Email
marli@uxpackt.com

INVALID EMAIL

* Full name
Marli Ritter

* Mobile number
+27 66 567 0990

* Email
marliuxpacktcom

⚠ It seems like the email address provided is not a valid email. Please check if you have entered it correctly.

Robust

The final principle, **Robust**, focuses on technology and to what extent user agents such as browsers, media players, and plugins can access content. Even though technology evolves rapidly, content should still be accessible through as many devices and user agents as possible. In short, the user should be able to access content as technology advances. This is an excerpt from WCAG 2.0:

"All web content and UI elements must be robust enough to be readable and correctly translated by a variety of user agents, such as assistive technology. It should also stay accessible through the evolution of these user agents and technologies in the future."

- **Maximize compatibility with current and future user tools:**
  To maximize compatibility with future user tools, the main focus should be to ensure that the way the website is built is based on known and credible technical standards. Within these technical standards arebasic guidelines such as ensuring that all elements have start and end tags and are nested accordingly. Each element should have a unique ID to avoid confusion, although keep in mind that some functionalities require duplicate IDs to make associations between certain sections within an element.

An overview of WAI-ARIA

The ARIA guidelines have a strong focus on ensuring scripted and dynamic content as well as interactive controls, such as sliders and menus, to be accessible with a keyboard. Most modern browsers and scripting libraries support ARIA, which consists of three main components, namely roles, properties, and states.

Roles

ARIA roles are an attribute given to elements to identify what their role or purpose is. Most HTML elements have a default role assigned to them, which can be overwritten to adjust the semantic context of the page structure and the elements that live within. In the following example, the `<role="menu">` was given to the `<ul>` tag to give context to the list, and ensure that the screen reader knows this is not a normal list of items, but in fact a menu:

```
<ul role="menu">
 <li><a href="index.html">Home</li>
 <li><a href="delivery-rates.html">Our delivery service</li>
 <li><a href="contact.html">Get in touch</li>
</ul>
```

Here are a couple of ARIA roles. The complete list can be found at `https://www.w3.org/TR/wai-aria/roles`:

- `<role="button">` allows for user-triggered actions
- `<role="menu">` offers a list of choices to the user
- `<role="search">` highlights the search functionality

Properties and states

ARIA properties define the properties of an element that can extend the meaning of the element beyond the default role. In the next example, the `aria-required="true"` property adds more context to the `<input>` tag, which is to notify the screen reader that this input field is required for successful validation:

```
<form action="post">
 <label for="username">Username</label>
 <input id="username" type="text" aria-required="true" />
 <hr/>
 <label for="password">Password</label>
```

```
<input id="password" type="text" aria-required="true" />
<hr/>
<input type="login" value="Login">
</form>
```

ARIA states define the current condition of an element. The state of an element can be dynamic and can change based on the user's interaction with the element. In the following example, the `<aria-disabled="true">` notifies the screen reader that the input state is disabled, although the user can change this state to `<false>` by interacting with the UI. This state is especially helpful when submitting forms; the screen reader needs to know that the `submit` button is disabled to allow the user to interact with the input fields. The `<aria-describedby="usernameError passwordError">` gives the screen reader descriptive information about the button:

```
<form action="post">
 <label for="username">Username</label>
 <input id="username" type="text" aria-required="true" />
 <hr/>
 <label for="password">Password</label>
 <input id="password" type="text" aria-required="true" />
 <hr/>
 <button type="submit" aria-disabled="true" aria-describedby="usernameError
passwordError">Login</button>
 </form>
```

Listed are a couple of ARIA properties and states. The complete list can be found at `https://www.w3.org/TR/wai-aria/states_and_properties`.

- `<aria-labelledby="label">` acts as an ID that can be referenced by many other elements
- `<aria-disabled="true">` gives the status of a form input element

Web accessibility requirements from a design perspective

The key to designing for web accessibility starts with proper planning of the design, its purpose, and the required outcomes. Creatives are passionate individuals who enjoy getting lost in their design process; unfortunately, some designs, as visually pleasing as they may be, they are not functional and will not adhere to the user's needs.

The following list gives some guidelines on what to keep in mind when designing for web accessibility:

1. **Keep to the logical structure**:
   As mentioned earlier in this chapter, the logical flow of elements in the HTML structure and the visual elements in the UI should be aligned and should follow a natural reading structure.

2. **Be mindful of typography**:
   As far as possible, make use of true text (text that's been added as HTML) to convey information as opposed to adding text to a flat visual element (text that's been added in an image and saved as a singular flat file), which cannot be read by assistive technology. The minimum font size that should be used is 10 points, and avoid using all caps in headings or content as this can be interpreted incorrectly by assistive technology.

3. **Ensure that contrast ratio is acceptable**:
   Contrast plays a critical role in making web content easier to read; the higher the contrast between the background color and the foreground text, the better the web content will be displayed; the lower the contrast, the more difficult it is to distinguish between colors and make out the outlines of visual elements and text. The **LEVEL A, AA**, and **AAA** criteria within WCAG standards requires a minimum contrast ratio background color, and the foreground text is based on a minimum text size for that specific contrast ratio. Here's a basic breakdown of these minimum requirements and their compliance to the success criteria:

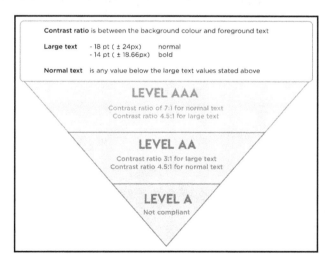

4. **Use animation and color-focused elements cautiously**:
When incorporating multimedia in a design, ensure that controls are accessible for the user to pause/stop the interactive elements. Flashing lights can cause seizures, and it's important for the user to have full control over such elements. As mentioned in the previous section, it is not advisable to use color only to display important information. Some users may use external tools to override color on a web page to suite their sight needs; in such cases, using a color only to communicate important information can be lost. Always ensure that important information has additional elements, such as iconography or text, to support the color.

Case Study - Booking.com analysis of design requirements for WCAG 2.0

The following is an example taken from the Booking.com website using the WebAIM browser extension called **WAVE** (**Web Accessibility Evaluation Tool**) to highlight contrast errors as well as guidelines on how to rectify them. Overall, the contrast ratios are good; it's only the light grey placeholder text in the input fields and the dark gray labels on the bright yellow background .

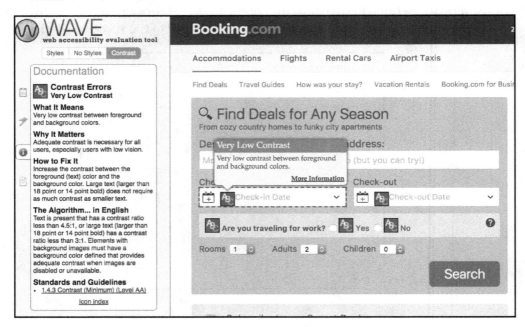

Another helpful online tool is **Checkmycolours**, which you can find at http://www.checkmycolours.com/.

By adding the domain name in the input field, Checkmycolours analyzes the website and gives an extensive report on every tag. Tags include all HTML tags with contrast attributes and their compliance with the WCAG 2.0 standards. The report includes the following components with IDs and classes to make it easier to find errors:

- **Node** is the HTML tag with the class or ID associated with it. This will help find the specific tag within the website.
- **Foreground** is the color value of the text.
- **Background** is the color value of the background on which the text is being displayed.
- **Sample** is a visual sample of what the text and background color combination looks like visually.
- **Contrast ratio** to comply with guideline 1.4 of the WCAG 2.0 should be at least as mentioned:
    - **LEVEL AA**: ratio 4.5:1
    - **LEVEL AAA**: ratio 7:1
- **Brightness and color difference** is based on WCAG 1.0 and calculated using this formula:

```
((Red value X 299) + (Green value X 587) + (Blue value X 114)) / 1000
The range for color brightness difference is 125.
The range for color difference is 500.
```

WAVE and checkmycolours are both tools used to analyze an existing website; **Sim Daltonism** is one of the many free online tools that can be used during the design process. As a designer with no limitations to their sight, it's difficult to know which color combinations are acceptable for specific color blindness. Sim Daltonism is a tool that simulates how the user with a specific color blindness will perceive a design. It's a good practice to keep a tool like this handy, to ensure that the direction of the design is in line with the accessibility standards. Here's an example of how Bitcoin's website looks through the eyes of the three main categories of color blind, **red-green confusion**, **yellow-blue confusion**, and **no color**.

You can download Sim Daltonism from `https://michelf.ca/projects/sim-daltonism/`:

Before we part ways

Designing a website that users love is all about focusing on usability. The effortless way in which users interact with the website despite limitations such as screen readers, how easily they recover from the errors they encounter, and how pleasing the design is to the senses, all play a vital role in the usability of a website. Applying basic UX principles using the **User-Centered Design (UCD)** process is key to always keeping the user in the center of all decisions made when creating a truly user-centric product.

A solid UX strategy is based on reliable data collected through user research to create useful personas with which the brand will be able to build an emotional connection and a credible long-term relationship. By understanding the users' behavior, motivations, and needs, these needs can besuccessfully addressed to leave the user with a satisfying user experience of the website. From the research phase, the concept within the UX strategy will be fleshed out using practical UX methodologies such as wireframes, task flows, user journeys, and prototypes to detect any possible flow issues, resolve basic functionality, UI interactions, and so on. User testing can be conducted at any time during this process to ensure that the website being built is in line with the value proposition and still focuses on the user's end goal.

After implementation, when the website has been published, it's crucial to continue to track the activity of the user with the website, conduct user research, and also do some A/B testing exercises to constantly improve the product. Always keep in mind that no perfect UX digital product exists; it's an endless iterative process of improvement that makes a website truly usable and enjoyable for users.

Summary

By complying with the WCAG 2.0 and the WAI-ARIA guidelines, digital products will inevitably be of a higher quality. The perception is that making a digital product accessible is not only costly, but also very time consuming, as you need developers and designers who specialize in web accessibility to implement these changes. This perception is not true. Even though some of these web accessibility guidelines seem quite complex, there are several free online tools available, of which the WAVE browser extension is exceptionally useful, to help find accessibility issues and provide guidelines on how to fix them. It's not about having a specialized skill in web accessibility, but in focusing on usability as a whole for all users.

Index